What's *Race*
Got To Do With It?

Darren E. Lund, Paul R. Carr, and Virginia Lea
Series Editors

Vol. 2

The Critical Multicultural Perspectives on Whiteness series
is part of the Peter Lang Education list.
Every volume is peer reviewed and meets
the highest quality standards for content and production.

PETER LANG
New York • Bern • Frankfurt • Berlin
Brussels • Vienna • Oxford • Warsaw

What's *Race* Got To Do With It?

How Current
School Reform Policy
Maintains Racial and
Economic Inequality

Edited by
BREE PICOWER and EDWIN MAYORGA

PETER LANG
New York • Bern • Frankfurt • Berlin
Brussels • Vienna • Oxford • Warsaw

Library of Congress Cataloging-in-Publication Data

What's race got to do with it?:
How current school reform policy maintains racial and economic inequality /
edited by Bree Picower, Edwin Mayorga.
pages cm. — (Critical multicultural perspectives on whiteness; Vol. 2)
Includes bibliographical references and index.
1. Discrimination in education—United States. 2. Education—Social aspects—United States.
3. Education—Economic aspects—United States. 4. Educational change—Social aspects—
United States. 5. Minorities—Education—United States. 6. Educational equalization—
United States. 7. Income distribution—United States. 8. United States—Race relations.
I. Picower, Bree, editor of compilation. II. Mayorga, Edwin, editor of compilation.
LC212.2.W44   370.80973—dc23   2014040433
ISBN 978-1-4331-2884-4 (hardcover)
ISBN 978-1-4331-2883-7 (paperback)
ISBN 978-1-4539-1476-2 (e-book)
ISSN 2166-8507

Bibliographic information published by **Die Deutsche Nationalbibliothek**.
Die Deutsche Nationalbibliothek lists this publication in the "Deutsche
Nationalbibliografie"; detailed bibliographic data are available
on the Internet at http://dnb.d-nb.de/.

The paper in this book meets the guidelines for permanence and durability
of the Committee on Production Guidelines for Book Longevity
of the Council of Library Resources.

© 2015 Peter Lang Publishing, Inc., New York
29 Broadway, 18th floor, New York, NY 10006
www.peterlang.com

Printed in the United States of America

Dedicated to our teachers, Jean Anyon and Suzanne Carothers.

Table of Contents

Acknowledgments

This book was born of many years of political struggle, political analysis, and teaching for social justice. We both want to thank our second family, the New York Collective of Radical Educators (NYCoRE). We have been core leaders in NYCoRE for more than a decade now and the shared organizing work, analysis development, and friendship that we have been privileged to be a part of are central to who we have become as scholar activists. We also want to recognize NYCoRE's network of sister organizations that make up the National Teacher Activist Groups (TAG): Association of Raza Educators, San Diego/Oakland; Education for Liberation Network; Educators' Network for Social Justice, Milwaukee; The People's Education Movement, Los Angeles; Teacher Action Group, Philadelphia; Teacher Activist Group, Boston; and Teachers for Social Justice, Chicago. It is through this network that we support each other in the struggle against the racist, neoliberal assault on schools, educators, and youth, in our local communities and across the country.

This book was initiated through a project funded by the Ford Secondary Education and Racial Justice Collaborative (FSERJC), under the guidance of Dr. Michelle Fine, Dr. john a. powell, Dr. Gina Chirichigno and Dr. Lauren Wells. This grant brought together a rare convergence of educators, scholars, youth, and activists who shared local work, gave feedback to one another, and provided small grants to spur the development of racial justice projects on both a local and national scale. We thank FSERJC for the intellectual, political, and financial support that it provided. For NYCoRE, this support launched an educator's study group titled *What's Race Got to Do With It*. Together we met once a month to more deeply understand the racial and economic structures of oppression that dominate current education reform. This study group was the root from which this book grew. We are forever grateful for the ideas, perspectives, new directions, and hunger for learning and teaching that the study group members brought to each meeting. Your work and your passion for justice are models of the transformative power and spirit of educator activists who do this work every day.

We would additionally like to thank William Waters, Grace Ahn, Simone Goldenstein, and Kelly Frazee for their support in the process of writing this book.

Edwin's Acknowledgments

First and foremost I want to thank my partner Jen, and our son, Teo, for dealing with my overcommitment. I've tried to step back over the last year, but even in step-back-mode, it is still too much. You two stick by me, in spite of it all. Jen, your steady love and support is an anchor. Teo, my desire to try to make the world we leave for you a little bit better, a little more just, drives why I do what I do. Thank you for being an inspiration for what my teacher, Jean Anyon, described as radical possibilities. I love you both.

I also want to acknowledge the teachers that have shaped my life as an educator-scholar-activist. My family, who have cheered me on at every step on my own path, and have been models of the good in humanity even in very difficult living conditions. Robyn Ulzheimer and colleagues at PS 87, and my colleagues at PS 165, who were there to support me as I stumbled around the work of teaching for social justice in the elementary school classroom. Jean Anyon, Michelle Fine, Ruth Wilson Gilmore, Steve Brier, Carmen Mercado, Pedro Pedraza, Wendy Luttrell, and Ofelia Garcia, for being researcher-scholars whom I have learned so much from, and have been my guide posts along my scholar-activist path. My scholar-friends, familia, at the Graduate Center of the City University of New York, including Jeremy Benson, Nelson Flores, Michela Bjork, Rachel Lambert, Jen Jack Gieseking, Ujju Aggarwal, Alejandro Carrion, Noah Golden, Ricardo Gabriel, Shannon Allen, Victoria Restler, and so many others. Your generosity and commitments to research for change inspire me everyday. My new colleagues and students at Swarthmore College, who have been so welcoming to my family as we have made the move to Pennsylvania, and have really made Swarthmore a wonderful place to teach. Finally I want to acknowledge my students in K–12 and higher education, and their families. It is they who, along with my son Teo, have challenged me, humbled me, and inspired me to work for justice.

Bree's Acknowledgments

I feel incredibly blessed that I have been able to craft a career based on my commitment toward antiracism in education. Through teaching, writing, and activism, I am incredibly lucky to be able to work toward educational justice as part of my "9–5" (or more realistically, my "24–7"). I'd like to thank the support of Montclair State University and specifically the Early Childhood, Elementary and Literacy Department for the academic freedom to be able to do this work as my livelihood and not just as an extracurricular activity.

In my work as an educator teaching about educational justice issues, I have had the honor of working with many students with whom I share a commitment to equity in education, whether they were students I encountered as elementary, undergraduate, or graduate students. While I have love for all such students, a few stand out and I'd like to thank them because their passion helps keeps mine lit: Johnny Phommasyha, my former 2nd/3rd grade student who now as a UC Berkeley graduate is dedicated to providing educational opportunities and ethnic studies for younger students from his Oakland roots. Daniel Hildreth, a former public school teacher who continues to share his commitment to children with special needs by returning to my classroom and preparing new teachers. And finally, Kathy Xiong, one of my first graduate students who has continued to inspire me with her groundbreaking teacher activist work that we now engage in shoulder to shoulder. Thank you all for keeping me motivated.

Mindy Kaling once said that "a best friend isn't a person, it's a tier" (2013). I honor those in this tier for their love, humor, support, cocktails, long phone calls, and cookies: Kristine Larsen, Anne Marie Marshall, and Rosa Rivera-McCutchen. And of course, I return the love of those who love me unconditionally: Barbara, Josh, Adam, Martika, and Chaka.

Race Against Time

Raising Black Boys

Neoliberal School Reform

(Whiteness) Two Sides of the same Coin

The Many Faces

Education

- White Supremacy

Reproduction of

Silencing Victims

Introduction

BREE PICOWER AND EDWIN MAYORGA

Often in educational justice circles and critical discussions of educational policy, researchers and activists are of two camps. Some (i.e., Apple, 2001; Compton & Weiner, 2008; Hursh, 2007) have importantly focused on the neoliberal turn in education reform. Such frameworks focus on how market-based reforms and privatization-driven policies have reproduced and expanded economic inequality. Other scholars (Frankenberg, 2012; Lynn, Yosso, Solórzano, & Parker, 2002) have centered on race and growing racial inequality as evidenced by opportunity gaps, the school-to-prison pipeline, and segregated schools. These analyses often happen in isolation from each other, continuing to divide those concerned with educational justice into "It's race!" vs. "It's class!" camps.

What's Race Got to Do with It is an attempt to bring together these often isolating frameworks to ask what role race plays in some of the hallmark policies of current school reforms such as school closing, high-stakes testing, and the proliferation of charter schools. Examining one individual policy strand of neoliberal school reform, each chapter in this book uses a lens similar to Leonardo's (2009) racial economic analytic framework, where "racial hierarchies and class exploitation occur in a symbiotic relationship and that changes in one produce changes in the other" (p. 8). By looking at these reforms through this racial economic framework, this edited volume complicates our analysis of how market-based reforms increase wealth inequality and maintain White supremacy. By analyzing current reforms through this dual lens, those concerned with social justice are better equipped to struggle against reforms in ways that unite rather than divide.

This book reveals the ways in which race, particularly Whiteness, is masked in hallmark neoliberal reforms, and how it operates in real ways to maintain racial and economic inequality. The chapters have similar structures:

Each traces the historical context of a singular reform, examines how that reform maintains Whiteness and economic inequality, and shares grassroots stories of resistance to these reforms. Each author was selected because of her or his cutting-edge racial economic analysis, understanding of corporate school reform, and active involvement in grassroots social movements aimed at increasing justice and equity in education.

Scholar Activism

The editors of this book, Bree Picower and Edwin Mayorga, are both teacher educators as well as core leaders in a grassroots, educational activist group called the New York Collective of Radical Educators (NYCoRE) for more than a decade. The seeds of this book grew from Bree and Edwin's shared work within NYCoRE, specifically with a grant that we received as part of a Ford Foundation funded project titled *The Ford Secondary Education and Racial Justice Collaborative* (FSERJC) (The Kirwan Institute for the Study of Race and Ethnicity, 2013).[1] Under the leadership of john a. powell, Michelle Fine, Lauren Wells, and Gina Chirichigno, FSERJC was a national project that convened and supported local-level working groups of educators, organizers, lawyers, advocates, and scholars from across the country to foster the creation of "more equitable and effective alternatives to current federal, state and local education reform initiatives" (The Kirwan Institute for the Study of Race and Ethnicity, 2013). Within this larger national project, Edwin and Bree used grant money to co-coordinate and facilitate a monthly series called *What's Race Got to Do with It* that engaged NYCoRE teachers in readings and discussions to examine the role that racism played in current school reform efforts such as school closings, charter schools, and high-stakes testing. As we began to center this analysis in more of NYCoRE's as well as our individual academic work, we saw the need to bolster and share our theoretical understandings of this phenomenon. As a result, we put together this volume by bringing together leading scholar activists' voices on how race and neoliberalism work in sync to maintain inequality across the country.

Having been educators, scholars, and activists within the New York City public school landscape for more than a decade, we conceive of our scholarly work as "engaged scholarship" (Hale, 2008) or "scholar-educator-activism" (Suzuki & Mayorga, 2014). From this perspective we, similar to Lipman (2011), feel that "research, and political engagement enrich each other, and that 'knowledge is vital to social action'" (Hale 2008, as quoted in Lipman, 2011). As former elementary school educators, and now teacher educators, we see our work as educators as central to what we mean by scholar activism.

As such, our academic work is centered on mapping the way: (1) dominance operates (Clarke, 2010) in teaching and education policy; (2) analyzing injustice; and (3) examining and using varied forms of resistance taken up by educators, youth, families, communities, and education advocates in schools and in the streets (Lipman, 2011; Picower, 2012). This documentary and analytic work is a beginning, rather than an end, for scholar activists. We direct our scholarship, teaching, and organizing toward supporting educators and education advocates in doing this critical work inside and outside the classroom (NYCoRE, 2002). This book is one way that we formulate and share conceptual frameworks to develop rich analyses of the racist capitalist education policy landscape in which we are situated to foster social justice (Anyon, 2009).

The Story of NYCoRE's Hydra

Coming together in 2002 at the start of the war in Afghanistan, NYCoRE sought to be a space for teachers to participate in the antiwar movement, within educational justice circles as well as in broader struggles for global justice. Focused on interrupting the multiple forms of injustice that intersect through schools, "NYCoRE is a group of current and former public school educators and their allies committed to fighting for social justice in our school system and society at large, by organizing and mobilizing teachers, developing curriculum and working with community, parent and student organizations" (NYCoRE, 2002).

Since its inception, NYCoRE has spent a great deal of time identifying key forms of oppression that affect the lives of educators, students, and communities. This has included military recruitment in secondary schools, the criminalization of youth, high-stakes testing, the rise of the charter school movement, and mayoral control of schools, to name but a few. In New York City, and across the country, NYCoRE saw these various oppressive policies and practices being rolled out one at a time in an individual fashion. However, the group understood that these policies were related to one another in cultural, political, and economic ways. In seeking to understand the connections, the group began to read literature and discuss notions of globalization, privatization, and neoliberalism. The readings and discussions gave the group more language to think about what was occurring in the New York City school system, and NYCoRE developed a metaphor for describing what was happening as an interconnected web of activity. Some NYCoRE members kept coming back to the notion that the attack on public education worked like a many-headed monster known as "the Hydra."

Those who are familiar with Greek mythology know that the Hydra was an immortal multi-headed creature. Any attempt to slay the Hydra was a struggle in futility and hopelessness, because if one head were removed, the Hydra would grow back two more in its place. Furthering NYCoRE's social justice metaphor, the Hydra was only finally able to be slain by Heracles because he worked together with an ally, his nephew, to remove all the heads at once, making it impossible for the decapitated heads to grow back.

NYCoRE made the connection that each of these Hydra heads was analogous to one of the market-based reforms unfolding in our city. The group observed that the school system was rolling out a variety of seemingly individual policies, or Hydra heads, one at a time, such as mayoral control, testing, charter schools, etc. The initial response by those concerned with educational justice was to furiously address each individual head by focusing time and energy on one after another. As the progressive education community became increasingly splintered and exhausted, NYCoRE observed that when one project was being addressed, other projects were lined up to continue moving a privatization agenda forward. The group realized that focusing on one head meant that our attention was often drawn away from the larger forces, or Hydra body, driving reform—namely, the form of capitalism that some describe as neoliberalism.

Since late 2010, NYCoRE has amplified this multi-headed analysis by looking at how racism in the United States is continually connected to neoliberal education reform. While there is rhetoric that the United States is living in a "post-racial" era where the material effects of race are no longer pertinent, the economic, political, and cultural problems of U.S. education continue to be tied to racial divisions. This book is a continuation of NYCoRE's efforts to better understand the Hydra of market-driven school reform.

Neoliberalism and Education

What's Race Got to Do With It is an attempt to undergird the Hydra metaphor with theoretical constructs that help those committed to educational justice better understand how seemingly individual education "reforms," or "Hydra heads," are all connected to a broader "body" that is pushing public education toward privatization. The following sections outline these theoretical constructs that are, in some ways, the internal organs of the Hydra: neoliberalism, structural racism, Whiteness and White supremacy, racial capitalism, and accumulation by dispossession.

Historical research on U.S. schools has demonstrated that schools and school systems are essential components of the work of the state[2] (Apple,

1996; Spring, 2001). On a basic level, schools and school systems have served as a site to meet the state's need for the development of individual members of its society. Whether the goal was educating individuals to participate in a democracy or to align with a particular social class, the focus of the school has been on producing people who fit the social order. Coupled with this notion of developing the individual is the school's position as part of the management of society. From the formation of centralized bureaucratic management systems (Tyack, 1974) to the struggles over racial desegregation (Spring, 2001), schools have been integral to social control projects created to meet varying and often conflicting economic, political, and societal needs (Spring, 2004). As such, current trends in school reform are part of a broader turn toward a capitalist, or market, view of organizing schools and the broader social order.

The school reform trends that have swept the nation over the last 15 years can be seen as part of what critical scholars have described as the rise of neoliberalism within education (Lipman, 2011). Neoliberalism, as a strain of capitalism, is a set of policies and practices that privilege market strategies over public institutions to redress social issues (Kumashiro, 2008). Such policies champion privatizing formerly public services, deregulating trade, and increasing efficiency while simultaneously reducing wages, deunionizing, and slashing public services (Martinez & Garcia, 2000; Tabb, 2001). Neoliberalism uses the ideology of individual choice to promote the idea of a meritocracy "that presumes an even playing field" (Kumashiro, 2008, p. 37). Lipman (2011) notes that "neoliberalism is an ensemble of economic and social policies, forms of governance, and discourses and ideologies that promote individual self-interest, unrestricted flows of capital, deep reductions in the cost of labor and sharp retrenchment of the public sphere" (p. 6). This is how neoliberalism creates a two-tiered system of education in which the people with control maintain power and opportunity by stripping it from already marginalized people—typically people of Color. Under neoliberal policies, groups of allies are broken up into individuals who are forced to compete against each other rather than work collectively. Within education, these policies work to challenge the legitimacy of public schooling by promoting vouchers, charters, and other quasi-private schools while privatizing services that were once the domain of public institutions, such as curriculum development and testing (Lipman, 2005).

Neoliberal school reforms share several trends: They increase privatization, slash public services, increase competition, and place both blame and success on individuals rather than systems. These trends use market-based rhetoric to take power from the majority of people and concentrate it in the hands of few while masking the processes that allowed this to happen. As

Lipman (2011) explains, "[i]n this framework, education is a private good, an investment one makes in one's child or oneself to 'add value' to better compete in the labor market, not a social good for development of individuals and society as a whole" (pp. 14–15). By focusing on the rights and responsibilities of individuals, neoliberal policies have resulted in increasing accountability systems that place blame on and then punish individual students and teachers rather than on the inequitable school systems that have inadequately served them. Rather than improving quality of education, this vicious circle creates school climates characterized by compliance, conformity, and fear.

As neoliberal education policies continue to push for competition and choice in city after city, the implications for the future of public education stands in the balance. As Lipman (2011) expounds, "Urban schools are wound up in privatization, public-private partnerships, demands for union 'flexibility,' teacher merit pay schemes, and mayoral takeovers, along with high stakes testing and restricted urban school districts, direct involvement of corporate actors and corporate philanthropies dictating school district policies—these are features of neoliberal governance dominating urban school districts" (p. 47). As a network of reforms, neoliberalism has spurred the privatization of education in a seemingly race-neutral yet highly racialized manner, resulting in the accumulation of capital and success for some and failure and dispossession for others. The following section elucidates the role that race plays in supporting this process.

Structural Racism, White Supremacy, and Whiteness

This book focuses on the neoliberal nature of market-based school reform while positioning neoliberalism within a system of racism. Derman-Sparks and Phillips (1997) argue that racism operates on three levels—institutional, cultural, and individual: "It encompasses a web of economic, political, social, and cultural structures, actions and beliefs that systemize and ensure unequal distribution of privilege, resources and power in favor of the dominant racial group at the expense of all other racial groups" (p. 10). In the literature that situates race as the organizing principle of such domination (Ladson-Billings & Tate, 1995; Omi & Winant, 1994; Stovall, 2006), it is critical to name this system and process of domination as White supremacy.

White supremacy is the way in which our society was founded and remains organized so that White people are at the top of the hierarchy of power. It is maintained through institutional, individual, explicit, and covert processes (Jensen, 2005; Leonardo, 2004). As defined by Jensen (2005) a [W]hite supremacist society is a society whose founding is based in an ideology of the inherent superiority of white Europeans over non-whites, an ideology that was used to justify crimes against indigenous people and Africans that created the nation. That ideology also has justified legal and extralegal exploitation of every non-white immigrant group, and is used to this day to rationalize the racialized disparities in the distribution of wealth and well being in this society. (p. 4)

It is this system of White supremacy, or White dominance over people of Color, that is protected and maintained by current racial ideology and policies. The following section highlights the role of "Whiteness" within this system of dominance.

Within this system, Whiteness is the ideology and way of being in the world that is used to maintain White supremacy symbolically and materially. Bush (2004) argues that Whiteness "reveals the ways in which Whites benefit from a variety of institutional and social arrangements that often appear (to Whites) to have nothing to do with race" (p. 15). Harris (1993), in her legal construction of "Whiteness as property," describes Whiteness as the "assumptions, privileges and benefits that accompany the status of being White [that] have become a valuable asset that whites sought to protect" and is thus protected by law (p. 6). In this construction of White supremacy in which Whiteness carries legal rights as protected property, Lipsitz (1998) explains his theory of the "possessive investment in whiteness":

> I use the adjective possessive to stress the relationship between whiteness and asset accumulation in our society, to connect attitudes to interests, to demonstrate that White supremacy is usually less a matter of direct, referential, and snarling contempt than a system of protecting the privileges of whites by denying communities of Color opportunities for asset accumulation and upward mobility. Whiteness is invested in, like property, but it is also a means of accumulating property and keeping it from others. (p. viii)

When Whiteness is seen as property and investment, the symbolic material effects of White supremacy are not only evident but are also more tangibly linked to the changing movements of capital. For example, Melamed (2011) argues that in the continuing expansion of a global capitalist system, the characteristics of the White supremacist system needed to adapt to be palatable as it helped to maintain a raced and classed social order. Whereas the 1980s and 1990s witnessed a striving for diversity and openness coupled with capital accumulation, the more immediate past has been marked by a focus on "economic freedom" and "consumerist diversity" (Melamed, 2011, p. 43) that obscured histories of racial and economic formations and arrangements.

Current school reforms follow this pattern and are typically framed in race-neutral or even co-opted civil rights language. This power erasure

(Kincheloe & Steinberg 1997), in which Whiteness remains masked from everyday consciousness, allows current school reforms to appear as equity measures while, in reality, such reforms have dire consequences for communities of Color. Leonardo (2004) explains how current school reform uses strategies of White supremacy through a particular process: "[Whites] set up a system that benefits the group, mystify the system, remove the agents of actions from discourse, and when interrogated about it, stifle the discussion with inane comments about the 'reality' of the charges being made" (p. 148). So while it may appear that race has nothing to do with reform, in fact, it is the driving force beneath it.

The current school reform of school closings can be used to illustrate this process. School closings are framed by reformers as a race-neutral strategy for equity; these closings are discussed as a way to protect children from having to attend failing schools. In reality, however, school closings have overwhelmingly affected students of Color, displacing them and forcing them into other overcrowded or underperforming schools, into schools in distant neighborhoods, or into the charter system. For example, in the 15 schools closed in Washington, D.C., in 2013, only two of the 2,700 students that were displaced by closings were White students (Rich, 2013). While school closings force the dislocation of thousands of students of Color, it clears the path for new charter schools and other education opportunities designed for White students in often gentrifying communities. This highly racialized process operates in ways that mask what race has to do with school reform while protecting and maintaining racial and economic hierarchies.

Racial Capitalism

Having explored economic, class-based analyses of education, critical theories of race, and Whiteness studies to examine current education reforms in the previous sections, this section moves toward the development of an integrated racial economic framework: the notion of racial capitalism. Leonardo (2012) notes that the goal in "performing a race and class synthesis is to privilege neither framework and, instead, offers an intersectional, integrated, or what I am calling a raceclass perspective" (p. 438). In other words, the analytic framework used in this book is one that seeks not to privilege one analysis (class or race) over the other. Rather the approach seeks to "trabajar en ambo," or to "work in both," as a way to better identify and examine the connections between capitalism and structural racism, or racial capitalism.

Racial capitalism, an idea drawn from Cedric Robinson's (1983) book *Black Marxism*, serves as a guide to thinking concurrently about structural racism and capitalism in schooling and education policy. Seeking not to reject Marxism, Robinson aimed to carve a distinct vision that linked Marxism with what he describes as the Black radical tradition. As Jodi Melamed (2011) points out, "Robinson's theory of racial capitalism clarifies the economic dimension, explaining that because 'the development, organization, and expansions of capitalist relations [have] pursued essentially racial directions [in modernity],' racialism is to be considered a 'material force' and a 'historical agency' of capitalism, with no outside between the two" (p. 8).

Over time, racial capitalism in the United States has shifted and adapted to protect capitalist accumulation and the supremacy of Whiteness. As Phelps (2014) points out, the United States is in the midst of its third great system of race and class, moving from chattel slavery to Jim Crow, and now to a system that "operates so subtly that it gives only the barest appearance of being a system" (p. 2). In this era of race and class defined by neoliberalism, institutions and actors have put into play various policies such as the privatization of public institutions, cuts in government services, and capital flight to low-wage countries (Lipsitz, 2011), in ways that are framed by proponents as "common sense" decisions (Kumashiro, 2008).

Commonsense rhetoric obscures from the discussion preexisting inequalities that have been shaped by race and class. Neoliberal policies actually decrease opportunities for upward mobility for most Americans while protecting capitalist accumulation. In this way class inequalities are obscured. But even more pertinent is that economic inequality is always already racialized. While wealth and power accrue, the language of individual responsibility for solving social problems and meritocracy turn a blind eye to those historical inequalities. In this third era of racial capitalism, the rhetoric of reform and justice is woven into the values of the market and becomes a veil for the protection of capitalist accumulation, the ongoing supremacy of Whiteness, and the continued dispossession and oppression of people of Color.

Accumulation by Dispossession

Much of the research that looks critically at corporate school reform examines the negative impact on communities of Color (Fabricant & Fine, 2012, 2013; Watkins, 2011). For example, such research tells the story of the amount of schools closed that disproportionately impact communities of Color, the services not provided to English Language Learners in charter schools, or the disproportionate impact of testing policies on African American students. This research helps paint a picture of institutional racism that is critical to dismantling a legacy of discrimination and deculturalization (Spring, 2004) brought forth by public education. However, missing in this picture are the ways in which these same reforms heap privilege, capital, and opportunities on White and middle-class students. Another goal of this book is to look at both sides of this same coin by examining how these reforms simultaneously oppress communities of Color while at the same time rewarding Whites.

Referred to as *accumulation by dispossession,* Harvey (2006) defines this process in which assets that belonged to one group are taken and put into circulation as capital for another group to profit from (Buras, 2011). Once such capital is within the market ready for investment and speculation, Harvey (2006) explains that "[n]ew terrains for profitable activity were opened up... Once in motion, however, this movement created incredible pressures to find more and more arenas, either at home or abroad, where privatization might be achieved" (p. 158). Within education, these reforms are often framed as meritocratic opportunities—or even civil rights measures, but in reality such reforms remove power, opportunity, and capital from people already marginalized by institutional racism and economic inequality and transfer it to those with power in a seemingly "race neutral" manner. Buras (2011) examined this process at work in post-Katrina New Orleans, now a 100% charter district, in what she described as a "strategic assault on black communities by education entrepreneurs" (p. 296).

Fine and Ruglis (2009) also build on Harvey's accumulation by dispossession to show how current neoliberal education policies dispossess poor students of Color from quality education. "As public educational funds are handed over to testing companies, publishing houses, private security, and policing organizations, the very conditions of teaching and learning degenerate and a discourse of individual responsibility for educational achievement permeates—especially in the most impoverished schools" (p. 21). This capital dispossessed from the public system accumulates in the hands of private corporations writ large, but also has implications for the lived experiences of racially diverse groups of students.

While Fine and Ruglis (2009) illustrate this process of dispossession, another example that concretely highlights the accumulative component of this cycle is that of school closures in New York City. Aggarwal and Mayorga (in press) illustrate that when a large comprehensive high school in a ritzy neighborhood was in the process of being closed, or phased out, and the mostly poor, emergent bilingual student population was being displaced, there was a parallel process of offering the now available space to new, more selective, small public schools and charter schools. These new schools would also have significant amounts of new funding funneled into remaking the building. In this particular case, the wealthy, often White, families from the neighborhood, as well as a branch of a local charter management organization, used the dispossession of students as an opportunity to demand neighborhood schools of their own. Ultimately a new school that fit this vision, and a more privileged student body, accumulated a large portion of the building and related funding.

The rapid-fire process of accumulation by dispossession under neoliberal school reform has profound implications for the permanence of racial and economic inequality. As Cheryl Harris notes, "the dialectical phenomena of White accumulation and Black disaccumulation—the incremental economic and social advantage for Whites and corresponding disadvantage for Blacks... aggregate[s] and compound[s] across generations" (as cited in Fine & Ruglis, 2009, p. 30). Lipsitz (2011) reminds us, "under these [economic] circumstances inherited wealth becomes even more important for those positioned to receive it" (p. 5). Throughout this book, each chapter author builds on this phenomenon, moving away from simply an identification of institutional racism to a more nuanced understanding of the maintenance of White supremacy in which the process of both racialized accumulation and dispossession through individual market-based reforms are made visible.

Seeing the Hydra Through the Heads

As the book editors, we want to also raise a point of caution as readers dive into each chapter. While we have invited each author to focus on a specific policy or set of practices, we caution against reading any of these as static, isolated, racialized neoliberal strategies. As Peck and Theodore (2012) assert, "neoliberalisation," as opposed to neoliberalism, is "a signifier for an always-contradictory process, and for an evolving/rolling programme of restructuring" (p. 179). A key characteristic of this current era of race and class is its undergirding logic of dynamism and adaptability. Some of the policies and practices that are discussed in the book, such as small schools, were not initially designed to move forward neoliberal logic. What underlying neoliberal logic does do is to encourage the re-appropriation of ideas like small schools and adapt them to achieving social goals.

What this demonstrates is that there is a connective tissue that is continually being forged between ideologies, intentions, and the formation of policies and practices. We refer back to NYCoRE's Hydra metaphor here, to remind the reader that the heads of the Hydra are not static, but evolving in relation to the underlying logic of racial capitalism and what is happening in the external world. When chapter authors were invited to look at a particular head of the Hydra, our intent was to give readers an opportunity to look broadly across the various, interconnected heads, while giving the authors an entry point for their analyses. Much like Jean Anyon (2014), who recognized that "education is an institution whose basic problems are caused by, and whose basic problems reveal, the other crises in cities" (p. 170), we are suggesting that an analysis anchored by one head of the Hydra helps reveal how it is connected to other heads and an underlying racial capitalist logic that has shaped the broader world. Understanding each of these policies and reform projects as part of a Hydra, or nexus (as Pauline Lipman suggests in this book), of racialized neoliberal policies and shifting strategies thus becomes a key component to resisting these oppressive forces. It is our hope that the thorough examination of each Hydra head will help the reader be able to better articulate what race has to do with each of these neoliberal reforms and the role it plays in maintaining racial and economic inequality.

Slaying the Hydra Through Social Movements

In creating this book, we asked our group of authors to end their chapters with discussions of resistance and social movements. A question we then ask ourselves, and may be asked by the reader, is, Why resistance? Or why social movement? We go back to the myth of the Hydra to think about this question. Heracles could not defeat the Hydra by himself, because he needed to take on individual heads of the Hydra and keep new heads from emerging. He called on Iolaus, his nephew, to help him. Every time Heracles decapitated a head, Iolaus would scorch the neck stumps to keep heads from regenerating. Iolaus's help allowed Heracles to begin attacking the Hydra's head and body altogether.

What the story of the Hydra foretells is that resistance to, or the slaying of, the Hydra will not be addressed through incremental policy changes, piece-meal reforms, or charitable giving by well-intentioned nonprofits. Rather, transformative change will require a coupling of policy/institutional work to social movements. Social movements are a vital social form where groups of people, or collectives, "give voice to concerns about the rights, welfare, and well-being of themselves and others by engaging in different forms of collective action and public protest" (University of California, Santa Barbara, Sociology, n.d.).

What the myth of the Hydra clarifies is that collective analysis and struggle are necessary in documenting how oppression works, articulating alternative perspectives on how the world should be, and taking actions that would improve the well-being of not just ourselves but those who are disproportionately harmed by structural inequality.

Since 2010 NYCoRE has used its meetings and political actions as generative spaces where members have an opportunity to discuss and analyze our social conditions and move toward taking individual and collective action in classrooms, in schools, in policy, and in the streets. It is NYCoRE's belief that by expanding collaborative struggles while maintaining a clear and compelling political analysis, the Hydra will eventually be slayed. Through the metaphor of the Hydra and this organizing work, NYCoRE has arrived at the following question: How might NYCoRE and others who are part of the educational justice movement develop a shared political analysis to defeat the Hydra of racialized neoliberal education reform?

It is in response to this question that *What's Race Got to Do With It* was formulated. It is also a rationale for why we asked authors to share and discuss potential and existing forms of resistance to their particular head of the Hydra and/or the Hydra as a whole. The chapter authors have come together to ask questions and generate answers and analyses of those questions. But asking those questions and analyzing research is only half the battle. Drawing on those analyses to inform action is what comes next. In education research, descriptions of social action are often missing from texts. Ironically, it is samples of action that are the pieces of research that readers are often most interested in learning from. In this book is analysis from an inspiring group of scholar activists who are not only writing and theorizing justice but also actually engaging with it every day in their localities. To ask them to document and analyze oppression and despair without providing examples of resistance and hope would have been a disservice to them and to the reader.

To us, this book and each chapter serves two purposes. First, this book and its chapters can serve as a guide to action. We encourage readers to facilitate these forms of inquiry to action in their own communities and across communities to slay the larger Hydra. Second, the book can remind people "the struggle for justice does not end when the school bell rings" (NYCoRE, 2002). The work of the scholar activist and teacher activist is daunting because it does not end when we leave our place of teaching or work. By providing the reader with artifacts of resistance, written by scholar activists, we want the reader to see that this work is about a deep love of humanity and seeing embers of hope glow ever brighter because of collective struggle.

Summary of Chapters

The first chapter of the book opens with an examination of high-stakes testing, a reform that in some ways serves as the lynchpin and justification for the others that follow. As NYCoRE activist Rosie Frascella stated at a rally against the punitive impact of testing, "Racism and privatization are destroying our schools, and standardized tests are the weapon." In this first chapter, **Wayne Au** traces how standardized testing has become the central tool for measuring education in the United States over the last 100 years. His chapter offers an overview of key concepts about high-stakes testing, provides a brief, modern-day history of high-stakes testing in education policy—including how our modern-day testing has roots in the racism of IQ testing and the eugenics movement—and reviews research evidence showing the disparate impacts of high-stakes testing on students of Color specifically. Using these lenses, Au argues that high-stakes, standardized testing operates as tool for the maintenance of White supremacy. Concluding with a brief description of the kinds of resistance building against high-stakes testing generally, Au also illuminates the White supremacist impulses embedded so deeply within the tests.

While the results of these tests continue to justify educational policy decisions, corresponding shifts in governance consolidate power in ways that decimate democratic local control. **David Stovall**'s chapter articulates a theoretical and praxis-oriented analysis of the realities of mayoral control through the broader ideology of Whiteness and the current project of neoliberal school reform. To understand mayoral control as ideology and policy, Stovall uses critical race theory (CRT) to gain a further understanding of its function as hegemonic machination of the state. Instead of resting solely on analytical critique of mayoral control, his contribution concludes with tangible examples of community opposition that has the potential for substantive change in the current landscape of city and educational politics.

Facilitated by the kinds of power consolidation described by Stovall, **Pauline Lipman**'s chapter that follows sheds light on one of the most formidable neoliberal reforms under mayoral control: school closings. Lipman situates school closings in the neoliberal and racial logics that drive the restructuring of public education in the United States. She argues that closing schools in communities of Color is a racialized policy of state abandonment that facilitates capital accumulation by dispossession. Racial ideologies and histories of White supremacy are central to this process. Yet, Lipman shows us that closing public schools is just one strategy of a shifting process of neoliberal experimentation. Thus, she argues for transformational education politics that incorporates opposition to school closings and other neoliberal strategies in a larger challenge to the underlying capitalist and racial logics that are remaking public education and cities. She concludes with the promise of an emergent grassroots movement and alternative agenda that centers the knowledge and experiences of parents, students, and communities of Color in strategies of school transformation and targets both corporate privatization and racial oppression.

Central to the project of power consolidation and closing schools is the ongoing corporate attack on teacher unions. While others have focused on the need for unions as one of the only united forces broad enough to push back against the privatization agenda, **Brian Jones**'s chapter sheds light on an often overlooked component of this attack: the impact on Black wealth and political power. He highlights a two-fold paradox of contemporary education reform, the first of which is that corporate reformers cast themselves as antiracist and antipoverty champions of Black youth while undermining trade unions that are a historic source of Black wealth and political power. The paradox only deepens when we notice that their attacks on teacher unions fall disproportionately on Black teachers. The second paradox Jones illuminates is that although Black teachers are, in many cities, being displaced by White teachers, White teachers are not the ultimate beneficiaries of this process. Jones argues that the attacks on Black teachers will have negative consequences for all teachers and for working people as a whole. In fact, Jones concludes that the faux "antiracism" of corporate education reform will ultimately benefit elites: politicians, business owners, ed-profiteers and some upwardly mobile middle-class professionals.

Using a historical lens to help trace the pathway that set contemporary reforms in motion, **Ujju Aggarwal** provides a critical genealogy of choice as a key principle of reform and management in education that emerged in the post-*Brown v. Board of Education* era. This genealogy illuminates that neoliberal restructuring dates back further than the 1980s, and can be understood as emerging in tandem with the Civil Rights Movement. By extending this timeline, Aggarwal illuminates that neoliberal restructuring in the United States is organized through race and is not reliant upon privatization mechanisms alone. Brown signified a moment when universal rights to education were won, thus indicating a different structure of citizenship than Jim Crow. However, Aggarwal argues, how universal rights were structured (as individual choices) became critical to understanding how the continuity of a tiered citizenship was both guaranteed and embedded within the capitalist state.

With the concept of choice now seamlessly embedded in mainstream ideology about educational "improvement," we have seen the expansion of charter schools and other reforms that frame quasi-private options as civil rights opportunities. **Terrenda White**'s chapter uses critical theories of Whiteness to understand proliferations of particular kinds of charter schools in urban communities of Color, such as No Excuses charter schools and charter schools with franchised models of private management and organization. As these schools have increasingly out-paced community-based charter schools in urban neighborhoods, it is unclear the racial and cultural significance of these shifts and its impact on everyday school practices. Using observations and interviews with regional directors, school leaders, and teachers in a charter school in New York City, White illustrates the ways in which Whiteness operates as a structuring force that shapes school norms, expectations, and practices. In doing so, readers will be able to identify what is at stake for teaching and learning of Black and Latino/a children whose schools have shifted drastically in light of market-oriented policies emphasizing choice and competition.

In keeping with Terrenda White's analysis that highlights how race and neoliberal reforms are experienced daily in schools, **Amy Brown**'s chapter also peeks inside a New York City School to examine the way that the dependence of current reforms on private dollars racializes relationships both inside and outside of schools. Based on two years of ethnographic teacher research at College Prep, a small, traditional public, New York City high school, Brown documents the ways in which the lived experience of privatization in urban education rearticulates race, class, and gender inequalities. Her findings at College Prep demonstrate a clear relation between philanthrocapitalism, White supremacy, and economic inequity. By tracing a brief history of what Ealy (2014) calls the "problem industrial complex," Brown connects this to a racialized political economy of education in New York City under former Mayor Michael Bloomberg. Through describing College Prep, and analyzing its relationship to funders, she demonstrates how the problem industrial complex intersects with the experience of College Prep teachers and students, concluding with possibilities for resistance.

While the majority of chapters in this volume focus on the neoliberal educational policy in the K–12 setting, **Barbara Madeloni** reminds us that institutions of higher education are not safe from such invasions from market-driven reforms. She situates teacher education as an essential site for the development of educators with the knowledge, commitment, and reflexivity to engage in social justice education. Recently, teacher education has seen the imposition of a standard national high-stakes assessment of student teaching, in the form of edTPA. In this chapter, Madeloni argues that the edTPA severely limits the possibilities for teacher educators to engage in teacher education for social justice. As an instrument of standardization and corporate education reform, Madeloni shows how the edTPA reproduces White supremacy by narrowing our understanding of teaching to simply what is measurable rather than the work that it truly is: complex, uncertain, and emerging within human relationships.

We end the book with *artifacts of resistance* to complement the set of examples of struggles for justice that are discussed throughout the book. They are the visual representations of action taken by the educators and youth doing this work every day. First there is a speech by **Asean Johnson** from when he was nine years old in 2013 in Chicago, Illinois. Asean has become a nationally prominent speaker against various aspects of racist neoliberal school reform in Chicago and beyond. His reprinted speech makes clear the devastating effects of school closures. **The Dreamyard Action Project** is a New York City–based youth organization, and their 10-point platform, modeled after the Black Panthers, was a critical response to the impact of mayoral control in their city. **The Teacher Activist Group (TAG)** platform provides a national scale response to current school reform. TAG is a network of educator-activist groups from different parts of the country, and of which NYCoRE is a member. The platform is an articulation of what these local organizations, collectively, believe to be the foundation for a just educational system for all youth, families, and educators. Finally, we have images and documents from the **Stand-Up-Opt-Out campaign** organized by the Prospect International High School in Brooklyn, New York. The teachers at the high school refused to administer state exams to their students who are all newly arrived immigrants and were set up to fail by this exam.

Collectively, these *artifacts of resistance* are a glimpse at the growing demands for educational and social justice that are emerging across the country, and of what Jean Anyon (2005, 2014) described as "radical possibilities." For Anyon the production of economic justice and just schools required the envisioning of another world and doing the collective work needed to make those visions a reality. Anyon (2005) wrote, "[i]f those of us who are angry about injustice can recapture this revolutionary spirit of democracy, and if we can act on it together, then we may be able to create a force powerful enough to produce economic justice and real, long-term school reform in America's cities" (p. 200). These artifacts, and chapters, are a testament to both the anger felt by many about the oppressive conditions in which education is situated, and the power of coming together to create change. We hope the book not only provides the reader an opportunity to deepen his or her thinking on what race has to do with these issues but also the inspiration to take part in the struggle for justice.

References

Aggarwal, U., & Mayorga, E. (in press). From forgotten to fought over: Neoliberal restructuring, public schools, and urban space. *The Scholar & Feminist Online*. Retrieved from http://bcrw.barnard.edu/publication-sections/sf-online/

Anyon, J. (2005). *Radical possibilities: Public policy, urban education, and a new social movement*. New York: Routledge.

Anyon, J. (2009). Progressive social movements and educational equity. *Educational Policy, 23*(1), 194–215.

Anyon, J. (2014). *Radical possibilities: Public policy, urban education, and a new social movement* (2nd ed.). New York: Routledge.

Apple, M. (1996). Power, meaning, and identity: Critical sociology of education in the United States. *British Journal of Sociology of Education, 17*(2), 125–144.

Apple, M. (2001). Comparing neo-liberal projects and inequality in education. *Comparative Education, 37*(4), 409–423.

Apple, M., & Aasen, P. (2003). *The state and the politics of knowledge*. New York: Routledge.

Buras, K. L. (2011). Race, charter schools, and conscious capitalism: On the spatial politics of whiteness as property (and the unconscionable assault on black New Orleans). *Harvard Educational Review, 81*, 296–331.

Bush, M. E. L. (2004). *Breaking the code of good intentions: Everyday forms of whiteness*. Lanham, MD: Rowman & Littlefield.

Clarke, J. (2010). Of crises and conjunctures: The problem of the present. *Journal of Communication Inquiry, 34*(4), 337–354.

Compton, M. F., & Weiner, L. (2008). *The global assault on teaching, teachers, and their unions: Stories for resistance*. New York: Palgrave Macmillan.

Derman-Sparks, L., & Phillips, C. B. (1997). *Teaching/learning anti-racism: A developmental approach*. New York: Teachers College Press.

Ealy, L. T. (2014). The intellectual crisis in philanthropy. *Society, 51*(1), 87–96.

Fabricant, M., & Fine, M. (2012). *Charter schools and the corporate makeover of public education: What's at stake?* New York: Teachers College Press.

Fabricant, M., & Fine, M. (2013). *The changing politics of education: Privatization and the dispossessed lives left behind*. Boulder: Paradigm.

Fine, M., & Ruglis, J. (2009). Circuits and consequences of dispossession: The racialized realignment of the public sphere for U.S. youth. *Transforming Anthropology, 17*(1), 20.

Frankenberg, E. (2012). *The resegregation of suburban schools: A hidden crisis in American education*. Cambridge, MA: Harvard Education Press.

Gramsci, A., Hoare, Q., & Nowell-Smith, G. (1972). *Selections from the prison notebooks of Antonio Gramsci*. New York: International.

Hale, C. R. (2008). Introduction. In C. R. Hale (Ed.), *Engaging contradictions: Theory, politics, and methods of activist scholarship*. Berkeley: University of California Press.

Harris, C. I. (1993). Whiteness as property. *Harvard Law Review 106*(8), 1710–1712.

Harvey, D. (2006). *Spaces of global capitalism: Towards a theory of uneven geographical development*. New York: Verso.

Hursh, D. (2007). Assessing No Child Left Behind and the rise of neoliberal education policies. *American Educational Research Journal, 44*(3), 493–518.

Jensen, R. (2005). *The heart of whiteness*. San Francisco, CA: City Lights.

Kincheloe, J. L., & Steinberg, S. R. (1997). *Changing multiculturalism*. Buckingham, UK: Open University Press.

The Kirwan Institute for the Study of Race and Ethnicity. (2013). The Ford Secondary Education and Racial Justice Collaborative. Retrieved from http://kirwaninstitute. osu.edu/the-ford-secondary-education-and-racial-justice-collaborative/

Kumashiro, K. K. (2008). *The seduction of common sense: How the right has framed the debate on America's schools*. New York: Teachers College Press.

Ladson-Billings, G., & Tate IV, W. F. (1995). Towards a critical race theory of education. *Teachers College Record, 97*(1), 47–68.

Leonardo, Z. (2004). The color of supremacy: Beyond the discourse of "white privilege." *Educational Philosophy and Theory, 36*(2), 137–152.

Leonardo, Z. (2009). *Race, Whiteness, and education*. New York: Routledge.

Leonardo, Z. (2012). The race for class: Reflections on a critical raceclass theory of education. *Educational Studies: Journal of the American Educational Studies Association, 48*(5), 427–449.

Lipman, P. (2005). Educational ethnography and the politics of globalization, war, and resistance. *Anthropology and Education Quarterly, 36*, 315–328

Lipman, P. (2011). *The new political economy of urban education: Neoliberalism, race, and the right to the city*. New York: Routledge.

Lipsitz, G. (1998). *The possessive investment in whiteness: How White people profit from identity politics*. Philadelphia, PA: Temple University Press.

Lipsitz, G. (2011). *How racism takes place*. Philadelphia, PA: Temple University Press.

Lynn, M., Yosso, T. J., Solórzano, D. G., & Parker, L. (2002). Critical race theory and education: Qualitative research in the new millennium. *Qualitative Inquiry, 8*(1), 3–6.

Martinez, E. & Garcia, A. (2000, February 26). *What is "neo-liberalism?" A brief definition*. Retrieved from http://www.globalexchange.org/campaigns/econ101/neoliberalDefined.html

Melamed, J. (2011). *Represent and destroy: Rationalizing violence in the new racial capitalism*. Minneapolis: University of Minnesota Press.

NYCoRE. (2002). Mission. Retrieved from http://www.nycore.org/nycore-info/mission/

Omi, M., & Winant, H. (1994). *Racial formation in the United States: From 1960's to 1990's*. New York: Routledge.

Peck, J., & Theodore, N. (2012). Reanimating neoliberalism: Process geographies of neoliberalisation. *Social Anthropology 20*(2), 177–185.

Phelps, C. (2014, February 24). *The tyee—Trayvon's legacy: How diversity hides racism.* Retrieved from http://thetyee.ca/Opinion/2014/02/24/Trayvon-Legacy/

Picower, B. (2012). *Practice what you teach: Social justice education in the classroom and the streets.* New York: Routledge.

Ravitch, D. (2010). *The death and life of the great American school system: How testing and choice are undermining education.* New York: Basic Books.

Rich, M. (2013, March 13). Rational decisions and heartbreak on school closings. *New York Times.* Retrieved from http://www.nytimes.com

Robinson, C. J. (1983). *Black Marxism: The making of the Black radical tradition.* London: Biblio Distribution Center.

Scott, J. C. (1998). *Seeing like a state: How certain schemes to improve the human condition have failed.* New Haven, CT: Yale University Press.

Smith, N. (2002). New globalism, new urbanism: Gentrification as global urban strategy. *Antipode, 34*(3), 427–450.

Spring, J. H. (2001). *Deculturalization and the struggle for equality: A brief history of the education of dominated cultures in the United States.* Boston: McGraw-Hill.

Spring, J. H. (2004). *American education.* Boston: McGraw-Hill.

Stovall, D. (2006). Forging community in race and class: Critical race theory and the quest for social justice in education. *Race Ethnicity and Education, 9*(3), 243–259.

Suzuki, D., & Mayorga, E. (2014). Scholar-activism: A twice told tale. *Multicultural Perspectives, 16*(1), 16–20.

Tabb, W. K. (2001). *The amoral elephant: Globalization and the struggle for social justice in the twenty-first century.* New York: Monthly Review Press.

Trouillot, M. (2001). The anthropology of the state in the age of globalization: Close encounters of the deceptive kind. *Current Anthropology, 42*(1), 125–138.

Tyack, D. B. (1974). *The one best system: A history of American urban education.* Cambridge, MA: Harvard University Press.

University of California, Santa Barbara, Sociology, (n.d.). *Social movements, revolutions & social change.* Retrieved from http://www.soc.ucsb.edu/research/social-movements-revolutions-social-change

Watkins, W. H. (Ed.). (2012). *The assault on public education: Confronting the politics of corporate school reform.* New York: Teachers College Press.

Note

1. www.fserjc.org/
2. The "state" refers to the constellation of processes, power relationships, and institutions that give shape to the formation of society. As such the state is a site through which power is distributed and fought over in relation to the society (See Apple & Aasen, 2003; Gramsci, Hoare, & Nowell-Smith, 1972; Scott, 1998; Trouillot, 2001.)

1. High-Stakes Testing: A Tool for White Supremacy for Over 100 Years

Wayne Au

Educators first began applying standardized testing to school children as early as 1848, but it was not until the early 1900s that such testing developed into a widespread tool for measuring students, teachers, and people more generally in the United States. Given the ubiquity of testing in education policy and practice today, it is critical to understand that when we look at standardized testing historically and how it is used as the central mechanism for accountability within education policy, high-stakes, standardized testing has operated as tool for the maintenance of White supremacy in the United States.[1]

In order to get to this understanding, in this chapter I first offer a basic overview of key concepts about high-stakes testing and then provide a brief, modern day history of high-stakes testing in education policy. I then follow with how our modern day testing has roots in the racism of I.Q. testing and the eugenics movement around the turn of the 20th century and continue with how such testing was introduced into education in the United States, including the ways that these tests support White supremacy through the guise of offering individual inequality and "objective" measures of students. I then give an overview of the research evidence showing the disparate impacts of high-stakes testing on students of Color specifically, and I conclude this chapter with a brief description of the kinds of resistance building against high-stakes testing generally, as well as the White supremacists impulses embedded so deeply within the tests.

Testing, the Basics

In the most basic terms a standardized test is any test that is developed, administered, and scored in a systematic, standardized manner. There are two general kinds of standardized tests: *norm referenced* and *criterion referenced*. A norm referenced standardized test compares one student's test score to other students taking the same test, essentially comparing how individuals scored relative to the average across all test takers (the norm). A criterion referenced standardized test measures a student's score against a set "criteria" of subject matter knowledge (Popham, 2001). Most standardized tests given in U.S. schools are now "high-stakes" tests in that students' scores are used to determine rewards and sanctions for students, teachers, principals, schools, and school districts. Standardized tests are also high-stakes because many test scores are published and shared with the public, making students, teachers, principals, and schools feel the weight of public pressure regarding student test performance, regardless of the actual complexity behind the scores (McNeil, 2000).

Our modern era of education policy wrapped around high-stakes testing began with the 1983 publication of the Reagan Administration's report on education, *A Nation at Risk: The Imperative for Education Reform* (National Commission on Excellence in Education, 1983). This alarmist report decried the poor quality of education in the United States. Even though much of the data used in *A Nation at Risk* was easily debunked (Berliner & Biddle, 1995), within a year of its release, 45 state level commissions on education were created and 26 states raised graduation requirements. By 1994 45 states implemented statewide, standardized tests for grades K–5. U.S. President George H. W. Bush, in conjunction with state governors, developed the groundwork for his America 2000 plan—focusing on testing and establishing "world class standards" in schools. U.S. President Bill Clinton and Vice President Al Gore committed themselves to following through on George H. W. Bush's plan, including a vocal commitment to pursuing a national examination system to meet new standards. By the year 2000, every U.S. state but Iowa administered a mandated, high-stakes, standardized test (Kornhaber & Orfield, 2001).

In 2001 President G. W. Bush advocated for federal education funding to be tied to test scores, and in 2002, the U.S. government passed the No Child Left Behind Act (NCLB) into law. NCLB notably required all students be tested in reading and math in grades 3–8 and once in high school, with future provisions that students be tested at least once at the elementary, middle, and high school levels in science. According to NCLB, if student standardized test scores did not meet stated goals for test score growth, schools faced penalties such as a loss of federal funding or the diversion of federal funds to pay for private tutoring, transportation costs, and other services (Karp, 2006). Upon taking office, President Obama selected Arne Duncan to lead the Department of Education and implemented the federal Race to the Top program, which included monies for more testing as part of a broader education reform package promoting the use of tests to evaluate teachers, attacks on teachers unions' right to collective bargaining, and the proliferation of charter schools (Kumashiro, 2012). Simultaneously, and as part of the Race to the Top agenda, national standards connected to high-stakes, standardized tests were developed as part of the Common Core State Standards as well (Karp, 2013, 2014).

Within the current context, high-stakes standardized tests function as the core for all education policy. From charter schools, to "value added measurement" and "student growth models" for teacher evaluation, to challenges to teacher tenure and collective bargaining, to school closings, to the use of undertrained and inexperienced Teach For America recruits in high needs and low needs schools, to the implementation of the Common Core national standards and tests, every current major educational initiative revolves around justifications associated with how different populations of students perform on high-stakes, standardized tests. These tests produce the data upon which important decisions about students, teachers, administrators, and schools are being made (Au, 2013). The centrality of high-stakes, standardized testing is the reason that it is important to understand their inherent racism and their role in enforcing White supremacy within the United States both historically and today.

A Brief History of High-Stakes Testing and White Supremacy in the United States

The origins of the use of standardized testing to assess and study large populations in the United States can be traced directly back to I.Q. testing and the eugenics movement of the early 1900s. Importing and distorting the work of French psychologist Alfred Binet, who developed the concept of "intelligence quotient," or I.Q., U.S. psychologists distorted Binet's original conception and use of I.Q. by injecting their own underlying presumptions about humans and human ability into their interpretations of test results (Au, 2009; Gould, 1996). For instance, as a psychologist and U.S. Army colonel in charge of the mental testing of 1.75 million recruits during World War I, in 1917 Robert Yerkes worked with Henry Goddard, Lewis Terman, and others to develop the Alpha and Beta Army standardized tests to sort incoming soldiers according to their "mental fitness." These cognitive scientists drew several dubious conclusions using this large pool of army recruit data, including that the intelligence of European immigrants could be judged according to their country of origin: The darker peoples of eastern and southern Europe were less intelligent than their fairer-skinned, western and northern European counterparts. They also asserted that, based on their test results, African Americans were the least intelligent of all peoples (Giordano, 2005). As Karier (1972) explains:

> Designing the Stanford-Binet intelligence test, Terman developed questions which were based on presumed progressive difficulty in performing tasks which he believed were necessary for achievement in ascending the hierarchical occupational structure. He then proceeded to find that according to the results of his tests the intelligence of different occupational classes fit his ascending hierarchy. It was little wonder that I.Q. reflected social class bias. It was, in fact, based on the social class order. (pp. 163–164)

With the authority granted by the supposedly "scientific findings" of these psychologists, eugenicists—who believed in the genetic basis for behavioral and character traits they associated with gender, race, national and class difference—rallied around the idea that race mixing was spreading the alleged inferior intelligence genes of African Americans, other non-White peoples, and immigrants (Selden, 1999). In this way, these early standardized tests clearly operated as a tool in the maintenance of White supremacy in the United States because they provided supposedly "scientific" evidence to claims of White superiority.

Such standardized testing, which proved so useful as a technology for sorting people efficiently by race and class under the justification of pseudoscience, and a well established White supremacist socio-political order, quickly moved into public education in the United States. As Tyack (1974) explains:

> Intelligence testing and other forms of measurement provided the technology for classifying children. Nature-nurture controversies might pepper the scientific periodicals and magazines of the intelligentsia, but schoolmen found IQ tests invaluable means of channeling children; by the very act of channeling pupils, they helped to make IQ prophecies self-fulfilling. (p. 180)

Then a Stanford University professor of psychology, and under the sponsorship of the National Academy of Sciences, the above-mentioned Lewis Terman played a key role in adapting the army tests into the National Intelligence Tests for schoolchildren in 1919, and by 1920 over 400,000 copies of these tests had been sold nationwide. Terman and others also created the Stanford Achievement Test in 1922, and by late 1925, he reported sales of this test to be near 1.5 million copies. Surveys in 1925, 1926, and 1932 found that the majority of cities in the U.S. with populations over 10,000 people were using these tests to classify and sort students in to ability groups in their schools (Chapman, 1988; Haney, 1984). As Karier (1972) explains:

> It was men like Thorndike, Terman and Goddard, supported by corporate wealth, who successfully persuaded teachers, administrators and lay school boards to classify and standardize the school's curriculum with a differentiated track system based on ability and values of the corporate liberal society. (p. 166)

Indeed, Karier's (1972) analysis highlights a disturbing parallel for today's context. Much in the same way that the Gates, Broad, and Walton Foundations, among others, influence education policy and reform in contemporary times (Barkan, 2011, 2012), Karier (1972) points out that:

> From the very beginning of the century, the new philanthropic endeavors of corporate wealth were directed at influencing the course of educational policy. John D. Rockefeller's General Education Board, which received its national charter in 1903, greatly influenced and shaped educational policy for Black America in the South, while the Carnegie Institute of Washington (1904) and the Carnegie Foundation for the Advancement of Teaching (1906) came to play a major role in shaping educational policy in both the South and the North. (p. 157)

These foundations were directly responsible for supporting the then-burgeoning movement for mass, standardized testing, and ironically the "values of the corporate and liberal society" to which Karier (1972, p. 166) refers, speaks to the ways that standardized testing was seen as a key to liberal notions of individual equality. These notions of individual equality and merit-based success based on hard work are deeply intertwined within the logics of standardized testing in the support of maintaining White supremacy, a topic I take up in the following section.

Standardized Testing, Meritocracy, and Whiteness

In what follows, I trace some of the critical, foundational logics that undergird high-stakes, standardized testing and its conceptual link to White supremacy through the ideology of meritocracy and the idea of aptitude. I begin here with a discussion of the ideology of meritocracy and its connection to the presumed objectivity of the tests. Using the SAT as an example, I then address how, despite explicitly race-neutral processes for test development, racism and White supremacy are embedded into the structures of such tests. I follow by discussing the strong correlation between the structural inequalities (e.g., poverty) in the lives of students of Color with educational achievement, test scores included, and I conclude this section by explaining how the rational logics of standardized tests functionally require failure of student populations—particularly populations under the duress of structural racism and White supremacy in their daily lives.

One of the key assumptions undergirding the use of standardized tests to measure, sort and rank students is the idea that these tests are measuring students objectively and accurately—for if the tests are objective, then they truly are assessing the individual merits of students. In turn the individual students who have worked the hardest and who have the most merit will rise to the top compared to their peers. This idea, that individual merit through hard work is what creates opportunity and success, is referred to as the idea of "meritocracy" (Lemann, 1999).

Despite producing clearly racist and classist outcomes, early standardized testing in the United States was viewed as providing a completely objective and value free measurement of human intelligence and ability (Au, 2009). This view of testing-as-objective-measurement has positioned these tests in a seemingly contradictory way: Despite the historical and structural inequality associated with the tests' outcomes, early advocates of standardized testing saw these tests as a means of challenging class privilege because they thought the tests were providing neutral, unbiased, and objective measures of individual effort and merit (Sacks, 1999). Under the assumption that standardized tests provide fair and objective measurement of individuals, such testing seemingly held the promise that every test taker is offered a fair and equal shot at educational, social, and economic achievement. The byproduct of this assumption was the masking of the racism and White supremacy that lay at the foundation of such testing at its outset. As Moore (2005) suggests,

> In terms of race, we assume that who is tested, what is tested, and how tests are administered and interpreted have all been bathed by neutrality through "testing conditions" that include sterile classrooms, "expert" test givers, and the use of inanimate computers and "color blind" standards. (p. 184)

The ideology of meritocracy undergirding the use of standardized tests effectively conceals structural inequalities associated with racism and White supremacy under the cover of "naturally" occurring aptitude among individuals (Bisseret, 1979).

Vis-à-vis the ideology of meritocracy, the low achievement on standardized tests of non-Whites (as well as working class people and some immigrant groups) can then be simply and neatly attributed to the failure of individual students, individual groups, or individual cultures, and not attributed to existing structural inequalities that support White supremacy. Even the SAT, as Hartman (2007) explains,

> ...failed to stray from past definitions of what it meant to be American. Sure, after the implementation of the SAT Blacks and other peripheral groups were able to gaze upon increased opportunity. But this gaze was merely an apparition

for most. The SAT, consistent with other integration projects, did not accommodate Black or female identities—in this case, differing learning styles. In order for a more fully integrated society to emerge from the SAT, the onus was placed upon Blacks to accommodate to American identity. The SAT further entrenched a seemingly elusive White identity as the de facto American identity. (p. 143)

In this sense the standardized tests operate as a tool of White supremacy simply because they make racist outcomes of the tests appear as a product of the way the world works objectively and naturally—they "scientifically" justify the existing racial order, and they do so within a false promise of measuring individuals equally.

A more modern look at research on the SAT illustrates how the "science" behind standardized test development can functionally hide White supremacist outcomes. Kidder and Rosner's (2002–2003) study of SAT questions finds significant White supremacist bias deep within the structure of test construction itself. In a study of over 300,000 SAT test takers, Kidder and Rosner examined the percentages of questions that Black, White, and Chicano (Mexican American) students answered correctly. Using calculations of average scores on each question by racial group, Kidder and Rosner determined what they called the "racial impact" of each test score question. For instance, if 50% of Whites and 30% of African Americans answered a particular SAT question correctly, the researchers assigned the question a 20% Black-White impact.

In their study, Kidder and Rosner (2002–2003) found that, "African Americans and Chicanos did not outperform Whites on any of the seventy-eight Verbal and sixty Math questions" (p. 148). Whites correctly answered 59.8% of the Verbal questions on average and African Americans correctly answered 46.4% of the Verbal on average, resulting in an overall 13.4% Black-White impact. Additionally Chicanos correctly answered Verbal test items at an average of 48.7%, giving an 11.1% Chicano-White impact. On Math questions Whites had an overall 58.4% correct answer rate, and African Americans had a 42% correct answer rate, giving an average disparate impact of 16.4%. Almost three out of ten Math questions averaged a 20% disparate impact between Whites and other groups. The average Chicano correct answer rate for Math questions was 46.5%, establishing an 11.9% Chicano-White impact.

Kidder and Rosner (2002–2003) find an explanation for these disparate test scores within the structure of the test design itself. The Educational Testing Service (ETS), who traditionally developed and administered the SAT at the time of the study, establishes statistically valid questions by using one section of the test as an experimental section, essentially trying out questions for possible use on future SATs. Based on the responses on the experimental test items, the SAT designers then make decisions to either keep a question and use it in the regular sections of future tests or discard it as an unusable, "invalid" test item. Kidder and Rosner compared some of the regular test items with the experimental ones and found an important pattern. For example, on one Verbal test item of medium difficulty, 62% of Whites and 38% of African Americans answered it correctly (for a 24% disparate impact). This question was a test item from one of the regular, non-experimental test sections. By comparison, an item of similar difficulty used in the experimental test section resulted in African Americans outperforming White students by 8% (that is, 8% more African American students answered the question correctly than White students). Test designers determined that this question, where African Americans scored higher than whites, was invalid and was not included in future SATs. The reason for this was that the students who statistically on average score higher on the SAT did not answer this question correctly enough of the time, while those who statistically on average score lower on the SAT answered this question correctly too often. Rosner (2003) explains this process of psychometrically reinforced racism:

> Each individual SAT question ETS chooses is required to parallel outcomes of the test overall. So, if high-scoring test takers—who are more likely to be white—tend to answer the question correctly in [experimental] pretesting, it's a worthy SAT question; if not, it's thrown out. Race and ethnicity are not considered explicitly, but racially disparate scores drive question selection, which in turn reproduces racially disparate test results in an internally reinforcing cycle. (p. 24)

At issue is the fact that statistically on average, White students outperform Black students on the SAT. Higher-scoring students, who statistically tend to be White, correctly answer SAT experimental test questions at higher rates than typically lower scoring students, who tend to be non-White, ensuring that the test question selection process itself has a self reinforcing, built-in racial bias. Couched in the language of statistical reliability and validity, the supposedly race-neutral process of test question development and determination ultimately structures in very race-biased results into the selection of the test questions themselves (Kidder & Rosner, 2002–2003), one that is arguably White supremacist in outcome regardless of the meritocratic impulses that in part defined the origin of the SAT. Further, it is worth noting that more recent research on the SAT has found other forms of racial and cultural bias built into the kinds of questions asked on the exam, where significant bias was found in the easier questions that appear earlier in the SAT test question sequence (Santelices & Wilson, 2010).

Similar to the SAT, other forms of modern day high-stakes, standardized testing have also proven not to be the paragons of meritocracy and have instead proven to recreate race and class based inequality. As Berliner (2012) explains, test scores in the U.S. are more determined by structural conditions affecting students than individual effort:

> Virtually every scholar of teaching and schooling knows that when the variance in student scores on achievement tests is examined along with the many potential factors that may have contributed to those test scores, school effects account for about 20% of the variation in achievement test scores...
>
> On the other hand, out-of-school variables account for about 60% of the variance that can be accounted for in student achievement. In aggregate, such factors as family income; the neighborhood's sense of collective efficacy, violence rate, and average income; medical and dental care available and used; level of food insecurity; number of moves a family makes over the course of a child's school years;... provision of high-quality early education in the neighborhood; language spoken at home; and so forth, all substantially affect school achievement. (n.p.)

While school does remain important, socio-economic factors outside of school—factors themselves that disproportionately impact communities of Color—simply have an overwhelming effect on educational achievement. However, this reality is effectively masked by the ideology of meritocracy embedded in high-stakes testing in the United States (Au, 2009).

The meritocratic assumptions of high-stakes testing in the United States are also belied by many of the logics that underpin the tests themselves. For instance, akin to systems of capitalist economics, systems of accountability built upon high-stakes, standardized testing cannot function if everyone is a "winner"—for both ideological and technological reasons. Ideologically, if everyone passed the tests there simply would be no way to justify elite status for any particular group: Every student would qualify for the most elite colleges and jobs, thereby rendering the very hierarchy of elitism obsolete. A high-stakes, standardized test that everyone passed would then function to challenge White supremacy, not maintain it. Additionally, and technically speaking, in order to remain statistically valid standardized tests generally require that some portion of students fail the test (Popham, 2001).

These ideological and technical points are critical for understanding how high-stakes testing fits into the discourse about race and class issues in the current education reform movement in the United States, which relies explicitly on the rhetorical goal of closing racial and economic achievement gaps in test scores (Ladson-Billings, 2006). There is a great irony within this discourse of framing education reform around the closing of test-based achievement gaps. Because the ways standardized tests require some amount of failure, closing the achievement gap does not mean having everyone be successful on high-stakes, standardized tests. Rather, closing the achievement gap actually means having proportional rates of failure and success amongst different groups. If education in the United States closed the high-stakes test score achievement gap among different groups it would simply mean that equal numbers of rich kids and poor kids pass and fail, equal numbers of White kids and African American kids pass and fail, etc. (Au & Gourd, 2013). Closing racial achievement gaps in high-stakes testing does not mean making sure all kids pass the tests, it simply means creating a racially proportionate underclass of students failing the tests.

White Supremacist Impact of Modern Day High-Stakes Testing

Up to this point in this chapter I have offered not only a history of high-stakes testing, but also an analysis of several key ways such testing operates in the maintenance of White supremacy. In the previous section I specifically highlighted how the concept of meritocracy has been coupled with the presumed objectivity of standardized tests to effectively mask structural racism and White supremacy within an explicitly race-neutral framework. In this section I turn to more empirical evidence of how high-stakes, standardized testing has a disparately negative impact on students of Color in classrooms and curriculum.

A look at the research evidence on the effects of modern day high-stakes, standardized testing on students of Color illustrates ways the tests function to support White supremacy in a variety of ways. Functionally high-stakes, standardized testing has served to support a White supremacist curriculum and classroom environment. Research has found that if a subject is not on the high-stakes test, it tends to get dropped from the curriculum that is taught in the classroom (Au, 2007). This phenomenon has a wide range of implications, but one of the critical issues that arises is that curriculum exploring issues associated with race and culture specifically is being ignored in response to the tests. Put differently, high-stakes testing evacuates multicultural, anti-racist perspectives out of the curriculum, creating a movement away from non-Whiteness toward a colorblind norm, a norm that ultimately supports Whiteness through racially disparate outcomes for students of Color (Au, 2009; Darder & Torres, 2004). Other research has found that high-stakes testing also promotes predominantly White, Eurocentric, and Western views in some U.S. states' world history, geography, and U.S. history tests (Grant, 2001). Toussaint (2000, 2001) tells the story of how, as an employee of a test scoring company, he was told to give higher scores to students who provided Eurocentric answers to test questions about Manifest Destiny and the colonization of the Americas. High-stakes, standardized tests also impose

Whiteness on teachers as well. Research has found that teachers who enter into the teaching profession with the stated goal of using multicultural, anti-racist content as a means to effectively teach the diverse students in their classrooms are giving up this goal in response to the curriculum pressures created by the tests (Agee, 2004). Since multicultural, anti-racist perspectives and content are not deemed legitimate by the tests, the end result is that within the high-stakes testing environment, multicultural, diverse, and non-White perspectives and content are being increasingly excluded from the classroom, thus acting as a tool for the maintenance of White supremacy.

The White supremacist curriculum enforced by high-stakes testing directly and negatively impacts students of Color. Research tells us that students learn best when they can connect themselves, their identities, their lives, and their experiences to their learning. This has proven to be true for students of Color in particular, especially those historically underserved by our school system: Curriculum that connects to students' cultures and identities fosters deeper connection to concepts and learning, and can lead to more academic success (Cabrera, Milem, & Marx, 2012; Romero, Arce, & Cammarota, 2009; Valenzuela, 1999). By legitimizing Whiteness through the delegitimization of non-Whiteness in curriculum and classroom environments, high-stakes tests explicitly include and exclude certain student identities in schools. Put differently, because high-stakes tests force schools to adopt a standardized, non-multicultural curriculum that structurally enforce norms of Whiteness, it ultimately silences the cultures and voices of children of Color, particularly if those voices, cultures, and experiences are not contained on the tests. High-stakes testing thus requires non-Whiteness to be subtracted from the curriculum (McNeil, 2000; Valenzuela, 1999) because of its emphasis on the standardization of a norm that enforces Whiteness. Indeed, diversity itself has become a threat to survival and success within the systems of high-stakes testing because it is antithetical to the process of standardization and challenges the Whiteness communicated within what is considered the "norm."

The White supremacy of high-stakes, standardized testing also manifests at the level of education policy implementation. At the state level the pressures of high-stakes, standardized testing are greatest in states with large, diverse populations of non-White students (Nichols & Berliner, 2005), and at the classroom and school level the narrowing of the curriculum is most drastic in schools with large populations of non-White students. For instance, the Center for Education Policy (Rentner et al., 2006) found that 97% of high-poverty school districts, which are largely populated by diverse groups of non-White students, have instituted policies specifically aimed at increasing time spent on reading. This is compared to only 55% to 59% of wealthier,

Whiter districts. In this way, high-stakes testing has produced more restrictive, less rich educational environments for non-White students.

Further, high-stakes, standardized test scores are increasingly being used as part of the decision-making for school closures in the United States, and these closures have disproportionately impacted communities of Color. For instance, according to the National Opportunity to Learn Campaign (2013), the population of the 54 public schools to be closed in Chicago in 2013 was 88% African American and 94% low income. In New York City, the population of the 26 public schools to be closed was 97% African American and Latino, and 82% low income, and in Philadelphia the 23 schools to be closed were 96% African American and Latino and 93% low income. School closings, as part of an extension of the use of standardized test scores to make high-stakes educational decisions, clearly function in a way that support institutionalized racism against working class Black and Brown kids.

High-Stakes Testing, Discipline, and the Schools-to-Prisons Pipeline

High-stakes, standardized testing also works within a system of education policy that seeks to discipline those who do not "fit" within the norms, and this too also works in the interest of White supremacy. High-stakes tests establish criteria through which those with power can define "failure" (transgression from the norm) and "success" (conformity to the norm), and then use those designations to rank students, teachers, schools, states, and countries. This enables the surveillance of those who do not "fit" within certain test-defined boundaries of success. This ever increasing web of surveillance (Hanson, 2000) works, in part, because categorically defined deficiencies, according to Lipman (2004), are made "visible, individual, easily measured, and highly stigmatized within a hierarchical system of authority and supervision" (p. 176).

The use of high-stakes, standardized tests as a tool to discipline through the evaluation and ranking of students, teachers, schools, and administrators enforces White supremacy in a very concrete way as well: It directly contributes to the schools-to-prisons pipeline. This happens along two pathways. The first is in the kind of school culture fostered by using high-stakes, standardized tests to evaluate teachers and students. Functionally such testing promotes a school culture of discipline and punishment (Foucault, 1995). Students and teachers are in essence surveilled by the tests, and when they step out of line by not performing well, they are punished. In this sense, within a high-stakes testing environment, teaching and learning are done under constant threat and fear. Not only are threat and fear not conducive to learning, such conditions also acculturate students to accepting more prison-like school culture. Further, this overall view of test-defined success and failure functionally pathologizes those who fail, and as I have discussed at length here, working class communities of Color have had persistently lower test scores historically. Thus, as Ekoh (2012) explains, this pathologizing of students and failure relates directly to the systematic functioning of institutions:

> If unable to thrive within the confines of the system, they [students] are pathologized and condemned as incompetent and lazy, for its not the system that fails them, but they, that fail the system. As such they must be re-made "healthy" and "reintegrated" into the oppressive status quo. Healthy, in this context referring to the state of mind that results when one has been successfully disciplined and "indoctrinated" into the dominant and oppressive system in such a way as to loose one's critical consciousness...(pp. 70–71)

Ekoh's point is critical for understanding the racial and racist relations I am attempting to pinpoint in my discussion here. The pathologizing and condemning of some groups within a system (in this case, education and schooling) simultaneously requires that other groups be deemed healthy and acceptable within that same system. Thus, if low income students of Color are pathologized, it is not simply a matter that White students are left to navigate a level or neutral educational playing field. Instead I'm suggesting that, in their function of supporting White supremacy, high-stakes standardized test also provide a pathway to success for affluence and Whiteness at the cost of the failure of low income students of Color. The system of testing is fundamentally structured not to support test-defined "success" for all, and instead requires the failure of some to prove the worthiness of others. The tests' role in this type of differentiation, or "distinction" in Bourdieu's (1984) terms, is illustrated by research that has found that high-stakes, standardized testing can contribute directly to the actual imprisonment of students of Color: A study by the National Bureau of Economic Research (Baker & Lang, 2013) found that standards-based high school exit exams increase the rate of incarceration by 12.5%. Put differently, kids who fail the exit exams (who are disproportionately non-White) have their options in life greatly limited, and one of the end results is a 12.5% increase in the chances that they might end up as a part of the criminal justice system. As this study illustrates, students who fail tests have opportunity taken away while passing students are allowed more opportunity. Given the racist and White supremacist functioning of the tests, this allows us to see how the tests are not neutral, and instead are an integral part of a system that supports affluent, White success.

Who's Benefitting From Testing?

A critical question to ask of all policies is, "Who benefits?" (Brantlinger, 2006). As I have argued in this chapter, the short answer is "Whiteness" and by extension, White people, if for no other reason than the role that high-stakes, standardized testing selectively supports the upward mobility of affluent White folks over others. However, there is another, very concrete answer to the question of, "Who benefits from the implementation of high-stakes testing?" According to the National Center for Educational Statistics (2013), the total expenditures for all education in the United States (public and private, from prekindergarten through graduate school) were estimated to be $1.2 trillion for the 2011–2012 school year, with U.S. elementary and secondary school expenditures being $700 billion of that total.

Free-market loving, corporate education reformers are very excited about the possibility of tapping into this huge market through the delivery of tests aligned to new standards, among other profit-making opportunities (Ravitch, 2013). This profit making orientation is illustrated by Joanne Weis (2011) in Ravitch (2013), who formerly served as the director for the Obama Administration's Race to the Top initiative and is currently U.S. Secretary of Education Arne Duncan's chief of staff, when she stated:

> The development of common standards and assessments radically alters the market for innovation in curriculum and development, professional development, and formative assessments. Previously these markets operated on a state-by-state basis, and often on a district-by-district basis. But the adoption of common standards and shared assessments means that educational entrepreneurs will enjoy national markets where the best products can be taken to scale. (p. 17)

High-stakes, standardized testing is one part of the free-market education reform puzzle, and there is money to be made. In his analysis for the Brookings Institution, Chingos (2012) offers an estimate of $1.7 billion being spent nationwide on the tests alone. This number is conservative, however, because it focuses on just the cost of the tests themselves and does not account for test-aligned textbooks, technology, and professional development often devoted to specific assessments. As Cavanagh (2013) explains, one estimate for technology-based testing and offshoot technology requirements to give the tests or prepare for the tests (e.g., new computers or tablets) was $1.6 billion for the year 2011, and that number was estimated to increase by 20% for 2012. According to Cavanagh, another estimate suggests that the total market for K–12 testing in 2012 was $3.9 billion, and it was expected to increase 4–5% every year to $4.5 billion by 2014. Within this mix companies like Pearson and McGraw-Hill are profiting both in developing and selling tests themselves (including administrative services like grading, analyzing, and reporting information) but also in selling textbooks and providing other services and materials in support of test preparation (Figueroa, 2013). So when we post the question of, "Who benefits from high-stakes, standardized testing?", in addition to the maintenance of status and upward mobility of affluent Whites, we also see the testing industry having enormous benefit for educational corporations in the United States.

Resistance to High-Stakes, Standardized Testing

Despite the ubiquity and hegemony of high-stakes, standardized testing in education policy today, it is important to understand that there has always been significant resistance. This resistance, however, has taken different forms in different times, and it was early resistance that looked to challenge the White supremacy of the tests most explicitly. For instance, Mexican American and African American educators critiqued the standardized test-based eugenics and I.Q. testing movements in the United States. One of the earliest African American educators to publicly challenge the findings of prominent psychologists involved in the I.Q. testing and eugenics movements was Horace Mann Bond, the director of the School of Education at Langston University in Oklahoma. In 1924 Bond critiqued I.Q. testing and eugenics in *Crisis,* the magazine of the National Association for the Advancement of Colored People (Au, 2009). George Sanchez (1940) argued about the racial bias in testing relative to Mexican American students in New Mexico, and in 1940, W. E. B. Du Bois, as quoted in Guthrie (1998), also recalled:

> It was not until I was long out of school and indeed after the (first) World War that there came the hurried use of the new technique of psychological tests, which were quickly adjusted so as to put black folk absolutely beyond the possibility of civilization. (p. 55)

However, this early resistance to I.Q. tests by educational leaders of Color did not prove to be enough to stop the ascendancy of standardized tests as a tool of White supremacy in the United States.

More recently there has been a surge of resistance to high-stakes, standardized testing, but this resistance has been more general in nature and less focused on the racism and White supremacy associated with the tests. One such organized resistance to the White supremacy of high stakes testing took place in 2003, when two community activist groups in California, Justice Matters and Youth Together, organized a campaign for the establishment of an alternative to the California High School Exit Exam (CAHSEE) for students in the Richmond School District, specifically because of the disparately racist impact of the CAHSEE on youth of Color and immigrant youth there. While the immediate campaign was unsuccessful in terms of changing policy, it was very successful at gathering students, parents, and community groups together as a coalition pushing for racial justice in California State testing (Gray-Garcia, 2012).

There have also been several individuals resisting the tests in the last decade, but this resistance has not been racially based and instead has focused on how high-stakes testing corrupts best practices for teaching and learning. In 2007 middle school teacher David Wasserman personally boycotted the Wisconsin Knowledge and Concepts Exam, but eventually gave in to district threats to his job and administered the test. In 2008 Seattle Public Schools middle school teacher Carl Chew also refused to give the Washington Assessment of Student Learning (WASL), and the district suspended him for his resistance. Juanita Doyon, a parent in Washington, also started a group, Mothers Against WASL, to organize Washington parents against what she saw as an assessment that was detrimental to education and learning. North Carolina teacher Doug Ward similarly boycotted the state test there on the grounds that it was inappropriate for students with disabilities, and he was fired for his actions (Oulahan, 2012). These smaller and individual acts of resistance, while not all "successful"—especially given the punishments resisters faced—were critical because the local and national stir created by their acts proved to be important for developing the community conversation around the broader issues of testing and educational justice.

In the last few years, however, particularly since the election of President Obama, the establishment of the Race to the Top initiative of his administration, and the implementation of the Common Core State Standards, resistance to high-stakes, standardized testing has grown exponentially. Perhaps most famously, in January 2013 all of the teachers at Seattle's Garfield High School boycotted the Measures of Academic Progress (MAP) test, causing a national wave of support both for their particular movement, but also around the problems with high-stakes testing generally. Teachers at six other Seattle public schools joined their colleagues at Garfield, and many saw this boycott as the beginning of the next wave of the movement against testing (Hagopian, 2013). While some of the leadership for the MAP test boycott clearly connected this test to the issues of racism and White supremacy (Hagopian, 2011), teachers boycotted this test for a variety of reasons not connected to race at all (Hagopian, 2013).

Indeed, 2013 saw a significant uptick in testing resistance generally. As FairTest (2013) summarizes in their report of test resistance at the time:

Students, parents and teachers engaged in boycotts, "opt-out" campaigns, and walkouts in Seattle, Portland, OR, Denver, Chicago and New York, with smaller events in other communities across the nation. Seattle teachers in several schools boycotted one test; most students, backed by their parents, did not take it when administrators gave it. Families boycotted at 40 schools in New York City and many outside the City...

Providence students staged a "zombie march," then organized a group of prominent adults to take the state graduation test, a majority of whom failed the math. Another effective action was a "play in" at Chicago Public Schools offices protesting the dozen or more standardized tests given to Kindergarten, first and second grade students. Demonstrations and rallies in New York, New Jersey, Texas, Chicago and elsewhere also garnered significant attention...

Legislative efforts took center stage in Texas, where parents led a successful charge to reduce high school end-of-course graduation tests from 15 to 5. In Minnesota, teachers unions and civil rights groups backed legislation that repealed the state's graduation exams. Bills were introduced in other states as a first step. Other concrete gains included a modest roll-back of testing in the early grades and high school in Chicago and of some Seattle tests. (n.p.)

Facebook groups of teachers fed up with testing and other aspects of the current education reform movement are growing, one of the biggest being the Badass Teachers Association (2014) which boast upwards of 38,000 supporters. Further, coalition groups of parents, teachers, and professors, like United Opt Out National (2014), are pushing to have their children "opt out" of taking the tests, much to the chagrin of administrators, officials, and policymakers. In February of 2014, for instance, an alliance of Chicago parents started a boycott of the Illinois State Achievement Test, as announced by another test resistance group, More Than a Score. This boycott launched with 500 students across 29 Chicago schools (Reid, 2014), and teachers at two Chicago public schools, Drummond Montessori and Saucedo Academy, voted as an entire faculty to boycott the same tests, despite promised reprisals from the district (Ahmed-Ullah, 2014). A collection of organizations nationally, including FairTest, Network for Public Education, Parents Across America, Save Our Schools, and United Opt Out National, along with several prominent anti-testing individuals, also launched a campaign and network called the "Testing Resistance & Reform Spring: Less Testing, More Learning," to continue to generate resistance to the testing in a more unified and coordinated way (Testing Resistance & Reform Spring, 2014). Thus, there is a significant test resistance movement growing (Rethinking Schools, 2014), even if much of that movement is not necessarily based on the pushback against the racism and White supremacy that high-stakes, standardized tests enforce within our system of education in the United States.

Conclusion

High-stakes, standardized testing has become universal in education policy, reform, and practice, and this universality has been established largely on commonsense understandings that avoid the faulty logics that lay at their foundations, deny the White supremacist history of such tests, and gloss over the racist outcomes of testing today. In this way we could argue that the imposition of high-stakes, standardized testing on public schools in the United States mirrors our larger discussion about education reform more generally: Despite all prevailing evidence about the ineffectiveness of these reforms, including ample evidence that these reforms are hurting kids and communities of Color, these backward policies continue to be advanced by politicians, pundits, and corporate leaders. Meanwhile the very real and very racist structural social, cultural, and economic inequalities that we know have a disproportionately high impact on the successes and failures of students of Color go untouched within mainstream public and political conversations.

However, as the testing juggernaut speeds ahead, one thing should give us all hope. The failures of the No Child Left Behind era are clear, the price of conceding to the requirements of Race to the Top is being questioned, and the popular pushback against the Common Core Standards (along with the impending threat of national testing that those standards bring) have all come together to shift the commonsense consciousness of many parents, teachers, and students. Locally and nationally, parents, teachers, and students—and yes, communities of Color included—are calling out injustices created by these tests (Rethinking Schools, 2014), and although inconsistent, these calls increasingly include the structural racism and White supremacy that high-stakes, standardized testing fundamentally supports.

References

Agee, J. (2004). Negotiating a teaching identity: An African American teacher's struggle to teach in test-driven contexts. *Teachers College Record, 106*(4), 747–774.

Ahmed-Ullah, N. S. (2014). 2nd CPS school votes to boycott state assessment test. *Chicago Tribune.* Retrieved from http://www.chicagotribune.com/news/local/breaking/chi-2nd-cps-school-votes-to-boycott-state-assessment-test-20140228,0,3961031.story

Au, W. (2007). High-stakes testing and curricular control: A qualitative metasynthesis. *Educational Researcher, 36*(5), 258–267.

Au, W. (2009). *Unequal by design: High-stakes testing and the standardization of inequality.* New York: Routledge.

Au, W. (2013). Coring the social studies within corporate education reform: The Common Core State Standards, social justice, and the politics of knowledge in U.S. schools. *Critical Education, 4*(5). Retrieved from http://ojs.library.ubc.ca/index.php/criticaled/article/view/182278

Au, W., & Gourd, K. (2013). Asinine assessment: Why high-stakes testing is bad for everyone, including English teachers. *English Journal, 103*(1), 14–19.

Badass Teacher Association. (March 11, 2014). Retrieved from http://www.badassteacher.org

Baker, O., & Lang, K. (2013). The effect of high school exit exams on graduation, employment, wages and incarceration (Working Paper No. 19182). Retrieved from National Bureau of Economic Research website: http://www.nber.org/papers/w19182

Barkan, J. (2011). Got dough?: How billionaires rule our schools. *Dissent, 58*(1), 49–57.

Barkan, J. (2012). Hired guns on astroturf: How to buy and sell school reform. *Dissent, 59*(2), 49–57.

Berliner, D. C. (2012). Effects of inequality and poverty vs. teachers and schooling on America's youth. *Teachers College Record, 116*(1). Retrieved from http://www.tcrecord.org (2014 paper publication).

Berliner, D. C., & Biddle, B. J. (1995). *The manufactured crisis: Myths, fraud, and the attack on America's public schools.* Reading, MA: Addison-Wesley.

Bisseret, N. (1979). *Education, class language and ideology.* Boston: Routledge & Kegan Paul.

Bourdieu, P. (1984). *Distinction: A social critique of the judgment of taste.* Cambridge, MA: Harvard University Press.

Brantlinger, E. (2006). An application of Gramsci's "who benefits?" to high-stakes testing. *Workplace, 6*(1). Retrieved from http://www.louisville.edu/journal/workplace/issue6p1/brantlinger.html

Cabrera, N. L., Milem, J. F., & Marx, R. W. (2012). An empirical analysis of the effects of Mexican American studies participation on student achievement within Tucson unified school district. Report to Special Master Dr. Willis D. Hawley on the Tucson Unified School District Desegregation Case, Tucson, AZ. Retrieved from http://works.bepress.com/nolan_l_cabrera/17/

Cavanagh, S. (2013). Demand for testing products, services on the rise. *Education Week.* Retrieved from http://www.edweek.org/ew/articles/2013/10/02/06testing_ep.h33.html

Chapman, P. D. (1988). *Schools as sorters: Lewis M. Terman, applied psychology, and the intelligence testing movement, 1890–1930.* New York: New York University Press.

Chingos, M. M. (2012). *Strength in numbers: State spending on K-12 assessment systems.* Washington, DC: The Brown Center on Education Policy at Brookings.

Chudowsky, N., Joftus, S., Kober, N., Renter, D. S., Scott, C., & Zabala, D. (2006). From the capital to the classroom: Year 4 of the No Child Left Behind Act. Center on Education Policy. Retrieved from http://www.cep-dc.org

Darder, A., & Torres, R. D. (2004). *After race: Racism after multiculturalism.* New York: New York University Press.

Delgado, R., & Stefancic, J. (2012). *Critical race theory: An introduction.* New York: New York University Press.

Ekoh, I. (2012). *High-stakes standardized testing in Nigeria and the erosion of a critical African worldview.* Doctoral dissertation, University of Toronto.

FairTest. (2013). *The spring 2013 testing reform uprising.* Retrieved from http://www. fairtest.org/sites/default/files/The-Spring2013-Testing-Reform-Uprising.pdf

Figueroa, A. (2013, August 6). 8 Things You Should Know About Corporations Like Pearson that Make Huge Profits from Standardized Tests. AlterNet. Retrieved from http://www.alternet.org/education/corporations-profit-standardized-tests

Fine, M. (2004). Witnessing whiteness/gathering intelligence. *Off white: Readings on power, privilege, and resistance,* 245–256. Psychology Press. In M. Fine, L. Weis, L. P. Pruitt, & A. Burns (Eds.), *Off white: Readings on power, privilege, and resistance* (2nd ed., pp. 245–256). New York: Routledge.

Foucault, M. (1995). *Discipline and punish: the birth of the prison* (A. Sheridan, Trans.; 2nd ed.). New York: Vintage Books.

Gillborn, D. (2005). Education policy as an act of white supremacy: Whiteness, critical race theory and education reform. *Journal of Education Policy, 20*(4), 485–505.

Giordano, G. (2005). *How testing came to dominate American schools: The history of educational assessment.* New York: Peter Lang.

Gould, S. J. (1996). *The mismeasure of man* (Rev. and expanded ed.). New York: Norton.

Grant, S. G. (2001). When an 'A' is not enough: Analyzing the New York State global history and geography exam. *Education Policy Analysis Archives, 9*(39). Retrieved from http://epaa.asu.edu/epaa/v9n39/

Gray-Garcia, T. (2012). Teaching is not testing: A community-led struggle to find an alternative to California's graduation exam. In W. Au & M. Bollow Tempel (Eds.), *Pencils down: Rethinking high-stakes testing and accountability in public schools* (pp. 183–188). Milwaukee, WI: Rethinking Schools, Ltd.

Guthrie, R. V. (1998). *Even the rat was white: A historical view of psychology* (2nd ed.). Boston: Allyn and Bacon.

Hagopian, J. (2011). Race and the (mis)measures of academic progress. Retrieved from http://seattleducation2010.wordpress.com/2011/05/17/race-and-the-mis measures-of-academic-progress/

Hagopian, J. (2013). Seattle test boycott: Our destination is not on the MAP. *Rethinking Schools, 27*(3). Retrieved from http://www.rethinkingschools.org/archive/27_03/ 27_03_hagopian.shtml

Haney, W. (1984). Testing reasoning and reasoning about testing. *Review of Educational Research, 54*(4), 597–654.

Hanson, A. F. (2000). How tests create what they are intended to measure. In A. Filer (Ed.), *Assessment: social practice and social product* (pp. 67–81). New York: RoutledgeFalmer.

Hartman, A. (2007). The social production of American identity: Standardized testing reform in the United States. *Socialism and Democracy, 17*(2), 131–164. doi: 10.1080/08854300308428369

Karier, C. J. (1972). Testing for order and control in the corporate liberal state. *Educational Theory, 22*(Spring), 159–180.

Karp, S. (2006). Leaving public education behind: The Bush agenda in American education. *Our Schools/Our Selves, 15*(3), 181–196.

Karp, S. (2013–2014). The problems with the Common Core. *Rethinking Schools, 28*(2). Retrieved from http://www.rethinkingschools.org/archive/28_02/28_02_karp.shtml

Kidder, W. C., & Rosner, J. (2002–2003). How the SAT creates "built-in headwinds": An educational and legal analysis of disparate impact. *Santa Clara Law Review, 43*, 131–212.

Kornhaber, M. L., & Orfield, G. (2001). High-stakes testing policies: Examining their assumptions and consequences. In G. Orfield & M. L. Kornhaber (Eds.), *Raising standards or raising barriers?: Inequality and high-stakes testing in public education* (pp. 1–18). New York: Century Foundation Press.

Kumashiro, K. (2012). *Bad teacher!: How blaming teachers distorts the bigger picture.* New York: Teachers College Press.

Ladson-Billings, G. (2006). From the achievement gap to the education debt: Understanding achievement in U.S. schools. *Educational Researcher, 35*(7), 3–12.

Ladson-Billings, G., & Tate, W. F. (1995). Toward a critical race theory of education. *Teachers College Record, 97*(1), 47–68.

Lemann, N. (1999). *The big test: The secret history of the American meritocracy.* New York: Farrar, Straus, and Giroux.

Lipman, P. (2004). *High stakes education: Inequality, globalization, and urban school reform.* New York: RoutledgeFalmer.

McNeil, L. M. (2000). *Contradictions of school reform: Educational costs of standardized testing.* New York: Routledge.

Moore, H. A. (2005). Testing whiteness: No child or no school left behind? *Washington University Journal of Law and Policy, 18*, 173–201.

National Center for Educational Statistics. (2013). *Digest of educational statistics: 2012* (No. NCES 2014–015). U.S. Department of Education, Institute of Educational Sciences, National Center for Educational Statistics. Retrieved from www.nces.gov/programs/digest/d12/

National Commission on Excellence in Education. (1983). A nation at risk: The imperative for educational reform. *United States Department of Education.* Retrieved from http://datacenter.spps.org/uploads/sotw_a_nation_at_risk_1983.pdf

National Opportunity to Learn Campaign. (March 4, 2013). The color of school closures. Retrieved from http://www.otlcampaign.org/blog/2013/04/05/color-school-closures

Nichols, S. L., & Berliner, D. C. (2005). The inevitable corruption of indicators and educators through high-stakes testing. Education Policy Research Unit, Education Policy Studies Laboratory, College of Education, Division of Educational Leadership and Policy Studies, Arizona State University, Tempe, Arizona. Retrieved from http://www.asu.edu/educ/epsl/EPRU/documents/EPSL-0503-101-EPRU-exec.pdf

Omi, M., & Winant, H. (1994). *Racial formation in the United States: From 1960's to 1990's.* New York: Routledge.

Oulahan, A. (2012). None of the above: Defiant teachers show they have had enough of high-stakes testing. In W. Au & M. Bollow Tempel (Eds.), *Pencils down: Rethinking high-stakes testing and accountability in public schools* (pp. 189–193). Milwaukee, WI: Rethinking Schools, Ltd.

Popham, W. J. (2001). *The truth about testing: An educator's call to action.* Alexandria, VA: Association for Supervision and Curriculum Development (ASCD).

Ravitch, D. (2013). *Reign of error: The hoax of the privatization movement and the danger to America's public schools.* New York: Alfred A. Knopf.

Reid, K. S. (2014). Chicago parents form coalition to promote state test boycott. Retrieved from http://blogs.edweek.org/edweek/parentsandthepublic/2014/02/chicago_parents_form_coalition_to_support_state_test_boycott.html

Rentner, D. S., Scott, C., Kober, N., Chudowsky, N., Chudowsky, V., Joftus, S., & Zabala, D. (2006). From the capital to classroom: Year 4 of the No Child Left Behind Act. Washington, DC: Center on Education Policy.

Rethinking Schools. (2014). The gathering resistance to standardized tests. *Rethinking Schools, 28*(3). Retrieved from http://www.rethinkingschools.org/archive/28_03/edit2283.shtml

Romero, A., Arce, S., & Cammarota, J. (2009). A Barrio pedagogy: Identity, intellectualism, activism, and academic achievement through the evolution of critcally compassionate intellectualism. *Race Ethnicity and Education, 12(2),* 217–233.

Rosner, J. (2003). On white preferences. *The Nation, 276*(14), 24.

Sacks, P. (1999). *Standardized minds: The high price of America's testing culture and what we can do to change it.* Cambridge, MA: Perseus Books.

Sanchez, G. I. (1940). *Forgotten people: A study of New Mexicans* (1996 Reprint ed.). Albuquerque: University of New Mexico Press.

Santelices, M. V., & Wilson, M. (2010). Unfair treatment?: The case of Freedle, the SAT, and the standardization approach to differential item functioning. *Harvard Educational Review, 80*(1), 106–133.

Selden, S. (1999). *Inheriting shame: The story of eugenics and racism in America.* New York: Teachers College Press.

Testing Resistance & Reform Spring. (March 11, 2014). Testing resistance & reform spring: Less testing, more learning. Retrieved from https://actionnetwork.org/event_campaigns/testing-resistance-reform-spring-less-testing-more-learning

Toussaint, R. (2000–2001). Manifest destiny or cultural integrity? *Rethinking Schools, 15*(2). Retrieved from http://www.rethinkingschools.org/archive/15_02/Test152.shmtl

Tyack, D. (1974). *The one best system: A history of American urban education.* Cambridge, MA: Harvard University Press.

United Opt Out National. (March 11, 2014). United Opt Out National: The movement to end corporate education reform. Retrieved from http://www.unitedoptout.com

Valenzuela, A. (1999). *Subtractive schooling: U.S. Mexican youth and the politics of caring.* New York: SUNY Press.

Note

1. I would like to be clear on how I am using the term "White supremacy" and how I am using racial categories like "White" in this chapter. The kind of White supremacy I refer to here speaks to what I see as the White supremacist outcomes of systematic and institutional racism in the United States in particular. As I argue here, as the expression of education policy and a pivotal apparatus for leveraging education reform in the United States, high-stakes, standardized testing functions as a tool for the maintenance of White supremacy. Additionally I want to be explicit in that I use "race" here not as a biological construct—since it has no factual basis in biology (Gould, 1996)—but as a social, historical, and political construction (Omi & Winant, 1994) that is used to sort and define human populations based on their perceived, and sometimes legally defined, racial identity in the United States.

2. Mayoral Control: Reform, Whiteness, and Critical Race Analysis of Neoliberal Educational Policy

David Stovall

The following chapter is an attempt to articulate theoretical and praxis-oriented analysis of the realities of mayoral control (MC) through the broader ideology of Whiteness and the current project of neoliberal school reform. To understand mayoral control as ideology and policy, critical race theory (CRT) is used to gain a further understanding of its function as hegemonic machination of the state. As a theoretical construct with beginnings in legal scholarship, CRT's utility in education reveals intersectional oppressions in the form of racist, neoliberal, corporate educational reform. Instead of resting solely on analytical critique of mayoral control, the following contribution concludes with tangible examples of community opposition that has the potential for substantive change in the current landscape of city and educational politics. Written through the lens of critical race praxis (CRP), the idea is to have readers engage the possibilities of interrupting mayoral control through concrete collective strategies.

The editors of this collection of writings have alerted us to the "Hydra" of neoliberal school reform. In its many iterations, one of the "heads" of the Hydra is mayoral control. If the body is neoliberal education reform, mayoral control should be considered one of the dangerous appendages, which in turn creates the formidable enemy that overtly argues for the end of public education as we know it. As strategy and practice, mayoral control operates on myriad assumptions primarily rooted in the belief that city residents are unable to make tangible decisions regarding quality education. At the current moment, its positioning as viable policy for large cities is slowly becoming the policy language championed by sworn enemies of publicly funded education (e.g., the Republican Party, American Enterprise Institute, Hoover Institute, Manhattan Institute, Broad Foundation, etc.).

In the attempt to structure the analysis of the following pages, the document is organized into the following sections: After a brief discussion of the use of CRT as a tool in policy analysis, section one provides a brief history of the origins of mayoral control in Chicago. The second section uses the analysis of educational theorists from a critical perspective to understand mayoral control as educational policy that reifies the ideology of Whiteness/ White supremacy. Section three provides an example of the complex arrangements that are facilitated under mayoral control, which pair housing and economic policy. Couched in the Chicago Housing Authority's (CHA) Plan for Transformation and the Renaissance 2010 policies of Chicago Public Schools (CPS), mayoral control centralizes power to solidify public/private partnerships, resulting in the further marginalization and isolation of low-income/ working-class African American and Latino/a residents in Chicago. The final section engages CRP to highlight current efforts to end mayoral control.

Critical Race Theory as Policy Analysis

For the remainder of this document I am utilizing the work of Solórzano (1997) in Yosso (2005) to conceptualize CRT in relationship to mayoral control as one of the "heads" on the Hydra of neoliberal education reform.

1. the intercentricity of race and racism with other forms of subordination
2. the challenge to dominant ideology
3. the commitment to social justice
4. the centrality of experiential knowledge
5. the use of interdisciplinary approaches (p. 73)

Tenets two, three, and four are of particular importance in understanding the political economy of mayoral control and its consequences for residents in urban areas. As CRT is traditionally rooted in counterstory, the intent is for those who engage the construct to begin to interrogate the underpinnings of policies that are purported as beneficial to the academic achievement of urban youth of Color from low-income, working-class communities. In excavating the counterstory in the convergence of the plans for mayoral takeover, CRT can be used to reveal the realities of such projects.

In the case of schools under mayoral control, inequity and disinvestment are ignored, equipping mayors with the ability to bypass the lack of necessary curricular and infrastructure support. By focusing on prepackaged results not the sources of inequity, changing curriculum and then restricting access to newly redeveloped schools makes "good sense" in the Gramscian meaning of the term: It is in the best interests of the state to shift curricular focus of schools and make them less accessible to the least desired segments of the population by way of mayoral control, which facilitates changes in academic admissions requirements, lottery systems (to regulate the number of "undesireables") and inaccessibility to housing. Mayoral control, while not the sole culprit in the progression of destabilizing and disenfranchising communities, operates as a crucial conduit in the process.

As mayoral control originates in Chicago, it has spread to New York; Boston; Cleveland; Washington, D.C.; Providence, Rhode Island; New Haven, Connecticut; and Harrisburg, Pennsylvania. In a similar arrangement, Baltimore and Philadelphia schools are jointly run by the mayor and the governor of the state (Lipman, 2011; Wong, 2007, 2003). This becomes problematic for cities as community voices are silenced through legislative means, limiting the ability to address issues for disinvested communities. When the mayor is the final authority on schools and is able to select members of her board, the appointed relationship allows for neoliberal policies to take shape. This most notably comes in the form of charter school proliferation, school closures, and union-busting measures such as merit-based teacher pay. In instances like the current situation in Philadelphia, shared governance between the mayor's office and state government creates an environment where community concerns are completely removed from school-based decisions.

In the newly "data-driven" mode of educational reform, there is an undercurrent that deserves conversation, which is heavily rooted in dispossession and the continued disenfranchisement of particular populations. These rationales render residents that have historically received less as disposable. If the national sentiment is that public education is a "broken" system, mayoral control provides the optimal condition by which to infuse wholesale changes to the system. However, instead of improvement for the masses, we get worse situations for historically disinvested communities of Color in large cities. From a national perspective, Chicago provides a prima facie example of the dangers of mayoral control under corporate neoliberal education reform.

Section One: Origins of Mayoral Control

Centered in the 1995 educational policy shift resulting in mayoral control of Chicago Public Schools (CPS), the mayor currently has sole authority in appointing the school board, which is responsible for final approval of

school-related issues (e.g., financial matters, curricular shifts, contract pro-
curement, approval of new schools, etc.). In addition to the ability to appoint
members of the school board, the mayor also has the ability to overturn any
decision made by the board. Facilitated under the 22-year mayoral tenure
of Richard M. Daley, the city has laid a blueprint for numerous cities in the
United States desiring to centralize control of its school system. In that time
frame, the number of educators on the school board in Chicago has decreased
significantly. Currently the board membership consists largely of people from
business, legal, and philanthropic sectors. This fosters a reciprocal relationship between the board and the mayor's office, as board members are usually
individuals or employees of entities that have contributed significantly to the
mayor's re-election campaign. Through the Illinois legislature, the mayor is
granted authority to replace an elected board with an appointed board. In
addition to appointing board members, the mayor is allowed to veto or overturn any decision made by the CEO of Chicago Public Schools, the Board of
Directors, or any localized leadership (Wong, 2006).

Chicago, as an epicenter for corporate education reform in the United
States, has global implications for state apparatuses seeking to end public education and replace it with neoliberal market-driven "reform." This is accom-
plished largely by way of public private partnerships. To secure said partnerships, mayoral control allows for the centralizing of decision-making power,
allowing for corporate influence in educational policy. On the ground, the
rhetoric of "choice" and "competition" operates as neoliberal devices that
provide an illusion that students, parents, and families are "choosing" options
focusing on educational improvement. Instead of improving the current
education conditions in low-income/working-class African American and
Latino/a neighborhoods, what we are witnessing is a return to a "more-of-
the-same" equation. Instead of the ability of these new instruments of reform
to contribute to wholesale academic improvement, students and families in
cities like Chicago are witnessing an entirely different dynamic.

Section Two: Mayoral Control and the Project of Whiteness

Leonardo (2009) reminds us that like capitalism, Whiteness is an all-
encompassing ideology that permeates thought and action in the Western
Hemisphere. Coupled with neoliberalism, the perfect storm of market ideology and racial oppression create a hegemonic apparatus that becomes difficult
to recognize or resist.

> In order for white racial hegemony to saturate everyday life, it has to be secured
> by a process of domination, or those acts, decisions, and policies that white

subjects perpetrate on people of Color. As such, a critical pedagogy of white racial supremacy revolves less around the issue of unearned advantages, or the state of being dominant, and more around direct processes that secure domination and the privilege associated with it. (p. 75)

Mayoral control secures such domination through a totalizing process that eliminates community input to the decisions that directly affect young people and families in public schools. As an overarching structure, mayoral control makes it nearly impossible for the most marginalized and isolated residents of a city to participate in a process to improve their educational well-being. By denying the majority of low-income/working-class residents of Color access to this process, they are rendered both invisible and disposable by city government. Pairing race and class, the wealthy—through control of the board of directors of public school systems—serve as rubber stamps to the mayor's agenda. If they resist, they will be removed instantaneously (Lipman, 2011). Coupled with the fact that there are few educators appointed to these mayor-appointed boards, the state (by way of the mayor's office) has secured a process by which to justify hardline tactics in the form of school closings under the rhetoric of "underperforming" or "underutilized." This has been evident in Chicago as it has shuttered or repurposed more than 150 schools since 2004. In 2013 49 schools were closed, constituting the largest single-year set of school closings in the history of the United States (Farmer et al., 2013).

Ideologically, mayoral control, like NCLB, is racialized upon closer examination. Returning to Leonardo (2009), his ruminations on NCLB should be considered a parallel assessment of mayoral control.

NCLB is an "act of whiteness" and perpetuates the innocence of whiteness as a system of privilege. It is a form of whiteness as policy. Its white common sense deems racial disparities as unfortunate outcomes of group competition, uneven social development, or worse, as stubborn cultural explanations of the inferiority of people of Color. (p. 127)

In Chicago, mayoral control was largely a revanchist attempt by the mayor to dislocate community power in schools from African American and Latino/a residents. Responding to the reforms of 1988 that created local school councils, the mayor (at this time Richard M. Daley) always felt that community control of schools in the form of budget appropriation and principal hiring was yielding too much control to "inept" community members. This process, as de facto racialized positioning by the mayor's office, was rationalized as the unfortunate realities of budget-strapped cities that have to make "tough decisions" regarding public goods. Such decisions are de-racialized and are removed from the historical realities of hyper-segregation, disinvestment, and destabilization in low-income neighborhoods. Rhetoric aside, the following section provides an example of how this ideology plays out in the lives of low-income/working-class African American and Latino/a residents in urban space.

Section Three: Mayoral Control, Neoliberal Education Reform, and City Policy—Renaissance 2010 and Quality Education for the Few

Documented extensively in the works of Lipman (2003, 2004, 2011), Saltman (2007, 2009) and Fabricant and Fine (2012), Chicago has been a hotbed for educational "reforms." I am particularly highlighting "reform" because the changes have been touted as positive changes, but they have also largely resulted in the further marginalization of low-income, working-class communities of Color. Largely rooted in the belief that free-market economies provide solution to the vast majority of social concerns, neoliberal reform is centered in the rights of the individual. The market is understood as correct and without fault, resulting in the rationale for privatization of public goods for the purpose of cost-effectiveness and the maximizing of profits. For low-income families of Color, this often results in a rhetorical charge that the market can solve the vast majority of political, economic, and social issues. Because these resources are falsely positioned as available to all, low-income, working-class families of Color are often blamed for not accessing said resources.

Deeply rooted in neoliberal ideology and rhetoric, this facilitated convergence of housing and educational policies. Centered in Chicago's attempt to market itself as a global city (attracting international investment from tourism and business ventures), housing has been paired with education as key components in the city's development. Dating back to 1971, Mayor Richard J. Daley (father of Richard M.) spearheaded a policy and planning initiative known as the Chicago 21 plan, targeting 21 wards (geographic and political districts) for redevelopment. Considered as part of the last wave of urban renewal strategies, the Chicago 21 plan should be understood as the blueprint for neoliberal reform in the city.

Fast-forward 41 years to the present, and actions by the mayor and other state actors to secure corporate contributions via free-market strategies has become the norm locally, nationally, and internationally. Sections of the Chicago model of reform have been duplicated in cities such as New York, Los Angeles, and Houston. Officials from all three cities have come to Chicago to study mayoral control (of the school board) and how to connect education and business with the intent to foster long-term development. Internationally, Chicago has been cited for its improvements in business, housing, and education. As a central hub for global finance, informational technological advancements, and management for systems of production, Chicago has fashioned itself as a viable competitor for investment from transnational global firms in business, industry, and entertainment (Smith & Stovall, 2008).

Through a collaborative of business interests known as the Commercial Club of Chicago, its Civic Committee developed a 2003 report known as "Left Behind." Included in this report was the notion that students in the United States are falling behind internationally in reading, math, and science. Their suggested solution was to retool the public educational landscape by infusing "innovation" from the business sector. Said innovations would be for the purposes of strengthening the U.S. workforce, returning the U.S. economy to supremacy in the global marketplace. The people best suited for leading reforms in this direction were those who possessed an intimate knowledge of free-market strategies to boost competition among education providers (Civic Committee of the Commercial Club of Chicago, 2003). Key to this strategy is the idea that competition is best to boost academic performance. Under free-market capitalism the belief is that if one school is performing well, it will push others to improve due to the interests of both institutions for students. Contrary to this understanding is the fact that each school serves a different set of students requiring a unique set of resources germane to that particular population. The competition strategy becomes ridiculous and absurd when accounting for the unique needs of students in a particular school. Granting one set of schools more resources than others will never encourage "competition." Instead, it guarantees the fact that schools without resources will remain without them. If poorly performing schools are asked to increase their academic performance without the necessary supports, it is the equivalent of asking someone to pull themselves up by their bootstraps when they do not have boots.

Nevertheless, the city moved forward with the policy and rolled out a plan in the summer of 2004 called Renaissance 2010. The idea promoted to the public was to implement the suggestions of the Civic Committee. By 2010 CPS proposed to target up to 70 "chronically underperforming" schools for "transformation" into 100 schools with the distinction of either charter, contract, or performance school. Where charters are granted by the state, contract schools have a different distinction in that they are a designation for individuals or groups that have secured individual contracts with the city to create schools. Where contract schools are a close cousin to charters with regard to funding formulas, the distinct difference lies in the direct partnership with the city, as charters are traditionally granted by the state. Currently the largest contract institution in Chicago is the Academy of Urban School Leadership (AUSL). Schools in the performance category were another manifestation of schools aimed at giving principals and teachers some levels of autonomy regarding curriculum and schedule. Simultaneously, the internal understanding was to lessen the city's financial commitment to education through the use of partners that could in turn use their contributions to education as tax subsidies (through the federal tax code's provision for charitable donations). Returning to the public sphere, said manifestations were posited to community residents as Chicago Public Schools moving to provide "choice" and "options" in the "education marketplace" (New Schools and Programs, 2013).

The first site of this experiment would take place in a collective of neighborhoods known as the mid-South region. Consisting of the geographic neighborhoods of Kenwood, Oakland, Grand Boulevard, and Douglass, 20 of the 22 schools in the four-neighborhood area were targeted for closure or restructuring in the aforementioned forms. Fortunately, due to the collective efforts of community organizations and a team of collaborating researchers, the first effort of the experiment was curtailed. Thanks to their efforts it was discovered that many of the schools targeted for reconfiguration were performing at or exceeding the standards set forward by the state. Discussed in detail in the next section, the desire was to couple school development with land development in the form of gentrifying the existing area. One specific community organization, the Kenwood Oakland Community Organization (KOCO), staged a sleep-in at CPS' central office building. Coupled with the work of Pauline Lipman, their efforts garnered attention resulting in the curtailing of the original rollout plan targeting 20 schools. Instead CPS targeted 10 schools, reconfiguring the vast majority to charters and contract schools.

Critical to this process is the intimate relationship to the housing market. Cited extensively in Arrastia (2007), Lipman (2003, 2011, 2012), and Smith and Stovall (2008) is the idea that because housing stock is key in attracting business interests in the city, schooling becomes an important conduit in solidifying long-term investment in schools. Because the main determinant of a family's home purchase are the schools in the perspective neighborhood, the mid-South region became a hotbed for gentrification, most notably through the mass destruction of public housing through the Chicago Housing Authority's (CHA) Plan for Transformation (Lipman, 2011). The mixed-income strategy employed to redevelop public housing in Chicago is a product of this thinking. Touted as a $1.6 billion plan, its aim is to redevelop areas once occupied by high-rise public housing as mixed-income communities. As housing stock in the redeveloped areas will be distributed in thirds among very low-income, moderate-income, and market rate homes, questions arise as dubious qualifications have been placed on the low-income group (Olivo, 2004). To receive any of the homes in the recent developments, public housing families have to go through a battery of screenings for health (specifically for substance abuse), employment (applicants must now work at least 30 hours per week unless they are not able or are in a training/educational program), and criminal activity (a person cannot rent an apartment if anyone in the household has a felony conviction). In the "Plan for Transformation" schools are framed as an important part of the plan, and the change in housing has been projected to mean an increase in families of moderate and affluent incomes. Because this requires strategic planning on the part of CPS, the converging of Renaissance 2010 and the Plan for Transformation is critical to bringing the larger neoliberal plan into fruition. Despite the provisions for low-income families in the new mixed-income communities, the aforementioned health, employment, and criminal compliances help to carefully sanitize the community marketed to newcomers. Schools, as the final frontier, provide the necessary push for buyers to take the final step in securing life in the city. Fortunately for the families that remain in some of the targeted areas, a collective of community organizations have been able to develop strategies to contest the efforts of CPS.

The residual effects of the convergence of Renaissance 2010 and the Plan for Transformation have been devastating for a growing number of African American and Latino/a communities in Chicago. According to the 2010 U.S. Census, Chicago lost 200,000 residents from 2000 to 2010 (Dahleen, Mullen, & Olivo, 2011). As the Plan for Transformation began in 1999, Renaissance 2010 was unveiled and first implemented in 2004. As the two policies converged during a six-year period, Chicago witnessed 178,000 African American residents depart from the city. Additionally, since the initial rollout of Renaissance 2010, 150 schools have been permanently closed, phased out (when students are no longer admitted), labeled as turnaround (when the existing staff is fired and an Educational Maintenance Organization [EMO] is hired to re-staff the school, usually with a new curricular focus). Coupled with the destruction of over 80% of public housing stock (whose population was 95% African American), many schools became depopulated while others were converted to "receiver schools." Institutions in this category would conduct an intake of students from the depopulated or closed schools.

As neoliberal educational reform, Renaissance 2010 as the byproduct of mayoral control has since morphed into numerous entities, securing private interests through organizations such as the Renaissance Schools Fund (a private philanthropic entity), the Chicago Public Education Fund (a phil-anthropic entity specifically for securing resources for charter and turnaround schools), and the Office of New Schools (an internal office to CPS). Coupled with new policy initiatives from the federal government (e.g., Race to the Top, No Child Left Behind reauthorization, etc.) this particular type of school reform has been touted as a replicable model over the last 17 years. In addition to CPS having five CEOs over the last 12 years, the rotating door of administration has created a central office structure with minimal trans-parency for communities that are demanding fair and equitable education for students of Color in low-income working-class areas of the city. Despite some slowing in the housing market due to the international economic downturn of 2008, the housing market in Chicago is trending upward despite periods of volatility. With Chicago's considerable loss of its African American population over the last decade, combined with the mass destruction of public housing, the current school restructuring plan has been able to move forward without significant stoppage. Discussed in depth in the final section, communities have been able to mobilize to challenge the trend largely exacerbated by may-oral control through Renaissance 2010.

As some would site the convergence of Renaissance 2010 and the Plan for Transformation as conspiratorial, I offer to take it a step further in that there is no longer a clandestine conversation surrounding policy aims. Instead, we should understand these policy machinations as public, where state actors and interested parties are supporting rhetorical rationales while materially imple-menting strategies to permanently remove particular residents from urban areas. The expressed public purpose of these policies are to attract a majority White affluent gentry from suburban areas in addition to investment from newly minted elites from international destinations (e.g., the Middle East, India, Southeast Asia, and mainland China). Coupled with the neoliberal push for privatization of the public sector, schools under mayoral control become the conduit for an illusion of progress for all, with the reality of prog-ress for some.

Conclusion: The Struggle Forward

It should be stated that the purpose of this chapter is not to contribute to a sense of hopelessness in those who have engaged in an epic battle for justice in the current educational landscape. Instead, the concern is to provide a critical analysis solely for the purpose of highlighting the necessity of resis-tance to mayoral control under the guise of corporate neoliberal education reform. Borrowing from Duncan-Andrade's notion of critical hope, I am of the understanding that hope must be supported by way of connection to the material conditions of the people we are accountable to and engaged with (Duncan-Andrade, 2009). In doing so we must be painfully honest with the realities of the current educational condition in urban areas. Chicago, as an emerging global city, by way of mayoral control, has set forth policies that are unfortunately becoming blueprints for cities in the United States and across the globe. Nevertheless, this reality does not have to be part and parcel of a foregone conclusion. The enormity of this reality should not be ignored. Instead, this current moment in education deserves specific action and reflection to develop the necessary tools for resistance.

As a framework for resisting these neoliberal educational trends moving forward, Yamamoto (1999) offers a way to think about our work with young people and families in the struggle for educational justice through critical race praxis (CRP). The following tenets have been critical in pairing the efforts of those in the research community with young people and families who are directly experiencing educational injustice under mayoral control.

- **Conceptual:** Examining the racialization of a controversy and the interconnecting influences of heterosexism, patriarchy, and class while locating that examination in a critique of the political economy.
- **Performative**: Answering the question as to what practical steps are responsive to the specific claim and who should act on that claim.
- **Material**: Inquiring into changes, both socio-structural and the remaking of the democratic structure of public institutions, in the material conditions of racial oppression. Examples would include access to fair housing, health care, quality education, employment, etc.
- **Reflexive**: Commitment to the continual rebuilding of theory in light of the practical experiences of racial groups engaged in particular anti-racist struggles. (pp. 130–132)

Because the current moment can seem so daunting, it is imperative to engage in collective strategies such as these to stabilize our efforts while continually working with others to reimagine and re-create education in cities. CRP, as a collection of tenets centered in action and reflection, allows us to contextualize the current moment in education with the responsibility of developing concrete strategies to challenge mayoral control. Despite the behemoth of corporate dollars that have come into education over the last 20 years, mayoral elections remind us that the only thing that has a chance against the Hydra is the ability of residents to organize, plan, and implement strategies that support inclusive, democratic structures for decision making.

In relationship to mayoral control, three examples of successful attempts to organize and implement transformative strategies are the 1983 and 1987 election of Harold Washington in Chicago and in the 2013 election of Chokwe Lumumba in Jackson, Mississippi. In reference to CRP, as *performative* campaigns, the central conduit to both electoral victories was the ability to mobilize new voters. A similar strategy underway is a push in the state of Illinois to pass legislation that will create an elected school board that will have the final say in educational decisions. Despite staunch opposition by corporate players, the *performative* and *material* elements of this campaign have come in the form of a groundswell of support for this measure as schools continue to close in African American and Latino/a low-income and working-class communities. As a democratic and representative process, an elected school board provides the opportunity for regions of the city that have historically been ignored to state their educational concerns while engaging with the board to locate viable alternatives. This process would allow for an explicit opportunity to challenge educational "reforms" that have the potential to further marginalize the aforementioned regions (e.g., overreliance on high-stakes testing, charter proliferation, de-unionization, etc.). Because these opportunities are not currently available under mayoral control, an elected school board would be a move toward equity in big-city educational decision-making.

While not a panacea by any stretch of the imagination, there are many issues that deserve attention regarding the conceptual and reflexive tenets of CRP if the elected school board legislation passes. One of the immediate concerns will be equitable representation for historically marginalized and disinvested communities. The city of Chicago, as a hyper-segregated metropolis plagued by rabid gentrification and joblessness in the aforementioned neighborhoods, does not have a history of equitable representation in its city council or on the board of trustees of CPS. Countering mayoral control, the current move for an elected school board provides the small spark of democracy that has the potential to ignite the masses.

Although the road forward may appear daunting, there are efforts across the United States and internationally that are fueling resistance to neoliberal education reform under mayoral control. Such efforts illuminate the type of critical hope Duncan-Andrade (2009) speaks of that supports the material realities of those who are working to collectively address their conditions. In 2011 the organization Stand For Children introduced legislation in Illinois that would limit the power of teachers to organize to address school conditions. The approved legislation requires a 75% approval vote of union membership to authorize a strike. Due to the organizing efforts of the Chicago Teachers Union (CTU), its delegation of community partners and its own

Caucus of Rank and File Educators (CORE), they were able to get 90% of their membership to authorize a strike vote. This has never happened in the history of large-scale organized labor in Chicago. Key to their success was CTU's ability to abandon tactics common to labor organizing. Instead, the CTU through CORE reached out to community partners to develop a strategy that centered the needs of students and parents as key in developing effective education reform.

Making the explicit claim to antiracist practice, the new leadership of the CTU has taken a collective stance against racism and White supremacy. Where the authorization of the strike vote is only one section of organizing, they have been tirelessly active in supporting community efforts to halt school closings and turnarounds (CORE, 2014). Currently the combination of the CTU and families represents a formidable entity with enough power to defeat a heavily funded set of politicians pushing for mayoral control and the end of public education. In this current moment, the only thing proven to beat heavily funded campaigns is a groundswell of new mobilized voters. If we pay attention to these current trends in organizing and intentional resistance, we are able to create clearer pathways to collectivize struggle against the hegemony of Whiteness in educational policy.

References

Arrastia, L. (2007). Capital's daisy chain: Exposing Chicago's corporate coalition. *Journal of Critical Education Policy Studies, 5*(1), 121–155.

Civic Committee of the Commercial Club of Chicago. (2003). Left behind: Student achievement in Chicago's public schools.

CORE. (2014). Retrieved from http://www.coreteachers.org

Dahleen, G., Mullen, W., & Olivo, A. (2011, February 18). Neighborhood population drain. Census shows central Chicago grew, while outlying areas lost. *The Chicago Tribune.* Retrieved from http://articles.chicagotribune.com/2011–02–18/news/ct-met-census-population-drop-20110218_1_decades-of-population-decline-hispanic-population-census-data

Duncan-Andrade, J. M. R. (2009). Note to educators: Hope required when growing roses in concrete. *Harvard Educational Review, 79*(2), 1–13.

Fabricant, M., & Fine, M. (2012). *Charter schools and the corporate makeover of public education: What's at stake?* New York: Teachers College Press.

Farmer, S., Klonsky, M., Konkol, P., Phillips, K., Pulido, I., & Stovall, D. (2013). *Research brief #5: Research brief on school closures.* Retrieved from www.createchicago.org

Leonardo, Z. (2009). *Race, whiteness, and education.* New York: Routledge.

Lipman, P. (2003). Chicago school policy: Regulating Black and Latino youth in the global city. *Race, Ethnicity, and Education, 6*(4), 331–355.

Lipman, P. (2004). *High stakes education: Inequality, globalization, and urban school reform*. New York: Routledge.

Lipman, P. (2011). *The new political economy of urban education: Neoliberalism, race, and the right to the city*. New York: Routledge.

Lipman, P. (2012). Neoliberal urbanism, race, and urban school reform. *The Assault on Public Education: Confronting the Politics of Corporate School Reform*, 33–54.

New Schools and Programs. (2014). Retrieved from http://www.cps.edu/NewSchools? pages?ONS.aspx

Olivo, A. (2004, September 17). New section 8 renters better off but ex-tenants of public housing face repair woes. *The Chicago Tribune*. Retrieved from http://articles. chicagotribune.com/2004-09-17/news/0409170262_1_public-housing-mixed-income-communities-new-section

Parents United for Responsible Education. (n.d.). Retrieved from http://pureparents.org

Saltman, K. J. (2007). *Capitalizing on Disaster: Taking and Breaking Public Schools*. Herndon, VA: Paradigm Publishers.

Saltman, K. (2009). The rise of venture philanthropy and the ongoing neoliberal assault on public education: The Eli and Edythe Broad Foundation. *Workplace: A Journal for Academic Labor, (16)*.

Smith, J. J., & Stovall, D. (2008). "Coming home" to new homes and new schools: Critical race theory and the new politics of containment. *Journal of Education Policy*, *23*(2), 135–152.

Solórzano D. (1997). Images and words that wound: Critical race theory, racial stereotyping, and teacher education. *Teacher Education Quarterly*, *24*(3), 186–215.

Wong, K. K. (2006). The political dynamics of mayoral engagement in public education. *Harvard Educational Review*, *76*(2), 164–177.

Wong, K. K. (2007). *The education mayor: Improving America's schools*. Washington, DC: Georgetown University Press.

Wong, K. K., & Shen, F. X. (2003). Big city mayors and school governance reform: The case of school district takeover. *Peabody Journal of Education*, *78*(1), 5–32.

Yamamoto, E. (1997). Critical race praxis: Race theory and political lawyering practice in post–civil rights America. *Michigan Law Review*, 821–900.

Yamamoto, E. (1999). *Interracial justice: Conflict and reconciliation in post–civil right America*. New York: New York University Press.

Yosso, T. J. (2005). Whose culture has capital? A critical race theory discussion of community cultural wealth. *Race Ethnicity and Education*, *8*(1), 69–91.

3. School Closings: The Nexus of White Supremacy, State Abandonment, and Accumulation by Dispossession

PAULINE LIPMAN

On May 22, 2013, Chicago's mayor-appointed Board of Education voted to close 49 neighborhood elementary schools and one high school, affecting around 40,000 students. The decision followed seven tumultuous months of protest in which literally tens of thousands of parents, students, teachers, and community members testified at public hearings, marched, picketed, sat in, held press conferences and vigils, and more to stop their schools from being closed. The 2013 closings were on top of more than 10 years of drastic school actions in which the board closed, phased out, consolidated, or turned around 105 neighborhood public schools. Massive school closings have similarly hit New York, the District of Columbia, Detroit, Philadelphia, and other urban districts (Gym, 2013; Pedroni, 2011; Vevea, 2013). Beginning in fall 2014, New Orleans will not have a single traditional neighborhood public school left (Layton, 2014b). At the same time, these districts have expanded privately operated charter schools and provided new selective enrollment schools targeted to affluent and White students.

This policy is remaking the race and class landscape of K–12 education in the United States as a constitutive part of the spatial, economic, and racial restructuring of cities themselves (Lipman, 2011). Understanding the social, economic, and political logics underlying this process, as well as its consequences for working-class students, families, and communities of Color, is crucial to develop strategies to resist these policies and to supersede them with a community and educator-driven agenda of educational equity and justice. While school closings are at the epicenter of community resistance as I write this, it is crucial to see them as an element of shifting, racialized neoliberal strategies to remake public education broadly.

In this chapter, I discuss school closings as a racialized policy of capital accumulation and state abandonment of communities of Color. Although school closings are affecting students of Color generally, as well as some White working-class students, their main target has been schools in African American communities. African American communities have also been the targets of general state abandonment through dismantling of public housing and other public services and through public disinvestment. Therefore, much of my discussion focuses on school closings in African American communities. I begin by describing the neoliberal and racial logics that are driving the restructuring of public education in the United States and briefly review the research on school closings. Next, I examine school closings in communities of Color as a form of organized state abandonment that facilitates turning over public schools to the market, and I discuss the racial ideologies that facilitate this process. Here I also interject a word of caution against reifying school closings as neoliberal strategy. I argue for a transformational education politics that incorporates opposition to school closings and other specific neoliberal strategies in a larger challenge to the underlying capitalist and racial logics that are remaking public education. I conclude with the promise of an emergent grassroots movement and alternative agenda that centers the knowledge and experiences of parents, students, and communities of Color in strategies of school transformation and that targets both corporate privatization and racial oppression.

Race, Neoliberalism, and the Restructuring of Public Education

Among education activists, parents, and students, it is becoming increasingly clear that actions to close public schools are part of a larger ensemble of policies that some refer to as "corporate education reform" but that can best be understood as the neoliberal restructuring of public education. Neoliberalism, a strategy of late capitalism, is an attempt to reinstitute the hegemony of market rule in every sphere of society (Harvey, 2005). Neoliberalism is not a fixed set of policies but rather a process of "creative destruction" of welfare statist economic, political, and ideological arrangements and construction of new arrangements that support free markets and capital accumulation. Neoliberalism is also path dependent; that is, it takes particular forms in different contexts in relation to specific histories and relations of social forces (Brenner & Theodore, 2002). In the United States, neoliberalism is a deeply racialized project. White supremacy has been central to the development, maintenance, and global expansion of U.S. capitalism, just as capitalism has provided the material and institutional basis for the entrenchment of White supremacy in every institution of U.S. society, albeit in multiple and fluctuating forms (Lipsitz, 1998; Melamed, 2011). Thus, it is important to situate school closings in this nexus of capitalist and racist logics.

Neoliberalism is a new regime of capital accumulation, characterized by what David Harvey (2005) calls "accumulation by dispossession"—the process by which capital cannibalizes spheres of production and social life that are public or held in common and turns them into commodities to be bought and sold in the market. Examples of this are everywhere—from selling off the Amazon rain forest, to patenting Mayan corn and the human genome, to privatizing education, public housing, public health clinics, roads, bridges, mass transit systems, public water systems, municipal fire departments, and on and on. In the United States alone, K–12 education is a $650 billion economic sector (Simon, 2012). Markets in charter schools, education services, curriculum, online classes, teacher training operations, the testing industry, tutoring services, branded university satellites, and more are now hot investment opportunities. Speculation in charter school bonds and charter school real estate is the topic of business publications, investor webinars, and bond trader and hedge fund news (Singer, 2014).

The basis to capitalize on education, particularly in cities, was laid through racialized policies that undermined public schools in communities of Color—cuts in federal funding to cities, the rollback of social welfare programs, and public and private disinvestment in African American and other communities of Color. These neoliberal policies were overlaid on a history of racial segregation and discrimination that robbed communities of Color of wealth and resources (Coates, 2014). Disinvested public schools in disinvested neighborhoods provided the material conditions and justification for a policy of closing schools. In particular, disinvestment in African American communities and their schools has opened them up as multimillion-dollar investment opportunities for real estate developers and charter school operators. In some cases, closing schools is part of a larger gentrification strategy (Lipman, 2011); in others it is part of a strategy of state abandonment, as I discuss below.

The post–World War II welfare state (based on full employment, expanding consumer sales, government spending, and a social welfare cushion) has been superseded during the past 25 years by a market-driven neoliberal state. The neoliberal state is weak when it comes to providing for social welfare but strong as a protector of capital and enforcer of social control. In a see-saw effect, the social welfare functions of government were gutted while the state's role in supporting markets where they exist and intervening to create new markets where they do not has expanded dramatically (Harvey, 2005).

This disproportionately affects African Americans and Latinos who, due to decades of social policy, lack the economic cushion of accumulated wealth that Whites are more likely to have (Coates, 2014). Moreover, many working-class African Americans, and some Latinos, have become expendable in the restructured neoliberal economy, more likely to be subject to racialized policing and containment than to economic and social opportunity. The end of the post–World War II welfare state era is also marked by a fusion of government and capital with a revolving door of corporate and political elites and public private partnerships. We see this in education in partnerships of elite corporate organizations and school districts to dismantle and privatize public schools, in takeovers of school districts and mayor-appointed school boards, and in the influence of billionaire venture philanthropists (such as Bill Gates and the Walton Family) (Lipman, 2014; Saltman, 2010).

Neoliberalism's ideological project is to produce new subjectivities and institutional practices, new notions of "citizenship," a new common sense— or a new social imaginary—in which the values and norms of markets, competition, personal responsibility, and individual choice saturate social institutions and shape who we are and how we act (Taylor, 2004). In the neoliberal world, each of us is expected to take responsibility for ourselves, to work on our own human capital and become an entrepreneur of ourselves. Our failure is our responsibility.

Race is at the core of this ideological project. The racialization of social welfare programs (e.g., public housing, Aid to Families with Dependent Children) was central to winning support for their elimination, with the trope of the African American "welfare queen" as racist representation. The hollowing out of the social state and shift to personal responsibility is premised on racialized "culture of poverty" theories and disciplining the "undeserving poor" (Lipman, 2009). Pathologization of Black urban space and devaluation of Black humanity are grounds to seize the land in Black communities, push out those who live there, and rebrand the area—including schools—as a space of Whiteness and civility, softening it up for a new round of investment and capital accumulation (Haymes, 1995).

Although the economic polarization produced by 25 years of neoliberalization has cut across race to affect working-class and some middle-class people, the effects are deeply racialized. Neoliberal shrinkage of the public sphere and weakening of unions, as well as attacks on affirmative action, reversed many of the gains wrested through the struggles of the civil rights and liberation movements of the 1960s and 1970s. The economic crisis precipitated by the collapse of the speculative housing bubble hit African Americans and Latinos/as particularly hard. From 2005 to 2009, median wealth of Latino/a households fell an incredible 66% and median wealth of Black households an equally incredible 53%, compared with just 16% for White households (Kochhar, Fry, & Taylor, 2011). This intensified the historical effects of White supremacy on Black families and communities (Coates, 2014).

In this context, school closings are yet another blow to communities of Color. Across the United States, school closings disproportionately affect students of Color, particularly African Americans, as dramatically illustrated by the National Opportunity to Learn's (2013) graphic, The Color of School Closures, showing that the vast majority of students affected by 2013 mass closings in Chicago, New York, and Philadelphia were students of Color, with African American students disproportionately affected. Shuttering schools in Black communities compounds the "education debt" owed to African American students for centuries of apartheid education (Ladson-Billings, 2006).

I draw on this framework to make sense of the mass closing of public schools, mostly in low-income, working-class communities of Color and to look ahead to strategies to contest these and other neoliberal policies.

Research on School Closings

Despite the U.S. Department of Education's emphasis on "evidence based" policy as grounds for assessing every aspect of education through a plethora of performance indicators (e.g., scores on standardized tests as measures of student achievement, Adequate Yearly Progress metrics as indicators of school failure/success, enrollment to capacity ratios as indicators of efficient use of school space), this methodology seems not to apply to assessing the efficacy of many of the department's neoliberal initiatives, including closing schools to improve students' educational opportunities and outcomes. Studies of school closings show that the vast majority of students do not experience improved academic performance as a result of transfers to other schools; only those students sent to the highest performing schools benefit academically (de la Torre & Gwynne, 2009). School closings are shown to have harmful effects in the year of the closing (de la Torre & Gwynne, 2009; Research for Action, 2013) and the year following closure (Research for Action, 2013). And recent longitudinal research in an unnamed urban district (Engberg, Gill, Zamarro, & Zimmer, 2012) found that students displaced by school closures experienced a persistent adverse effect on achievement gains and attendance. Only students relocated to schools of substantially higher quality (75th percentile change in Student Performance Score) experienced no significant *drop* in achievement.

In fact, students of Color affected by school closings are not being transferred to the schools districts rank as their best. Most have been transferred to schools the same or only marginally better on district measures of quality (de la Torre & Gwynne, 2009).[1] In Chicago's 2013 school closing plan, 87.5% of the moves were not to top-performing schools. In our study of parents' experiences with school closings in Chicago (Lipman, Vaughan, & Gutierrez, 2014), parents said school closings had a negative academic impact on their children, and most believe their new schools are not better than the schools that were closed. Some reported increased class sizes, loss of resources, and loss of relationships with trusted adults that negatively affected their children's educational experiences.

School closings also create mobility and have damaging social and emotional consequences. Research shows that students lose at least four months of academic gains every time they change schools (Kerbow, 1996). This is why districts enact policies to limit mobility, yet school closings are a form of forced mobility. Even schools that are closed and then taken over by a "turn around" operator produce mobility effects. In turnaround schools, all the adults in the building are dismissed, and the turnaround operator brings in new staff, curriculum, and policies. As a result, students lose connection with trusted adults and familiar programs that provide stability. There have also been increased violence and safety concerns as a result of students having to travel long distances, across dangerous streets or out of their neighborhoods, when their schools are closed.

School closings are an assault on children, families, and communities, a form of displacement that breaks the web of sustaining human connections that coalesce in the school. Yet, nowhere in the discourse about the efficacy of this policy is this human dimension mentioned. Indeed, the process of closing schools is itself dehumanizing to African American, Latino/a, and other parents who are excluded from any real decision-making, whose knowledge is disregarded, and who are treated like numbers on a spreadsheet. The decision is made elsewhere, by those with little or no connection to or knowledge of the communities affected. It is this dehumanization that most sharply reveals the racism at the center of a policy to close schools purportedly to advance educational goals.

In our study of school closings (Lipman, Vaughan, & Gutierrez, 2014), narratives of parents and caregivers, most of whom were African American, were filled with both the pain of the closings and the insight and expertise of those deeply knowledgeable about the schools their children attend. Parents talked about damaging social and emotional impacts of closing a school—children's deep sense of loss, anxiety, and insecurity. One parent said, "the kids were grieving. It was just like somebody had died and it had. The school died" (p. 13). Both parents and children had deep personal ties to their schools. Many described the schools as like "family." When they were closed, that family connection was broken. School closings were also a loss to the community as a whole. Many of the schools that were closed had been anchors in their communities and spaces of intergenerational relationships. Many parents were actively engaged in their schools as volunteer teaching assistants, assistant coaches, school monitors, unofficial community liaisons, elected local school council representatives, and more. Some anchored whole programs. When schools closed not only did the schools lose these parental resources but the parents lost the meaning their involvement had for them. For a number of parents and caregivers, participating in their schools was a way of "giving back" to their communities. Not only had they been excluded from decisions about school closings, some were now excluded from participating in their children's new schools.

School Closings: Organized State Abandonment

This disregard for African American and Latino/a children and adults reflects the wholesale abandonment of some African American and Latino/a urban areas that are largely superfluous from the point of view of corporate and financial interests. Urban communities that have been demonized in the White racial imagination, and persistently disinvested in by the state over the past 25 years, are now the targets of organized state abandonment (Lipman, 2013; Lipsitz, 2014). Schools are at the center of this strategy through school closings, charter school expansion, and takeovers of public schools by private management organizations. This collusion of the state and capital to dispossess people of Color of their schools is part of a larger process of dispossession of homes, land, and historical "home places" (Haymes, 1995) through dismantling public housing, foreclosure of homes and rental units, closing public clinics and hospitals, and privatization of other public services.

State abandonment of public schools is evident in cities across the United States. The Journey for Justice Alliance (2014) reports that, in recent years, Detroit, New York, and Chicago have all closed more than 100 public schools. Columbus (OH), Pittsburgh, St. Louis, Houston, Philadelphia, Washington D.C., Kansas City, Milwaukee, and Baltimore have all closed more than 25. The District of Columbia closed 39 neighborhood public schools since 2008; Newark closed 13 since 2009. As of fall 2014, every traditional neighborhood public school in New Orleans will have been closed. The district will be 100% charter.

These closings have disproportionately affected African American students. In Chicago, since 2001, more than 150 neighborhood public schools were closed, phased out, consolidated, or handed over to private managers. Schools with more than 99% students of Color, what the Chicago Teachers Union calls "Apartheid schools," have been the principle target of these actions (Caref, Hainds, Hilgendorf, Jankov, & Russell, 2012). In the 2013 closings, 79% of the students affected by closings, co-locations of charter schools in neighborhood public schools, and turnaround schools were African American although 40.5% of the students in the district are African American. Most of the remaining students were Latino/a. After over a decade of school closings, there are some African American areas of the city that are now public school deserts—they have almost no neighborhood public schools left. In five of these community areas, more than 60% of children are attending schools outside their neighborhoods (Karp, 2013).

In Philadelphia, after a barrage of protest, in summer 2013, the Board of Education closed 23 schools, one quarter of the schools in the district. Over 80% of the students were African American though the school district student population is 58% African American. Just 4% of the students affected were White (Lee, 2013b). The majority of closings were in the heavily African American North and West sides of the city. Washington D.C.'s closure of 15 schools in 2013 affected about 2,700 students; just two students (less than 0.01%) were White, although White students make up 9% of the D.C. public school student population. Of the total affected students, 93% were African Americans although 72% of the students in the district are African American (Khalek, 2013). In Detroit dozens of school closings have primarily affected African American students who make up most of the school population.

The impact of school closings extends beyond the loss of educational institutions. In Chicago and elsewhere, protests against school closings emphasize that they are more than bricks and mortar. Many are anchors of stability and community resources in African American areas that have experienced economic impoverishment, public and private disinvestment, dismantling of public housing, and home foreclosures. School closings are a form of mass displacement that further destabilizes these communities. In Chicago, many of the neighborhood schools that have been closed served generations of the same families and were the center of their communities. Whatever their failings—and parents have proposals for how their schools could improve (Lipman, Vaughan, & Gutierrez, 2014)—parents testified at school closing hearings that each school that was closed had strengths that went beyond typical academics—arts and sports programs, a stellar science curriculum, a core of excellent teachers, community partnerships, or parent activities that would be lost when it was closed. Schools that were closed also have histories as cultivators of African American cultural and intellectual achievements as well as histories of struggles for racial justice. Shuttering schools named for African American cultural and intellectual leaders such as Mahalia Jackson, Benjamin Banneker, Marcus Garvey, and Mary McCloud Bethune (as was done in Chicago) unmistakably signals disregard, if not disdain, for that history and those who have inherited its legacy.

School closings are generally the endgame of a slow slide toward educational abandonment through years of persistent disinvestment and destabilization. Many of the closed schools that served low-income, working-class African Americans, Latinos/as, and other students of Color in Washington D.C., Chicago, Detroit, New York, Philadelphia, and elsewhere had already experienced cuts in resources and programs and multiple rounds of destabilizing neoliberal experiments, including a revolving door of school leaders and various external oversight bodies, teacher-proof curriculum, and other failed, top-down "reforms" (see, for example, Gutierrez & Lipman, 2012). Some schools had been effectively downgraded to minimalist test-prep schools (Lipman, 2004). While gentrified and upper-middle-class areas of Chicago have new state-of-the-art selective enrollment and specialty schools, many schools in African American and Latino/a low-income areas lack adequate material and educational resources such as full-time music and art teachers, up-to-date science labs, school nurses, adequate counselors, and libraries (Chicago Teachers Union, 2012). In 2009, when parents in a Chicago immigrant Mexican community occupied their school field house for 43 days to pressure Chicago Public Schools (CPS) for a school library, Chicagoans learned that 140 public elementary schools did not have libraries; 100 of them were in African American and Latino areas of the city. In December 2011, CPS's Chief Operating Officer admitted that CPS did not intend to invest in schools that would be closed in the next 5–10 years (Ahmed-Ullah, 2011). The economic crisis, beginning in 2007, provided the impetus to abandon these schools altogether on grounds of purported budget deficits.

In Chicago, African American and Latino parents and students who testified at school closing hearings and spoke to the media, and those who we interviewed (Lipman, Vaughan, & Gutierrez, 2014), were quite clear that shuttering their schools was an organized process of racist public abandonment. As one parent put it, "You know, I feel they don't care about the African American communities. They don't care if we get an education" (p. 22). Dyett High School student Walter Flowers said, "It just feels like they don't care as much as we want them to. It's been heartbreaking. CPS just turned its back on us" (Lee, 2013a). The board voted to phase out Dyett in 2012 after years of disinvestment and destabilization despite parent and community organizing to bring resources into the school. Before the board voted to close Dyett, the school had been so stripped of resources that there were no Advanced Placement classes, only a rudimentary schedule of science and math classes, and students had to take their mandatory art credit online, plus, many college preparatory and mentoring programs were lost when CPS refused to continue funding them (Gutierrez & Lipman, 2012).

Apparently following the Eli Broad Foundation's school closing manual (Broad Foundation, 2009), school district leaders and mayors in Philadelphia, Chicago, Detroit, and other cities claimed schools had to be closed because they were under-enrolled, that is, not operating at efficient capacity. This rationale treats significant changes in student enrollment as a natural process of demographic change. But population shifts are shaped by public policies that are driven by intertwined logics of capital and race. Loss of student enrollment is the product of selective (public and private) disinvestment and reinvestment in urban space. It is produced in the nexus of public policy and private investment, for example, policies to dismantle public housing, overheated real estate markets and gentrification, corporate decisions to deindustrialize and outsource jobs, and education policies that support some public schools and destabilize or starve others of resources or expand charter schools (Lipman, 2011). This policy nexus accounts for the reduction of Detroit's population by more than 50% over the past 20 years and the loss of thousands of school-age children, the eviction of thousands of African Americans from New Orleans after Hurricane Katrina, and the loss of 181,000 African Americans in Chicago from 2000 to 2010. The shuttering of a school is yet another form of public disinvestment and state abandonment, compounding the effects of these policies and further driving out low-income African Americans and some Latino/as.

As Aiwah Ong (2006) points out, neoliberal governments protect those people who are valuable to capital and make vulnerable those who are not. In Chicago, disposability of working-class, low-income communities of Color is paired with the over-valuing of gentrified and upper-middle-class White areas of the city that have new state-of-the-art selective enrollment and specialty schools (Lipman, 2004). Even as Chicago Public Schools closed 50 schools serving African American and Latino/a low-income students on grounds of budget deficits, they planned another new selective enrollment public high school in the gentrified area that was home to the demolished Cabrini Green Public Housing development. Named for President Obama, the school is just a stone's throw from another premier selective enrollment public high school. These two schools, in an area known as the "gold coast" for its affluent population, contrast with the historical African American Bronzeville area that will have no neighborhood public high school if Dyett High School is closed.[2]

Accumulation by Dispossession

A well-organized, lavishly-funded ensemble of corporate and political forces is aggressively pushing a neoliberal program to gear all aspects of education to workforce preparation, U.S. competitiveness, and capital accumulation (Gutstein, 2009). Wall Street bankers, hedge fund operators and other financial speculators, and large corporations such as Microsoft, Dell, and Pearson recognize the enormous profits to be made from privatizing every component of public schools. In a form of disaster capitalism, the economic crisis has provided an opening to accelerate this agenda through mass school closings and charter school expansion. Nationally, from 2000–2012, the percentage of charter schools increased from 1.7 to 5.8%, and the total number of charter schools increased from 1,500 to 5,700. The percentage of U.S. students attending charter schools increased from 0.7 to 4.2% (U.S. Department of Education, 2014). The expansion of charter schools in school urban districts is particularly striking. From 2005–2006 to 2012–2013, 20 large urban school districts (including Detroit, Los Angeles, Newark, Baltimore, and Houston) had a 35% increase in charter school enrollment, and charter enrollment more than doubled in 13 of the districts (National Alliance of Public Charter Schools, cited in Journey for Justice Alliance, 2014, p. 3). Funding and advocacy of billionaire venture philanthropists such as Bill Gates, Eli Broad, and the Walton family; support from the U.S. Department of Education; and the shift in resources from public schools to charters have bolstered charter school expansion.

Over the past decade, Chicago Public Schools lost roughly 30,000 students and added more than 50,000 charter school seats (Black, 2013). In some African American community areas that have had large losses in K–12 student population, and in which individual schools have also lost substantial enrollment, CPS nonetheless authorized more charter schools while closing public schools. The disruption of closing one neighborhood school has a ripple effect on others in the area, creating a downward spiral of destabilization. This churn in neighborhood schools creates opportunity for well-funded charter schools to recruit students, further contributing to declines in public school enrollment and justifying more school closings. In some areas of Chicago, the few remaining neighborhood schools are surrounded by charter schools. In one African American area of the city that has experienced multiple rounds of school closings, turnarounds, phase outs, and charter expansion, only 40% of elementary school students attend their neighborhood school, compared with 60% 10 years ago. A third of the students who don't attend their neighborhood school attend a charter school (Karp, 2013). In areas with virtually no public schools left, charter schools have become the default education option.

"Underutilized" and "failing" schools in communities of Color are a form of distressed property to be cannibalized by corporate and financial elites as a new source of profit. As in post-Katrina New Orleans, "forceful expulsion" of African Americans, in particular, by seizing their schools (Buras, Randels, & Salaam, 2010) and replacing them with charter schools constitutes accumulation by dispossession. In this process, African American and Latino/a children are cast as both consumers of charter schools and commodities in a growing speculative investment sector. Charter school operators float bonds to fund their expansion and these bonds are then bought and sold in international bond markets as speculative investments. For example, the Wells Fargo investment company reported in 2011 that there were 478 charter school company bond issues, amounting to more than $5 billion, in the 13-year period 1997–2010 (Wells Fargo, 2011, p. 3), an average of $10 million per bond. In other words, financial speculators are making millions of dollars off of bonds sold by charter school companies that in urban areas primarily enroll students of Color. Many of these students were dispossessed—"robbed"—of their public schools by city governments and appointed school boards, essentially to be turned over to charter school operators. In short, through the collusion of the state and capital, closing public schools facilitates the private appropriation of African American and other public space for predatory capital accumulation.

The violence and racism of this process is becoming quite clear to parents and children who are experiencing it. As one African American Chicago parent put it, "The reason they closing the schools so they can fade out our schools and open charter schools and push the people out of our communities" (Lipman, Vaughan, & Gutierrez, 2014, p. 23). The Journey for Justice Alliance, a national alliance of 36 grassroots community, youth, and parent-led organizations of Color in 21 U.S. cities, notes in its report on school closings (2014):

> the policies being implemented have unquestionably been racially discriminatory. That is not to say that the individuals responsible are "racists" who are deliberately closing schools in our communities and expanding the use of charter schools because they want to harm our children. What it does mean is that within the set of political, economic, and social forces that are producing these changes,

there are strong tendencies to treat our communities differently than other communities would be treated. Racism, in this form, has consistently and repeatedly manifested itself by the "reformers"... There is simply no way our communities would be losing our public school systems were it not for the pervasiveness of these biases. (p. 5)

Racial Ideologies and Neoliberal Markets

Mass closing of public schools in African American and other communities of Color is justified on the grounds of fiscal austerity. Essentially, cities propose to balance budgets on the backs of children of Color. This devaluation of Black humanity and other people of Color is masked by the duality of discourses that, on the one hand, racially code communities of Color as dysfunctional, chaotic, violent, and unable to govern their own affairs, while, on the other hand, laud colorblind markets as the "civil rights movement of our generation" (Ballasy, 2011).

For neoliberals, all that is public is "bad" and all that is private is "good," with the public coded as "Black" and that which is private coded "White" (Haymes, 1995). This racially coded neoliberal discourse provides a warrant to demolish public housing, privatize public hospitals, and close, turn over to private operators, or convert to charter schools public schools in African American and other communities of Color. At the same time, closing public schools is legitimated by recourse to neoliberal antiracist discourses (Melamed, 2011) that equate equity with markets, for example, school choice as the path to equitable education. If parents do not take advantage of these choices they are responsible for the outcome. Against charges of racism surrounding school closings, the state resorts to colorblind rationales. The closing of 50 schools disproportionately affecting African American students is cast as simply the outcome of applying a set of colorblind criteria (enrollment ratios and academic achievement) that select for schools that disproportionately happen to be African American. Race is not a criterion; therefore, the decision to close schools is not racist, as Chicago Public Schools contended in their defense against Chicago parents' efforts obtain a court injunction against the 2013 school closings on grounds of disparate impact on African Americans.[3]

Although the target is people of Color, race is central to broader neoliberal goals of capital accumulation. George Lipsitz (2014) explains that race is even more critical to neoliberalism than it was to earlier stages of capitalism:

The ideology of contemporary capitalist neoliberalism needs to disavow the idea of race, because race references historical social identities not reducible to market relations... [yet] neoliberalism needs race even more than previous stages of capitalism did. By making public spaces and public institutions synonymous with communities of Color, neoliberals seek to taint them in the eyes of white working-class and middle-class people, who then become more receptive to privatization schemes that undermine their own stakes in the shared social communities that neoliberalism attempts to eliminate. (p. 11)

An account of closing schools as the solution to "failed" and under-enrolled schools does not account for how they came to be this way. It fails to account for the disinvestment and destabilization of schools and communities of Color or the political and economic policies that robbed people of their assets, pushed people out of their neighborhoods, and gentrified them (Coates, 2014). It does not account for centuries of racial segregation and the advantages of wealth accumulation by Whites. Nor does it account for the "education debt" owed to Black children—the decades of unequal funding, inadequate facilities, and virulent discrimination coupled with benefits bestowed on White children through policies that advantaged their parents economically and spatially (Ladson-Billings, 2006). As Lipsitz (2011) points out,

The long history of rewards for racism and subsides for segregation disappears from this equation. The wealth that whites inherit from previous generations is rarely mentioned. We do not acknowledge the cumulative vulnerabilities that Black individuals and communities face from centuries of impediments to asset accumulation, decapitalization, and discrimination. (p. 245)

In contrast, Lipsitz encourages us to draw from the "Black spatial imaginary" to "see that how 'things are' is, at least in part, a consequence of how they came to be" (p. 245). Yet even with an understanding of this political and economic racial history, many parents, faced with closed and/or disinvested neighborhood public schools, are left with few real choices but to send their children to charter schools.

Shifting Neoliberal Strategies

Although I focus on school closings as a particularly draconian education policy, I want to caution against reifying this policy as neoliberal strategy. Neoliberalism is not a fixed regime or social settlement, but a constantly evolving process of experimentation (Peck & Theodore, 2012). Neoliberalism as a political, economic, and ideological process provided a strategic response to the crisis of capitalism in the mid-1970s and has evolved and remade itself as a "roiling" process of opportunistically capitalizing on crises, including those neoliberal policies created. The privatization of schools in New Orleans following Hurricane Katrina and the response of bankers and investors to the collapse of the speculative housing bubble in 2008 are cases in point. Since the 2008 crash, despite the discrediting of deregulated capitalism, neoliberals have reengineered their strategies and found new ways to speculate and privatize—a potential speculative boom in education investments is one such strategy. In education we have seen a variety of neoliberal experiments: vouchers, charter schools, turnaround schools, virtual schools, Teach For America, value-added assessment of teachers, No Child Left Behind, recovery districts, portfolio districts, intensified racialized discipline and outsourcing of youth prisons, privatized alternative schools for school push outs, the Common Core industry, and more. Moreover, Melamed (2011) demonstrates that the flexible appropriation and incorporation of various antiracisms has been central to extend the life of U.S. capitalism and to expand capital accumulation. Thus, to see school closings in isolation or as a fixed strategy is myopic and misses the underlying racialized, neoliberal logics of late capitalism that are at the root of the problem.

In Chicago, when the Board of Education closed 50 schools, the CEO of CPS promised there would be no school closings for five years. Nine months later the Board turned over three elementary schools in Black communities to a private turnaround operator—school closings by another name. Hedge fund operator and virulent critic of the Chicago Teachers Union Bruce Rauner is running for governor of Illinois as the Republican candidate. His program is to give each child vouchers to use in a full-scale market of private education options. The large Chicago charter school chain run by the United Neighborhood Organization (UNO), whose schools are concentrated in Latino/a communities, is on the ropes for flagrant cronyism and corruption and is carrying an unsustainable load of debt on its bonds. This has led to pressure for charter school accountability. Closing a few irresponsible charter schools might demonstrate even-handedness, undermining claims that the real agenda is privatization, and might suggest that closing neighborhood schools in Black and Latino/a communities is actually a colorblind policy.

This shifting terrain is the minefield education activists have to negotiate. Understanding neoliberalism as an unruly, opportunistic process is crucial for developing strategies to contest and defeat it. Fixating on any one policy in isolation leaves us constantly reacting to neoliberal initiatives. Missing the larger racial agenda would divide and disarm opponents. We must see school closings as part of a nexus of racialized neoliberal policies and shifting strategies. While parents, students, and educators work to defend their schools from being closed, we need a program for teacher-community driven school transformation, community/public accountability, and an articulation of the kind of public schools we want. Otherwise we're constantly chasing neoliberals' tails. One way to think about this is "non-reformist reforms"—reforms that weaken the underlying system and create structures, grassroots organization, and reframing ideologies that move us toward the education and society we want. We need to ask: How do we contest the nexus of neoliberalization, capitalism, and material and cultural racism itself as it manifests in specific policies and ideologies?

Conclusion: The Promise of an Emerging Grassroots Movement

Closing schools in communities of Color is essentially a colonial policy funded by billionaires Bill Gates, Eli Broad, the Walton family, and others who deploy their enormous wealth and influence to steer education policy. A well-organized ensemble of corporate and political elites, think tanks, venture philanthropies, and corporate "reform" groups is making decisions about the education of low-income students of Color (Saltman, 2010). Under the guise of "we know what is best for you," they facilitate the appropriation of Black and Latino/a public space for capital accumulation and racial exclusion and control. They operate from the ideology that whatever is good for business is good for schools, but the unspoken assumption is that working-class children of Color are suited for the low-wage jobs that make up the largest growth sector of the labor force and should therefore have schools appropriate to disciplining them for these roles (Lipman, 2011). Moreover, much profit can be made from privatizing schools for Black and Latino/a children.

These actions are *done to* families and communities of Color who are assumed to have nothing to offer toward educating their children. While the testimony of parents and emergent research reports catalogue the injustices and human suffering caused by school closings, a way forward is also emerging. Committed parents, students, and community members are a fundamental resource to not only improve but also transform schools (Communities for Excellent Public Schools, 2010; Journey for Justice Alliance, 2014; Lipman, Vaughan, & Gutierrez, 2014). In organized resistance to school closings across the United States, parents and students and their committed teacher allies have claimed, "we are the people who can save our schools." Parents have demonstrated they are a rich resource for school improvement and source of educational vision. Their knowledge, expertise, and actual participation in their schools contrasts with the distance and lack of knowledge of the hired "experts" and officials who make decisions for them (Lipman, Vaughan, & Gutierrez, 2014).

Mass school closings, perhaps more than any other single neoliberal strategy, have produced organized grassroots resistance locally and nationally (Journey for Justice, 2014). School closings have spawned grassroots coalitions of parents, students, and teachers, led by people of color. Along with the significant emergence of social movement teacher unionism (Gutstein & Lipman, 2013) in Chicago and Milwaukee in alliance with parents and students, these coalitions are offering an analysis that penetrates the intersection of race and capital and advances alternatives to neoliberal, White supremacist education policies (e.g., Chicago Teachers Union, 2012; Journey for Justice, 2014; Schools and Communities United, 2014). The starting point for this alternative is the desires and knowledge of parents and communities of Color and committed teachers.

Not willing to simply defend schools as they are, parents who are opposed to school closings also want something more. In our research, parents voiced their desire for a rich, challenging, humane, holistic education for all children. They want respectful public schools where young people can develop not only academically but also as thoughtful, caring, and just human beings (Lipman, Vaughan, & Gutierrez, 2014). Their broad vision dwarfs the narrow, impoverished neoliberal notion of schools as an aggregate of test scores, bodies with future job skills, and obedient subjects. This vision and emergent organization is a basis for a transformational education politics that prefigures the kind of society we want—and desperately need.

References

Ahmed-Ullah, N. S. (2011, December 15). CPS: Poorer-performing schools less likely to get funds. *Chicago Tribune*. Retrieved from http://articles.chicagotribune.com/2011–12–15/news/ct-met-cps-buildings-20111215_1_urban-schoolleadership-cps-operating-officer-tim-cawley

Ballasy, N. (2011, January 17). U.S. Secretary of Education: Education is the civil rights issue of our generation. cnsnews.com. Retrieved from http://cnsnews.com/news/article/us-secretary-education-education-civil-rights-issue-our-generation

Black, C. (2013, May 13). Closing schools, cutting resources. Chicago Newstips. Community Media Workshop. Retrieved from http://www.newstips.org/2013/05/closing-schools-cutting-resources/

Brenner, N., & Theodore, N. (2002). Cities and the geographies of "actually existing neoliberalism." *Antipode, 34*(3), 349–379.

Broad Foundation. (2009). School closure guide: Closing schools as a means for addressing budgetary challenges. Retrieved from failingschools.files.wordpress.com/2011/01/school-closure-guide1.pdf

Buras, K. L., Randels, J., & Salaam, K. (2010). *Pedagogy, policy, and the privatized city: Stories of dispossession and defiance from New Orleans*. New York: Teachers College Press.

Caref, C., Hainds, S., Hilgendorf, K., Jankov, P., & Russell, K. (2012) *The Black and White of education in Chicago's public schools*. Chicago Teachers Union. Retrieved from http://www.ctunet.com/questcenter/research/position-papers/privatization-the-black-white-of-education-in-chicagos-public-schools

Chicago Teachers Union. (2012). *The schools Chicago students deserve*. Author. Retrieved from http://www.ctunet.com/

Coates, T. (2014, May). The case for reparations. *The Atlantic*. Retrieved from http://www.theatlantic.com/features/archive/2014/05/the-case-for-reparations/361631/

The Color of School Closures. (2013, April 23). National Opportunity to Learn Campaign. Retrieved from http://www.otlcampaign.org/sites/default/files/color-of-closures.jpg

Communities for Excellent Public Schools. (2010). *A proposal for sustainable school transformation*. Washington, D.C.: Author. Retrieved from http://www.ceps-ourschools.org

de la Torre, M., & Gwynne, J. (2009, October). *When schools close: Effects on displaced students in Chicago public schools*. Consortium on Chicago School Research. Retrieved from http://ccsr.uchicago.edu/sites/default/files/publications/CCSRSchoolClosings-Final.pdf

Engberg, J., Gill, B., Zamarro, G., & Zimmer, R. (2012). Closing schools in a shrinking district: Do student outcomes depend on which schools are closed? *Journal of Urban Economics* (71), 189–203.

Gutierrez, R. R., & Lipman, P. (2012). The 3 D's of Chicago school reform. Collaborative for Equity and Justice in Education, University of Illinois at Chicago. Retrieved from htttp://www.uic.ceje.edu

Gutstein, E. (2009). The politics of mathematics education in the US: Dominant and counter agendas. In B. Greer, S. Mukhopadhyay, S. Nelson-Barber, & A Powell (Eds.), *Culturally responsive mathematics education* (pp. 137–164). New York: Routledge.

Gutstein, E., & Lipman, P. (2013). The rebirth of the Chicago Teachers Union and possibilities for a counterhegemonic education movement. *Monthly Review, 65*(2), 1–12.

Gym, H. (2013). School closures rock Philadelphia. *Rethinking Schools, 27*(4). Retrieved from http://www.rethinkingschools.org/archive/27_04/27_04_gym.shtml

Harvey, D. (2003). *The new imperialism*. Oxford: Oxford University Press.

Harvey, D. (2005). *A brief history of neoliberalism*. Oxford: Oxford University Press.

Haymes, S. N. (1995). *Race, culture and the city*. Albany: SUNY Press.

Journey for Justice. (2014). *Death by a thousand cuts*. Author.

Karp, S. (2013, Spring). A sign of stability. *Catalyst Chicago, 24*(3), 11–15.

Kerbow, D. (1996). Patterns of urban student mobility and local school reform. *Journal of Education for Students Placed at Risk, 1*(2), 147–169.

Khalek R. (2013, May 31). Racist school closings in Washington, DC. *Truthout*. Retrieved from http://www.truth-out.org/news/item/16672-racist-school-closings-in-washington-dc

Kochhar, R., Fry, R., & Taylor, P. (2011). Wealth gaps rise to record highs between Whites, Blacks, Hispanics. Pew Research: Social and Demographic Trends. Pew Charitable Trust. Retrieved from http://www.pewsocialtrends.org/2011/07/26/wealth-gaps-rise-to-record-highs-between-whites-blacks-hispanics/

Ladson-Billings, G. (2006). From the achievement gap to the education debt: Understanding achievement in U.S. schools. *Educational Researcher, 35*(7), 3–12.

Layton, L. (2014a, May 13). Activists file civil rights complaints. *Washington Post.* Retrieved from http://www.washingtonpost.com/local/education/2014/05/13/1a0d3ae8-dab9-11e3-b745-87d39690c5c0_story.html

Layton, L. (2014b, May 28). In New Orleans, major school district closes traditional public schools for good. *Washington Post.* Retrieved from http://www.washingtonpost.com/local/education/in-new-orleans-traditional-public-schools-close-for-good/2014/05/28/ae4f5724-e5de-11e3-8f90-73e071f3d637_story.html

Lee, T. (2013a). Amid mass school closings, a slow death for some Chicago schools. MSNBC. Retrieved from http://www.msnbc.com/msnbc/dont-call-it-school-choice

Lee, T. (2013b). Mass school closings' severe impact on lives of black, Latino students. MSNBC. Retrieved from http://nbclatino.com/2013/10/15/mass-school-closings-severe-impact-on-lives-of-black-latino-students/

Lipman, P. (2004). *High stakes education: Inequality, globalization, and urban school reform.* New York: Routledge.

Lipman, P. (2009). The cultural politics of mixed income schools and housing: A racialized discourse of displacement, exclusion, and control. *Anthropology & Education Quarterly, 40*(3), 215–236.

Lipman, P. (2011). *The new political economy of urban education: Neoliberalism, race, and the right to the city.* New York: Routledge.

Lipman, P. (2013). Economic crisis, accountability, and the state's coercive assault on public education in the USA. *Journal of Education Policy, 28*(5), 557–573.

Lipman, P. (2014). Capitalizing on crisis: Venture philanthropy's colonial project to remake urban education. *Critical Studies in Education.*

Lipman, P., Vaughan, K., & Gutierrez, R. R. (2014). Root shock: Parents' perspectives on school closings in Chicago. Collaborative for Equity and Justice in Education, University of Illinois at Chicago. Retrieved from http://www.ceje.edu

Lipsitz, G. (1998). *Possessive investment in Whiteness: How White people profit from identity politics.* Philadelphia: Temple University Press.

Lipsitz, G. (2011). *How racism takes place.* Philadelphia: Temple University Press.

Lipsitz, G. (2014). Introduction: A new beginning. *Kalfou: A Journal of Comparative and Relational Ethnic Studies, 1*(1), 7–14. Retrieved from http://tupjournals.temple.edu/index.php/kalfou/article/view/7

Melamed, J. (2011). *Represent and destroy: Rationalizing violence in the new racial capitalism.* Minneapolis: University of Minnesota Press.

National Opportunity to Learn Campaign. (2013). Retrieved from http://www.otlcampaign.org/

Ong, A. (2006). *Neoliberalism as exception: Mutations in citizenship and sovereignty.* Durham, NC: Duke University Press.

Peck, J. & Theodore, N. (2012). Reanimating neoliberalism: Process geographies of neoliberalisation. *Social Anthropology, 20*(2), 177–185.

Pedroni, T. (2011). Urban shrinkage as a performance of Whiteness: Neoliberal urban restructuring, education, and racial containment in the post-industrial, global niche city. *Discourse: Studies in the Cultural Politics of Education, 32*(2), 203–216.

Research for Action. (2013, March). Issue brief school closing policy. Pennsylvania Clearinghouse for Education Research (PACER). Retrieved from http://www.researchforaction.org/wp-content/uploads/2013/03/RFA-PACER-School-Closing-Policy-Brief-March-2013.pdf

Saltman, K. (2010). *The gift of education: Public education and venture philanthropy.* New York: Palgrave.

Schools and Communities United. (2014). *Fulfill the promise: The schools and communities our children deserve.* Milwaukee: Author.

Simon, S. (2012, August 1). Privatizing public schools: Big firms eyeing profits from U.S. K–12 market. *Huffington Post.* Retrieved from http://www.huffingtonpost.com/2012/08/02/private-firms-eyeing-prof_n_1732856.html

Singer, A. (2014, May 20). Why hedge funds love charter schools. *Huffington Post.* Retrieved from http://www.huffingtonpost.com/alan-singer/why-hedge-funds-love-char_b_5357486.html?view=print&comm_ref=false

Taylor, C. (2004). *Modern social imaginaries.* Durham, NC: Duke University Press.

U.S. Department of Education. (2014). National Center for Education Statistics. *The Condition of Education 2014* (NCES 2014–083), Charter School Enrollment. Retrieved from http://nces.ed.gov/programs/coe/indicator_cgb.asp

Vevea, B. (2013, May 22). CPS Board votes to close 50 schools: Chicago Public Schools plans in the largest scale closing in American history. WBEZ 91.5. Retrieved from http://www.wbez.org/news/cps -board -votes -close -50 -schools -107294

Wells Fargo. (2011). Charter school investments: How risky are they? Wells Fargo Securities Municipal Research Report. Retrieved from http://www.wellsfargo.com/research

Notes

1. These measures are problematic because they rely heavily on standardized test scores, attendance, and graduation rates and other flawed measures that fail to account for unequal opportunity to learn. However, even on their own measures, school districts are not transferring students to their "best" schools.
2. As I write this in June 2014, parents and students and broad coalition of community organizations and institutions continues to fight for the renewal of Dyett High

School as an open-enrollment neighborhood school focused on Global Leadership and Green Technology.

3. Transcripts of court proceedings, in *Swan, McDaniel, Newman v. Barbara Byrd-Bennett, CEO, Board of Education of the City of Chicago*. Available from author.

4. Keys to the Schoolhouse: Black Teachers, Privatization, and the Future of Teacher Unions[1]

BRIAN JONES

Introduction: Locked Out

It was one of those days when I arrived at my elementary school in East Harlem so early that the building was locked. I suspected as much from a block away because I could see two of my coworkers standing outside with their coats and bags. These two women were African American and were old enough to have children my age. Each of them had taught in the school for more than a decade. I had been a teacher in Harlem for eight years at this point, but I was only in my fourth year of teaching in this particular school. My coworkers rang the bell again when I arrived, and we chatted, waiting for someone from the maintenance staff to open the door. After a few more minutes went by, a young White woman (younger than me, at least) approached. I suspected she worked at the charter school co-located in our building, but I did not recognize her. This was not too unusual, though, since I observed frequent turnover in the charter school staff and even administration throughout the school year. There were always new faces in the building. "It's locked?" the young woman asked as she approached. "Well," she continued, "you're in luck!" She reached into her bag, pulled out a key, and proceeded to open the building for us.

The arrival of a young White teacher with less than a year's experience working in the school and in possession of a key to the building did not, however, indicate our "luck." Rather, it signaled one of the distinctive features of what is called education "reform" today: the privileging of White teachers over teachers of Color. White teachers are given literal and metaphoric "keys" to open the schoolhouse door, while teachers of Color are increasingly locked out.

This chapter will highlight a two-fold paradox of contemporary education reform. First, corporate reformers say they want to rectify the legacy of racism in schooling and claim the mantle of the Civil Rights Movement. At the same time, their free-market orientation leads them to undermine an important movement victory: public sector unionization for African Americans. Thus, the first paradox is that the "antiracism" of education reform actually reduces the wealth and power of Black people. The second paradox is that White teachers—like the young woman with a key to my school building—who are ostensibly the winners in this scenario, may actually be losers in the long run, since the erosion of union strength will make it harder for them to make a living, raise families, and retire as teachers. The main beneficiaries of weakened teacher unions will ultimately be social elites for whom union power is a threat. Thus, the fate of African American teachers should be a central concern to all who wish to defend and improve both public schools and teacher unions.

Civil Rights and Public Sector Unions

The leading figures in the *actual* Civil Rights Movement explicitly challenged the idea that the free market could deliver Black people from racism. Many of them were socialists or social democrats (Ella Baker, Bayard Rustin, Stokely Carmichael, to name a few) and strongly supported unions (LeBlanc & Yates, 2013). Rosa Parks made use of trade union resources to build the famous Montgomery Bus Boycott (Theoharis, 2013). Ella Baker, who helped to found the Southern Christian Leadership Conference and the Student Nonviolent Coordinating Committee, studied Marxism and dreamed of "the day when the soil and all of its resources will be reclaimed by the its rightful owners—the working masses of the world" (Ransby, 2003).

From the beginning of his career, Dr. Martin Luther King Jr. was focused on unions as essential vehicles for social advancement. "The negro people are by and large a laboring people," he said. "The forces that are anti-negro are by and large anti-labor" (Honey, 2011). King consulted regularly with top union leaders such as Walter Reuter of the United Auto Workers (UAW) and A. Phillip Randolph of the Brotherhood of Sleeping Car Porters. Randolph, also a socialist, was officially the lead organizer of the 1963 March on Washington, although Rustin did most of the strategic and logistical work. King often spoke to union audiences and in union halls. A version of his famous "I Have a Dream" speech was, in fact, first rehearsed two months earlier at a UAW-sponsored march in Detroit (Honey, 2011).

To be clear, unions have not been flawless vehicles of justice or antiracism in this country. At their worst, unions have been outright racist and many explicitly excluded African Americans for a long time. However, the ideology of White supremacy has always been an Achilles' heel of the union movement—a weakness. At its high points, when it has grown in strength and size, radical activists have pushed the unions to include Black workers and to take up their special demands. The explosive growth of the Congress of Industrial Organizations in the late 1930s is one of the best examples (Smith, 2006).

Given the opportunity to participate, African Americans continue to be the most enthusiastic union supporters for one simple reason: Political rights mean little without rights at work (Ramirez, 2012). The conditions of work determine most of one's conditions of life. How much money a person will have, how much free time, one's health and longevity are, for the most part, determined by the nature and conditions of work. Given historic patterns of racist discrimination in hiring, job assignments, promotions, pay, and so on, it is not surprising that African Americans—more than any other group—have historically sought to control these processes through collective bargaining. As of this writing, Black workers continue to have a higher union membership rate (13.6%) than White workers (11.0%), Asian workers (9.4%), or Hispanic workers (9.4%) (Bureau of Labor Statistics, 2014).

Corporate Education Reform, Unions, and Civil Rights

K–12 teaching is the most unionized (non-uniformed) occupation in the country. In 2013 there were almost three and a half million K–12 teachers in the United States, and 40% of them belonged to one of two national parent teacher unions: the National Education Association (NEA) or the American Federation of Teachers (AFT)—a higher percentage of union membership than any other occupation, according to the Bureau of Labor Statistics (2014).

Corporate education reform favors privatization and "free market" solutions to school governance ("running schools like a business" and so on) and is, therefore, necessarily antithetical to the ethos of trade unions and of collective bargaining. The struggle over teacher unions is a cornerstone of a larger contest over restructuring (or, more accurately, reducing) public sector services. The public sector is almost five times more unionized than the private sector, which means the project of austerity and service cuts faces a highly organized opponent: the unionized employees who provide those services. Since unionized teachers are so numerous, they represent a potentially formidable obstacle to the privatization of public education in particular, and to neoliberal restructuring in general, and therefore, from the perspective of the current "reform" consensus, they have to be weakened, neutralized, or destroyed (Harvey, 2005; Klein, 2007; Welner, 2013).

This general framework explains the broad support we find across the political spectrum for significant attacks on teacher unions among educational and political leaders (including liberals and the Democratic Party). Not unlike the way that President Ronald Reagan's firing of 11,000 air traffic controllers signaled a general antiunion offensive, a wave of recent mass firings has marked the rise of the corporate education reform movement. President Barack Obama praised the firing of 93 teachers in Central Falls, Rhode Island, in 2010 (Greenhouse & Dillon, 2010). That same year Michelle Rhee fired 600 teachers in Washington, D.C., for low test scores, including 240 in one day (Toppo, 2013). And when 7,000 teachers were fired in the wake of a devastating flood in Louisiana, U.S. Secretary of Education Arne Duncan said, "I think the best thing that happened to the education system in New Orleans was Hurricane Katrina" (Bruce, 2010).

Today's application of "free market" principles to schools represents a variation on a historic theme. This is not the first time business leaders and like-minded politicians have seized hold of the idea that schools need to be restructured in their own image. Roughly 100 years ago a similar process unfolded in an "efficiency" movement, when the "brightest minds" of the day became convinced that the factory should serve as a model for the schoolhouse (Callahan, 1964). But today's business craze in schooling has a unique twist: The corporate education reformers portray themselves as the second coming of the American Civil Rights Movement. These wealthy and powerful people compare themselves, over and over again, to that great social struggle, and they cast themselves as activists challenging an entrenched power. They are fighting, they claim, not for profit and riches, but to end a great injustice born of racism and inequality in American schooling. They are particularly concerned about young people of Color, and often the plight of African American youths forms the emotional center of their appeals.[2]

There are many examples of this pattern. In 2009 a banker from Goldman Sachs was quoted at a fancy casino-style fundraiser for charter schools in New York City (where teachers mostly do not have unions) referring to charter schools as "the civil rights struggle of my generation" (Haas, 2009). That same year, then New York City schools Chancellor Joel Klein (who has since moved on to work for Rupert Murdoch's Wireless Generation education division, selling tablets and apps to schools) praised charter school chain CEO Eva Moskowitz as literally fulfilling the promise of the Supreme Court's historic *Brown v. Board of Education* decision (Jones, 2009). The opening of the film *Waiting for Superman*, which blamed teacher unions for protecting bad teachers and ruining public education, was hailed by Arne Duncan as a "Rosa Parks moment" for education (Allan, 2010). One of the stars of that film was Geoffrey Canada, the founder of the Harlem Children's Zone, a network of social services covering a 100-block radius in Harlem and including two charter schools. Since then, Canada has become probably the most famous African American educator (arguably the most famous American educator, period). He has appeared in television programs on every major network, in countless feature articles in magazines, on radio programs, and even in a television commercial. He is frequently introduced as an "activist" and talks frankly about the tough circumstances facing young African Americans today, including unemployment and mass incarceration.[3]

Surveying these public statements, it is noticeable that for someone who speaks so often about poverty and racism, Canada never criticizes banks, subprime mortgage lenders, employers, or even police for their respective roles in the plight of African American families and youth. His most caustic and venomous public statements are instead aimed at teacher unions. In a book based on *Superman*, Canada was quoted to say:

> [O]ne of the by-products of the strong teachers' unions in this country is that teacher contracts define with excessive specificity what a teacher can and cannot do in the classroom. And once you define everything that happens in a school—how many hours teachers work, how many classes they teach, how long their lunch breaks and bathroom breaks are, and the details of their compensation structures—you deprive the leader, the principal, the director, and even the teachers themselves of the ability to try new things, thereby strangling any hope of innovation. (Weber, 2010, p. 198)

Here we have a classic exposition of the kind of "business model" ethos of corporate education reform. Hope for "innovation" lies (mostly) with management. Workers cannot innovate. And if they can, they certainly cannot do it with collective bargaining. In fact, if they are allowed to bargain collectively, all hope for innovation is "strangled." At one of the first screenings of *Superman* in New York City, Canada participated in a panel discussion afterward, where he said, not just of teacher unions, but of unions in general: "I'm sure there are things the unions have done to help children. I just can't think of any" (Heilemann, 2010).

For Canada and corporate reformers like him, the legacy of the Civil Rights Movement has been carefully detached from its historic roots in trade unionism. This chapter contends that this rhetorical combination—antiunion on the one hand, and antipoverty and antiracist on the other—is profoundly misleading and ironic at best, and dangerous at worst. Unions in general, and public sector unions in particular have been central to wealth accumulation and social mobility for African Americans. Every move to attack unions and to privatize the public sector is deleterious to African American prosperity. In this way, the antiracism of corporate education reformers paradoxically serves White supremacy and institutional racism.

African Americans and Public Sector Unions

The public sector has historically been in advance of the private sector when it comes to desegregated staffing and equality of opportunity. The dramatic expansion of the public sector over the 20th century, combined with the growing political influence of African Americans, opened up opportunities for Black workers in the public sector far earlier than the private sector. As early as 1928, for example, Black employees were estimated to be 15–30% of the workforce at the largest urban post offices (Parks, 2011). At the end of the 20th century, African Americans were 21% of the postal work-force—nearly twice their percentage of the overall civilian labor force (U.S. GAO, 2003).

Far more than manufacturing, public sector employment became *the* economic niche for African Americans, especially after World War II. When President Kennedy allowed collective bargaining for federal employees in 1962, municipalities nationwide followed suit. Public sector union members quickly became the majority of union members nationwide. From the mid-1960s to the early 1970s, public sector union membership more than quadrupled (Freeman, 1986). Whereas professional and managerial employment for White people grew in the public sector by 34% between 1960 and 1975, the corresponding figure for African Americans was 55% (Brown & Erie, 1981). In 1970 nearly half of all Black male professionals and two-thirds of all Black female professionals worked in the public sector (Freeman, 1986; Parks, 2011). Black people working in the public sector earn more money than they do in the private sector. This is even more true for Black women than for Black men. The median income public/private sector differential in 2000 was 15% for Black men and 19% for Black women. That year, almost half of all Black women (43%) worked in state or state-related industries (Katz, Stern, & Fader, 2005).

In a study published in *The Journal of American History,* Michael Katz and his co-authors (2005) show compelling evidence that public sector employment was much more central to the security, wealth, and mobility of Black workers than manufacturing, which is often assumed to be the bedrock of mid-century Black wealth. They conclude: "Public employment... has been the principal source of black mobility, especially for women, and one of the most important mechanisms reducing black poverty" (p. 356). Why are the wages and benefits higher in the public sector? The higher rate of unionization is certainly one important factor. In 2008 roughly 37% of all government employees were unionized compared to 8% in the private sector (Parks, 2011). Public sector workers can also pressure their employers as voters. Only in the public sector can employees elect their employers! Thus, for Black people, public sector unions have also been a source of political power. Conversely, attacks on public sector unions are also attacks on Black political power.

So while Canada "just can't think of" anything that unions have done for children, the 20th century provides evidence of some pretty big ones: Unions in general, and public sector unions in particular, meant wealth, security, and political power for African American families.

The Rise and Fall of Black Teachers

The story of African Americans and the teaching profession has its own unique dynamic within the larger context of public sector employment. Historically, teaching was one of the only professional careers available to educated Black men and women. In the early part of the 20th century, as more African Americans sought higher education, they swelled the ranks of the teaching force. In the second half of the century, the number of Black teachers precipitously dropped. In part, there was a good reason: Black people with college degrees were able to find other kinds of work. The other part was the often unacknowledged effect of desegregation in the South—Black teachers had a harder time finding work in integrated schools, where White people were in charge and did not want to hire them. One survey estimates that the historic 1954 Supreme Court decision to desegregate the nation's schools—*Brown v. Board of Education*—led 40,000 Black teachers to lose their jobs by 1972 (Parker, 2008). After World War II, 79% of Black female college graduates were teachers. By the mid-1980s, that number dropped to 23% (Zumwalt & Craig, 2005). The desegregated job market for Black teachers was not a "free" market. In New York City, for example, the standardized testing system helped Jewish applicants break into the profession (previously dominated by the Irish), but despite their claim to "objectivity" the tests blocked the rise of Black and Latino teachers. By 1965 only 3% of NYC public school principals and only 8% of its teachers were Black—while Black youth already comprised 50% of the student population (Brier, 2014).

Despite the post-*Brown* drop, the K–12 system expanded massively, as did the number of teachers, including the number of African American teachers. From 1940 to 2000 the number of Black male teachers increased by 481% and the number of Black female teachers increased by 56% (Katz et al., 2005). Although the *number* of Black teachers increased, the expansion of the system as a whole meant that the *percentage* of Black teachers has actually fallen and the teaching force overall, since the 1960s at least, has been predominantly composed of White people (Snyder & Hoffman, 2002). White teachers are roughly 84% of the K–12 workforce today, while Black teachers are only 7% (Feistritzer, Griffin, & Linnajarvi, 2011).

Given that this chapter argues that public sector employment, particularly unionized public sector employment, and especially unionized public sector employment *as teachers* matters greatly to Black wealth and prosperity, then we need to spend a moment looking at that very small number: 7%. It would be easy to point to the fact that more than 80% of teachers are White—and have been for a while—to explain why teacher unions have, in some cities, been indifferent or hostile to the needs and aspirations of Black students and their families. It is true that many northern Black migrants in the 20th century found their children herded into overcrowded ghetto-ized schools, and often faced intense racism and abuse from White teachers.[4] It is also true that in some places this same dynamic persists. But this is a political story, not just a demographic one.

In New York City, for example, many educators in the 1930s joined the Teachers Union (TU), which was also mostly White (at the time, predominantly Jewish). TU teachers fought side by side with Black parents to remove racist depictions of African Americans from the official curriculum, to elevate the teaching of Black history, to improve conditions in the schools, to ensure that racist principals were fired, and more. They agitated for and won the construction of two new school buildings in Harlem in 1938 (Murphy, 1990). Why would a group of mostly White teachers prioritize challenging White supremacy? The answer is political—TU was led by members of the Communist Party, people who believed deeply that the struggle against racism went hand in hand with trade unionism (Naison, 1983). Several decades later, when the TU was crushed in the McCarthyist witch-hunts, the more conservative United Federation of Teachers (UFT) became the exclusive bargaining agent for teachers in the city. Tragically, in 1968 the UFT took its members out on a series of strikes *against* a section of the Black community that was trying to exercise greater control over their neighborhood schools.

So in the same city and the same school system, with a similar teacher demographic, we see two different political relationships between White teachers and Black families. Genuine solidarity between these groups has not been automatic, but neither has it been impossible.

Yet even though teacher unions are dominated by White members, it is still true that the survival of those unions is of no small import to Black communities nationwide. Although African American teachers are only roughly 7% of the national K–12 public school teaching force, they tend to work in large, urban school districts that serve predominantly students of Color. Thus, *to the communities where they work,* the employment of African Americans as teachers matters greatly. Black teachers are 19% of the K–12 staff in New York City, for example, 21% of public school teachers in Boston, and 26% in Chicago (CTU, 2011; NYC, 2014a; Vaznis, 2014). In some places, these percentages actually represent a decline. The New York City Independent Budget Office found that the percentage of newly hired Black teachers between 2008 and 2013 dropped from 13.8% to 11.6% (NYC, 2014b). As recently as 1995, for example, 45% of teachers in Chicago were African American (Simon & Kelleher, 2012). Still, the pattern of geographic concentration remains, and therefore policies that disproportionately affect these concentrations of Black teachers take on a greater significance in those locations.

A Threat to Black Wealth

Black teachers are concentrated in large urban school districts, and they tend to work in schools largely populated with Black students (Boser, 2011). Since some of the most dramatic attacks on unionized teachers have taken place in large urban districts and have targeted schools with high concentrations of Black students, corporate education reform has had a disproportionate effect on Black teachers. Despite representing a quarter of all educators in Chicago public schools, Black teachers were 65% of teachers in schools targeted for closure in 2011 (Caref, Hainds, Hilgendorf, Jankov, & Russell, 2012). In Newark, researchers found that Black teachers in that city teach twice as many Black students and were more than twice as likely to work in schools that faced punitive "consequences" (such as closure) as a result of the "One Newark" reform plan (Weber, Baker, & Oluwole, 2014).

A news report on the mass firing of teachers in New Orleans after Katrina reveals a similar dynamic:

> Beyond the individual employees who were put out, the mass layoff has been a lingering source of pain for those who say school system jobs were an important component in maintaining the city's black middle class. New Orleans' teaching

force has changed noticeably since then. More young, white teachers have come from outside through groups such as Teach for America. And charter school operators often offer private retirement plans instead of the state pension fund, which can discourage veteran teachers who have years invested in the state plan. (Dreilinger, 2014)

Education Week reported that from 2007 to 2013, the percentage of African American teachers in New Orleans plummeted from 73% of the workforce to 49%, while the percentage of White teachers nearly doubled (Zubrzycki, 2013).

Other writers have emphasized that privatization and the neoliberal restructuring of schools hurts children of Color—and African American children in particular—through overuse of standardized testing, staff turnover, disruption of community schools, zero tolerance policies, and so on (Hursh, 2007; Lipman, 2011; NCFOT, 2007; Noguera, 2009). I agree with those critiques and would like to add another dimension. The corporate education reformers rhetorically position schools as a solution to poverty. This chapter contends that they are partly right, but for a different reason. Schools *can* do something about poverty—they can hire people and treat them like human beings. In neighborhoods where African Americans are struggling to find jobs, schools can hire local residents and give them the kinds of salaries and benefits that actually have, historically, lifted people out of poverty.

The combination of unions and public sector employment continues to be important to economic security for African Americans. A 2014 study from the Center for Economic and Policy Research concludes that overall Black people in union jobs earn almost 27% more than Black people in non-union jobs (Jones & Schmitt, 2014). At the end of the 20th century, 82% of all Black men in the public sector had employer-provided health insurance, and 76% had a pension plan. In the private sector the comparable figures for Black men are 55% and 41% (Parks, 2011). A school reform "movement" that attacks unions and the public sector represents a mortal threat to Black wealth, power, and mobility. Weakening or eliminating teacher unions would have profound consequences for the rest of the union movement and for the public sector as a whole. All working people—and Black workers in particular—will be in a weaker position vis-à-vis their employers if these attacks are successful.

The ultimate beneficiaries of weakened or destroyed teachers' unions include people who benefit from the lubricated process of capital accumulation: politicians, business owners, ed-profiteers, and upwardly mobile middle-class professionals. Politicians confront teachers as employees. If the teacher union in their area is weakened, then municipal leaders have a stronger hand at the bargaining table with teachers *and* with other groups of public sector workers, such as bus drivers, firefighters, sanitation workers, and so on. Since teacher unions are a large part of the union movement nationwide, business owners stand to benefit as well. If teacher unions are weaker, then the labor movement as a whole is weaker, and the large owners and employers are in a stronger position in general (Sustar, 2013). Those who stand to profit directly from the privatization of schools—school operators, contractors, real estate developers, consultants, textbook publishers, testing developers, and so on—also benefit from the weakening of teacher unions because the environment in which they sell their wares will be less regulated by union contracts, and workers will have less say in the governance of schools (Ravitch, 2013).

Finally, upwardly mobile professionals who are (mostly, but not entirely) White may also gain from the weakening of teacher unions. Through organizations like Teach For America, upwardly mobile middle-class college graduates who are mostly White are able to get master's degrees that are subsidized, expand their business contacts and networks, and pad their résumés, whether their long-term career goals are in the field of education or not. In the 2007–2008 school year, TFA's secondary school teachers were 89.1% White, higher than the corresponding percentage in schools nationwide: 83.5% (Clark, Chiang, Erbe, McConnell, Silva, & Sonnenfeld, 2013). Likewise, the expansion of standardized testing and the role of "big data" in education has created enormous employment opportunities for highly educated developers and consultants (Au, 2008). To the extent that teachers unions represent a vehicle for resisting the above mentioned trends, politicians, business owners, ed-profiteers, and upwardly mobile middle-class people will continue to benefit from the weakening or outright destruction of teacher unions.

The Fates of Teachers and Students Are Linked

The corporate reformers want to pit teachers against students, claiming that the rights of teachers stand in the way of justice for students. As this chapter went to press, a California court ruled that teacher tenure was unconstitutional (*Vergara v. State of California*, 2014). The plaintiffs (funded by a Silicon Valley millionaire) argued that tenure protections hurt children. In finding for the plaintiffs, the judge invoked the legacy of *Brown v. Board of Education* (Medina, 2014). A similar lawsuit has recently filed in New York (Layton, 2014).

Where White unionized teachers seem indifferent or even hostile to the concerns and aspirations of Black students and families—by ignoring, dismissing, or downplaying parent or student concerns about teaching methods,

scipline policies, to give some examples—the agents of pri-
too easily aim parent anger at teacher unions, while posing
as courageous antiracists. In other words, it is not always clear to a parent who
your ally is if it seems like the teachers do not care about your child, while
the reformers profess to care a great deal. In some cases, White teachers may
feel uncomfortable bringing up issues of racism, whereas corporate reformers
boldly declare that racism must be challenged. In such tough circumstances,
it may seem nearly impossible that teachers, students, and their families will
ever see each other as allies.

The long-term trends bear out the idea that teachers, parents, and students have an interest in finding a way to stand together. For example, one
trend is that the manner in which schools treat adults is ultimately related
to the way they treat children. The corporate reformers want teachers to be
disposable and to work with a proverbial sword over their heads. Students in
these highly pressurized schools end up in a similar position. In a test-centric
school culture, teachers and students both live and die by their performance
numbers. Reformers who celebrate staff turnover, who rejoice at mass
firings, who want to treat adults as interchangeable, disposable cogs will
inevitably treat children the same way. In 2009 Geoffrey Canada expelled
an entire eighth-grade class of students because their test scores were too
low. One Harlem Children's Zone board member explained the decision as
"trimming the sails." He said: "[I]f the board hadn't trimmed the sails, and
a year later the school was still in trouble, it could have been a disaster for
the agency's public profile… it would have affected the Harlem Children's
Zone brand, and that is a very important brand to protect" (Tough, 2009).
Apparently it is not just teachers who get in the way of Canada's "innovations"; students do, too. There is considerable evidence that many other
charter schools resort to similar methods to protect their respective brands
(Welner, 2013)

The notion that privatization and union-busting can be weapons in a
new Civil Rights Movement does violence to history. Many people recall
that Dr. King was assassinated in Memphis in 1968. However, most forget
that the reason he had traveled to Memphis was to support the struggle of
1,300 sanitation workers who were fighting for the right to form a public
sector union. To King, their movement was inseparable from the cause of civil
rights. The sanitation workers were Black, and the mayor was White. Like
many employers of Black migrants, the mayor more or less saw them as field
hands and himself as the master. The famous slogan the workers carried on
placards—"I Am a Man"—spoke volumes about the real content of the struggle for public sector unions. For a White supremacist power structure to grant

union rights and to have to sit at a table and bargain collectively with Black garbage workers required acknowledging their equality as human beings.

Oppression and exploitation have always been the terrible twins of working life for African Americans. For that reason, to escape poverty and find some measure of justice, they have, *more than any other group in this country*, sought the protection of unions. The corporate education reformers want us to believe that the struggle against racism and against economic exploitation are separate. They claim to challenge racism by ratcheting up exploitation. The whole history of struggle against White supremacy in this country—including the actual Civil Rights Movement!—proves the opposite. King's claim that "[t]he forces that are anti-Negro are by and large anti-labor" is still true. There is no way to challenge racism without challenging economic exploitation and vice versa. Likewise, there is no way to save the children by beating up on the adults (Anyon, 2014). To the extent that neoliberal education reform succeeds in shredding public sector services and weakening or eliminating unions, it will, contrary to its rhetoric, have taken away from Black people essential means of challenging both racism and poverty.

Social Movement Unionism

Today, unions represent a small part of the overall population. Only 11% of all American workers are in unions, down from 20% in 1983 (Bureau of Labor Statistics, 2014). The overall decline in the rate of unionization in the United States means that fewer people are familiar with the potential benefits of joining or making common cause with trade unions. The two main umbrella unions for teachers—the NEA and AFT—have too often been passive (at best) or complicit (at worst) in the face of the corporate reform agenda (Sustar, 2013). Thus, parents and students are not the only ones who may be disengaged from the importance of the labor movement; many unionized teachers are as well.

The process of turning this situation around is going to be challenging and complicated. As of this writing, some union leaders have become more rhetorically militant, connecting teacher and community interests, and making a straightforward case against reforms that are harmful for teaching and learning (American Federation of Teachers, 2013; Roekel, 2014). In some cities, groups of unionized teachers who grasp the danger presented by corporate education reform have also concluded that antiracism is a strategic imperative for their survival. In some cases these groups have been elected to lead their local unions, while in other places they exist as activist groups (and/or caucuses) within the union. These are hopeful indicators of change.

But when parents and students perceive teacher unions as having selfishly defended their members' interests (narrowly conceived) for decades, militant rhetoric alone won't create overnight solidarity. Genuine solidarity can only be forged in practice, in the context of a common struggle that brings parents, teachers, and students together to fight for the schools our children deserve.

That phrase—*the schools our children deserve*—has been on the lips of educators and activists nationwide ever since it appeared in the title of a report published by the Chicago Teachers Union (CTU) in 2012. Preparing to negotiate a new contract with the city, *The Schools Chicago's Children Deserve* put the CTU on the ideological offensive by highlighting the union's positive vision for public education. The document is full of demands that resonate with parents and students, such as smaller class sizes, well-rounded curricula, and quality school facilities. In strong language, the document condemned inequality in resources and funding in Chicago's public schools, and specifically noted the pattern of racial discrimination:

> Students and their families recognize the apartheid-like system managed by CPS. It denies resources to the neediest schools, uses discipline policies with a disproportionate harm on students of Color, and enacts policies that increase the concentrations of students in high poverty and racially segregated schools. (CTU, 2012)

The CTU also matched words with deeds. When a new union leadership (the Caucus of Rank and File Educators—CORE) was elected to executive leadership in 2010, they decided to change the union's relationship to its members, and to the school communities. Members were encouraged to mobilize themselves alongside community members to challenge gentrification, school closings, privatization, and in response to many other issues that directly affected teachers and community members alike. However, not all actions were led by the union. At times, the union followed the lead of community members. When community groups initiated an occupation of a school building slated for "turnaround," CTU members joined the action. Civil disobedience, disruptions of public hearings, and even sit-ins became part of the life of the union (Uetricht, 2014). This strategy paid off when the CTU went on strike in the fall of 2012. The benefits of an aroused, active membership showed in the strike vote. With 92% of CTU members participating, 90% voted to authorize the strike. The legacy of common struggle with community members made it impossible for the mayor to pit parents against teachers. Ninety-one percent of students in

CPS schools are children of Color. Despite the major inconvenience to Black and Latino/a parents, they overwhelmingly supported the strike—63% of African Americans and 65% of Latinos/as, according to a poll conducted on the third day of the strike. A majority of White residents (52%) disapproved (Moser, 2012).

Nationwide, other groups of educators and union activists are trying to follow the CTU's lead. In Portland, the Portland Association of Teachers (PAT) released a document in advance of their 2014 contract negotiations titled, "The Schools Portland's Children Deserve" (PAT, 2013). The PAT took their case to the public. They made class size a central issue in their contract campaign, which helped bring parents and students into the contract fight on the union's side. PAT activists also made alliances with organized groups of students. The Portland Student Union put out a statement called "The Schools Portland Students Demand," which they read aloud in a protest at a Portland School Board meeting (PD x SU, 2014). When the teachers voted to authorize a strike, students walked out of classes in several high schools to show solidarity. One of those schools was Jefferson High School, where the student body is majority Black. Students marched out of classes chanting: "No more racist school closures," "We support our teachers," "More art, less OAKS [Oregon's standardized test]," and "Black student power" (Levy, 2014a). In the end, the union's militant stance and solidarity from parents and students forced the city to back down, and the strike was averted. The attempts to pit parents of Color against the union failed. The NAACP, the Black-led Portland Parent Union, and other community groups publicly stood with the union (Levy, 2014b). Through this struggle, the PAT won 150 new hires to reduce class size, more planning time for elementary school teachers, and modest salary increases.

Although many groups of change-oriented teacher unionists are not in elected executive positions within their respective unions, two more groups did come to power in 2014: Educators for a Democratic Union member Barbara Madeloni was elected president of the Massachusetts Teachers Association, and Alex Caputo-Pearl of the Union Power caucus was elected to lead the United Teachers of Los Angeles (Blume, 2014; Jaffe, 2014).[5] Whether you call it "social justice unionism" or "social movement unionism" (there is not space here to discuss the distinctions), these groups of educators are trying to rebuild their unions from the bottom up.[6] They emphasize democratic decision-making and grassroots organizing, and recognize the centrality of directly confronting corporate education reform, institutional racism, and White supremacy in our schools.

The Stakes

Parents have the right to place their child in a public school. There is no corresponding right to attend most charter schools. Admission is often by lottery. In many "free market" models, no school has any obligation to serve any particular child. Parents approach each school as shoppers but have no guarantee their child will be admitted anywhere. Why would any parent cede that right?

Corporate education reformers have often targeted communities that feel the least well-served by the public education system. They approach frustrated parents with a Faustian bargain: "Give up your democratic rights as citizens and join us in calling for the blood of the unions, and we will give you better schools." Those of us who want to defend and improve public education cannot lay blame with parents who take up that bargain. But neither do we have to concede the terrain of the debate. By listening to, and making common cause with, some of our most neglected and oppressed communities, we can leverage the potential power of unions to actually improve public schools for the people who need them most.

As demonstrated above, Black teachers are *disproportionally* affected by corporate education reform. The whitening of the teaching force, if it advances, will not only herald the weakening of teacher unions, it will also make strengthening teacher unions more difficult. This is especially true in cities with large concentrations of Black students and other students of Color. When Black teachers are locked out, then solidarity is locked out, and community is locked out. If Black teachers are locked out, replaced by rotating cohorts of temporary teachers from Somewhere Else, the struggle to develop the kind of teacher-community relationships required to save our schools is set back immeasurably.

If the privatization of K–12 education advances, the weakening of the public sector will likewise have negative consequences for White working people and again, disproportionately for Black workers, too. The attack on Black teachers, disguised as an antiracist initiative, is part of the larger attack on unions. In the long run, only social elites (often dubbed "the 1%") stand to gain from this process. Historically, racism has been an effective tool for dividing the laboring population and preventing it from uniting and making common demands. Now, corporate education reform has mobilized faux "antiracism" to the same end. What is at stake is nothing less than the balance of power between capital and labor in the United States. In this struggle to defend and improve public education, we ignore the centrality of racism and the special position of African American teachers at great peril.

References

Allan, N. (2010, September 30). Arne Duncan: Education documentary is a "Rosa Parks Moment." *The Atlantic*. Retrieved from http://www.theatlantic.com/politics/archive/2010/09/arne-duncan-education-documentary-is-a-rosa-parks-moment/63867/

American Federation of Teachers. (2013, May 1). AFT calls for moratorium on Common Core consequences. Retrieved from https://www.aft.org/newspubs/news/2013/043013commoncore.cfm

Anyon, J. (2014). *Radical possibilities: Public policy, urban education, and a new social movement* (2nd ed.). New York: Routledge.

Au, W. (2008) Between education and the economy: high stakes testing and the contradictory location of the new middle class. *Journal of Education Policy, 23*(5), 501–513.

Blume, H. (2014, April 29). Alex Caputo-Pearl wins runoff to lead L.A. teachers union. *Los Angeles Times*. Retrieved from http://www.latimes.com/local/la-me-utla-election-20140430-story.html

Boser, U. (2011). Teacher diversity matters: A state-by-state analysis of teachers of color. *Center for American Progress*. Retrieved from http://files.eric.ed.gov/fulltext/ED535665.pdf

Brier, S. (2014). The ideological and organizational origins of the United Federation of teachers' opposition to the community control movement in the New York City public schools, 1960–1968. *Labour/Le Travail, 73*, 179–193.

Brown, M. K., & Erie, S. (1981). Blacks and the legacy of the great society: The economic and political impact of federal and social policy. *Public Policy, 29*(3), 229–330.

Bruce, M. (2010, January 29). Duncan: Katrina was the "best thing" for New Orleans school system. *ABC News*. Retrieved from http://abcnews.go.com/blogs/politics/2010/01/duncan-katrina-was-the-best-thing-for-new-orleans-schools/

Bureau of Labor Statistics. (2014, January 24). Press Release: "Union Members—2013". Retrieved from http://www.bls.gov/news.release/pdf/union2.pdf

Callahan, R. (1964). *Education and the cult of efficiency*. Chicago: University of Chicago Press.

Caref, C., Hainds, S., Hilgendorf, K., Jankov, P., & Russell, K. (2012). *The black and white of education in Chicago's public schools*. Chicago: Chicago Teachers Union.

Chicago Teachers Union. (2011). Teacher demographics on school closings. *New York Sun*. Retrieved from http://www.nysun.com/new-york/fewer-blacks-more-whites-are-hired-as-city/86580

Chicago Teachers Union. (2012). The schools Chicago's students deserve: Research-based proposals to strengthen elementary and secondary education in the Chicago public schools. Retrieved from http://www.ctunet.com/blog/text/SCSD_Report-02-16-2012-1.pdf

Clark, M., Chiang, H., Erbe, A., McConnell, S., Silva, T., & Sonnenfeld, K. (2013). The effectiveness of secondary math teachers from Teach For America and the teaching fellows programs. *U.S. Department of Education Institute for Education Sciences.* Retrieved from http://ies.ed.gov/ncee/pubs/20134015/pdf/20134015.pdf

Dreilinger, D. (2014, January 16). 7,000 New Orleans teachers, laid off after Katrina, win court ruling. *Greater New Orleans Times-Picayune.* Retrieved from http://www.nola.com/crime/index.ssf/2014/01/7000_new_orleans_teachers_laid.html

Economic Policy Institute. (2012, May 21). Education needed in 2020 workforce and education levels of the 2011 workforce. *The State of Working America.* Retrieved from http://stateofworkingamerica.org/chart/swa-wages-figure-4a-education-needed-2020/

Feistritzer, C. E., Griffin, S., & Linnajarvi, A. (2011). Profile of teachers in the US, 2011. *National Center for Education Information.*

Freeman, R. (1986). Unionism comes to the public sector. *Journal of Economic Literature, 24,* 41–86.

Greenhouse, S., & Dillon, S. (2010, March 6). School's shake-up is embraced by the president. *New York Times.* Retrieved from http://www.nytimes.com/2010/03/07/education/07educ.html?pagewanted=all

Haas, N. (2009, December 4). Scholarly investments. *New York Times.* Retrieved from http://www.nytimes.com/2009/12/06/fashion/06charter.html?pagewanted=all&_r=0.

Harvey, D. (2005). *A brief history of neoliberalism.* Oxford: Oxford University Press.

Heilemann, J. (2010, September 5). Schools: The disaster movie. *New York Magazine.* Retrieved from http://nymag.com/news/features/67966/

Honey, M. K. (2011). *Going down Jericho road: The Memphis strike, Martin Luther King's last campaign.* New York: Norton.

Hursh, D. (2007). Assessing no child left behind and the rise of neoliberal education policies. *American Educational Research Journal, 44*(3), 493–518.

Jaffe, S. (2014, May 13). In upset, reform candidate wins Massachusetts teachers association presidency. *In These Times.* Retrieved from http://inthesetimes.com/working/entry/16692/barbara_madeloni_massachusetts_teachers_association

Jones, B. (2009, November 13). The charter school charade. *Socialist Worker.* Retrieved from http://socialistworker.org/2009/11/13/charter-school-charade

Jones, J., & Schmitt, J. (2014). *Union advantage for Black workers* (No. 2014–04). Center for Economic and Policy Research (CEPR).

Katz, M. B., Stern, M. J., & Fader, J. J. (2005). The new African American inequality. *The Journal of American History, 92*(1), 75–108.

Klein, N. (2007). *The shock doctrine: The rise of disaster capitalism.* New York: Metropolitan Books.

Layton, L. (2014, July 28). Campbell Brown takes on teacher tenure in New York. *Washington Post.* Retrieved from http://www.washingtonpost.com/local/education/campbell-brown-takes-on-teacher-tenure-in-new-york/2014/07/28/135010e4–16a1–11e4–9e3b-7f2f110c6265_story.html

LeBlanc, P., & Yates, M. (2013). *A freedom budget for all Americans: Recapturing the promise of the civil rights movement in the struggle for economic justice today*. New York: Monthly Review Press.

Levy, S. (2014a, January 13). Jefferson demands respect. *Socialist Worker*. Retrieved from http://socialistworker.org/2014/01/13/jefferson-demands-respect

Levy, S. (2014b, February 25). Portland teachers prove the power of solidarity. *Socialist Worker*. Retrieved from http://socialistworker.org/2014/02/25/portland-teachers-prove-power

Lipman, P. (2011). *The new political economy of urban education: Neoliberalism, race, and the right to the city*. New York: Routledge.

Medina, J. (2014, June 10). Judge rejects teacher tenure for California. *The New York Times*. Retrieved from http://www.nytimes.com/2014/06/11/us/california-teacher-tenure-laws-ruled-unconstitutional.html?_r=0

Moser, W. (2012, September 17). Poll shows substantial CPS parent, racial divide on Chicago teachers strike. *Chicago Magazine*. Retrieved from http://www.chicagomag.com/Chicago-Magazine/The-312/September-2012/Poll-Shows-Substantial-CPS-Parent-Racial-Divide-on-Chicago-Teachers-Strike/

Murphy, M. (1990). *Blackboard unions: The AFT and the NEA, 1900–1980*. Ithaca: Cornell University Press.

Naison, M. (1983). *Communists in Harlem during the depression*. New York: Grove Press.

National Center for Fair and Open Testing. (2007, August). How standardized testing damages education. *FairTest*. Retrieved from http://fairtest.org/how-standardized-testing-damages-education-pdf

New York City. (2014a). 2013 Workforce profile report. Retrieved from http://www.ibo.nyc.ny.us/iboreports/2013workforceprofilereport.pdf

New York City. (2014b). Teachers newly hired each year (from Independent Budget Office Analysis of DOE Teacher Files). Correspondence with IBO Director.

Noguera, P. A. (2009). *The trouble with Black boys:… And other reflections on race, equity, and the future of public education*. San Francisco: John Wiley & Sons.

Parker, W. (2008). Desegregating Teachers. *Washington University Law Review, 86*(1), 14–15.

Parks, V. (2011). Revisiting shibboleths of race and urban economy: Black employment in manufacturing and the public sector compared, Chicago 1950–2000. *International Journal of Urban and Regional Research, 35*(1), 110–129.

Peterson, B., & Charney, M. (1999). *Transforming teacher unions: Fighting for better schools and social justice*. Milwaukee, WI: Rethinking Schools.

Portland Association of Teachers. (2013, April 18). PAT initial bargaining proposal: Summary of proposals designed to create the schools Portland students deserve. Retrieved from http://media.wix.com/ugd/892fbe_cc3e36c1554d349b1dc0e1ddf-7dc85fc.pdf

Portland Student Union. (2014, January 14). The schools Portland students demand. Retrieved from http://portlandstudentunion.org/2014/01/14/the-schools-port land-students-demand/

Ramirez, R. (2012, October 16). Poll: Minorities view labor unions more favorably. Retrieved from http://www.nationaljournal.com/thenextamerica/workforce/poll-minorities-view-labor-unions-more-favorably-20121016

Ransby, B. (2003). *Ella Baker and the Black freedom movement: A radical democratic vision.* Chapel Hill: University of North Carolina Press.

Ravitch, D. (2013). *Reign of error: The hoax of the privatization movement and the danger to America's public schools.* New York: Random House.

Roekel, D. V. (2014, February 19). NEA president: We need a course correction on common core. Retrieved from http://neatoday.org/2014/02/19/nea-president-we-need-a-course-correction-on-common-core/

Simon, S., & Kelleher, J. (2012, September 10). Analysis: Striking Chicago teachers take on national education reform. *Reuters.* Retrieved from http://www.reuters.com/article/2012/09/10/us-usa-chicago-schools-analysis-idUSBRE8890VS20120910

Smith, S. (2006). *Subterranean fire: A history of working-class radicalism in the United States.* Chicago: Haymarket Books.

Snyder, T. D., & Hoffman, C. M. (2002). Digest of education statistics, 2001 (NCES 2002–130). U.S. Department of Education. *National Center for Education Statistics.* Washington, DC: U.S. Government Printing Office.

Sustar, L. (2013). Teachers unions at the crossroads: Can the assault on teachers be rebuffed? *New Labor Forum, 22*(2) 60–68.

Theoharis, J. (2013). *The rebellious life of Mrs. Rosa Parks.* Boston: Beacon Press.

Toppo, G. (2013, April 11). Memo warns of rampant cheating in D.C. public schools. *USA Today.* Retrieved from http://www.usatoday.com/story/news/nation/2013/04/11/memo-washington-dc-schools-cheating/2074473/

Tough, P. (2009). *Whatever it takes: Geoffrey Canada's quest to change Harlem and America.* New York: Mariner Books.

Uetricht, M. (2014). *Strike for America: Chicago teachers against austerity.* New York: Verso.

United States Government Accountability Office. (2003). U.S. Postal Service: Data on Career Employee Diversity. Retrieved from http://www.gao.gov/assets/100/92171.pdf

Vaznis, J. (2014, January 20). Officials in Boston seeking Black teachers. *The Boston Globe.* Retrieved from http://www.bostonglobe.com/metro/2014/01/20/boston-public-schools-seeks-more-diverse-teaching-force/PweKkx5C6NQmaSGXDmmccJ/story.html

Vergara vs. State of California (2014). Superior Court of the State of California. Case No. BC484642. Retrieved from http://www.documentcloud.org/documents/1193670-tenative-vergara-decision.html

Weber, K., (2010). *Waiting for Superman: How we can save America's failing public schools.* New York: Perseus Books.

Weber, M., Baker, B., & Oluwole, J. (2014). *"One Newark's" racially disparate impact on teachers.* Retrieved from http://njedpolicy.files.wordpress.com/2014/03/weber-baker-oluwole-staffing-report_3_10_2014_final2.pdf

Weiner, L. (2012). *The future of our schools: Teachers unions and social justice.* Chicago: Haymarket Books.

Welner, K. G. (2013). The dirty dozen: How charter schools influence student enrollment. *Teachers College Record.* Retrieved from http://www.tcrecord.org

Zubrzycki, J. (2013, April 19). TFA alumni aid new teachers in New Orleans. *Education Week.* Retrieved from http://www.edweek.org/ew/articles/2013/04/19/29neworleans_ep.h32.html

Zumwalt, K., & Craig, E. (2005). Teachers' characteristics: Research on the demographic profile (Eds.), *Studying teacher education: The report of the AERA panel on research and teacher Education.* Mahwah, NJ: Erlbaum.

Notes

1. Special thanks to the Lannan Foundation, the CUNY Graduate Center's Office of Educational Opportunity and Diversity Programs, and the Syracuse University School of Education for support. Thanks are also due to Chloe Asselin for critical feedback, and to Joshua Freeman, Edwin Mayorga, Delisa Saunders, Keeanga-Yamahtta Taylor, and Eric Zachary for research assistance. Jean Anyon made this work possible in countless ways, and remains a source of guidance in memoriam.

2. For this reason, this chapter will focus on the particular history of African American teachers and workers in the 20th century. I use the terms *Black* and *African American* as self-reported categories interchangeably, usually following the style of the source cited.

3. I analyze Canada's public rhetoric in an unpublished manuscript titled "Washington and Canada: Free Market Uplift in the Era of Social Defeat."

4. The White teacher in Mason, Michigan, who told Malcolm Little (later known as Malcolm X) that it wasn't "realistic" for a "nigger" to aspire to be a lawyer was probably displaying a nicer, paternalistic version of the racism Black migrants experienced in northern schools. See Malcolm X, 1964. *The Autobiography of Malcolm X.* New York: Ballantine.

5. The following sample of social justice oriented teacher union groups are, as of this writing, not elected to executive leadership: the Movement of Rank and File Educators (MORE), New York; Social Equality Educators (SEE), Seattle; New Caucus, New Jersey; Educators for a Democratic Union (EDU), San Francisco.

6. Peterson and Charney explain social justice unionism for teachers in *Transforming Teacher Unions: Fighting for Better Schools and Social Justice* (1999). Lois Weiner argues that "social movement unionism" is a better term in *The Future of Our Schools: Teachers Unions and Social Justice* (2012).

5. School Choice: The Freedom to Choose, the Right to Exclude

UJJU AGGARWAL

It's a Tuesday afternoon in February, and Tasha has arrived early for a workshop that is organized at the Head Start center where her four-year-old child attends preschool. The workshops are held every Tuesday afternoon and focus on public school access for low-income parents. This is Tasha's first time in attendance. There's a drip in the classroom sink that, alternating with the "bloop" of the small fish tank, provides a percussion-like background as she waits. Soon, two more women trickle in. Like Tasha, both Nicole and Edith also have children who currently attend the Head Start center. Next year, their children will exit the Head Start center and enter kindergarten. In preparation, both women also regularly participate in the weekly workshops. They have been meeting together since October.

This Tuesday, the rose-colored tiles that cover the floors take on a darker hue, as there is not much sun that makes it through the cinder-block glass windows. Outside is Aberdeen Avenue, and the thick glass provides a barrier between the small children inside and the "big kids" outside who attend the two middle schools across the street. The middle schools are housed in one building, Adam Clayton Powell (ACP), which takes up an entire block. Edon is the honors middle school program for Community School District 3 in New York City.[1] The other school, STRIVE, otherwise known as ACP, serves a "general" student population. As a reviewer for Insideschools's popular education website put it, "A single middle school serving two different student populations, Adam Clayton Powell School... at times seems to have a split personality." The mental health prognosis results from the structures inside the school, which ensure that students who occupy different race and class positions are separated from one another. Their separation is rationalized by standardized tests, which are said to measure their academic ability.

And so it happens, on Aberdeen Avenue as elsewhere in the United States more than half a century after *Brown v. Board of Education* (1954), that two groups of students—one largely Black and Latino/a and one largely White—who see each other every day, rarely meet. The students of Edon and STRIVE do not even eat lunch together. More recently, their interactions outside of the building have been further elided after complaints from Edon students and their parents resulted in different dismissal times for the two schools. Aberdeen Avenue was once deemed a "gang" area, and ACP students have historically been associated with this characterization. Although the avenue has been changing over the past years as gentrification moved through the neighborhood, there are still security cameras outside of preschool, providing a veneer of safety. And it is the precariousness, or lack of security, for the futures of their children that has brought Tasha, Nicole, Edith, and the other mothers from the Head Start center together.

New York City's Community School District 3, the district in which these women have come together to navigate kindergarten admissions, is one of the most racially and economically diverse districts in the nation's largest school system (Kucsera & Orfield, 2014). It is also one of the most segregated and unequal districts in New York City and the district that provides the most choice, or options, to parents as to where they might send their child to school. Choice-based programs in District 3 include dual language programs, magnet programs, districtwide choice programs, gifted and talented education, and more. In this chapter I propose that these characteristics of District 3—diverse, segregated, unequal, and choice-based—are joined together by design.

As they settle themselves into the small wooden chairs made for the three-year-olds who occupy the room during the day, Nicole and Edith start sharing updates with one another about the public elementary school tours that they have recently attended. After some time of listening to the women's detailed assessments, Tasha interjects, "Wait a minute, can I ask a question?...What are these meetings *about?*" In response, the women share what they do together every week: The members of the group work to help each other find good schools for their children, and make sure all schools are good and serve the community. They learn about their rights and they go on school tours together. "Going together is better," Nicole adds, "because the schools in the district are racism and discrimination. They do not want the families who are not rich and White—they do not want our children." Tasha responds, "So... what's new... I mean haven't they *always* done that? I mean, you know... that's the way it's always been... So are they doing something *different now?*"

Over the course of several years of conducting outreach as a community organizer, I met many parents who asked similar questions: *Why care? What's new? Isn't that the way it's always been?* Rather than indicative of an apathetic disposition, such questions can be better understood as reflective of Ruth Wilson Gilmore's (2007) observation that "for African Americans there is nothing new in realizing, once again, second-class status (Du Bois [1935] 1992; Sykes 1988; Fields 1990). But while repetition is part of the deadly drama of living in a racial state, the particular challenge is to work out the specific realignments of the social structure in a period of rapid change" (p. 214).

In this chapter, I examine how choice, as a key principle of reform and management in education, ensures that diversity is joined by segregation and inequality; and as such, it is critical to working out a post-*Brown* realignment among the state, the market, and rights. This realignment becomes critical to addressing the critique found within Tasha's question of "*What's new?*" and to understanding the modes through which segregation, inequality, and neoliberal restructuring are inextricably connected.

Historicizing Choice

Choice-based education policies have become increasingly critiqued and associated with neoliberal education reform, which many scholars and activists mark as having begun with the publication of the 1983 report, *A Nation at Risk: The Imperative for Educational Reform* (Gardner, 1983). The thrust of this trajectory of scholarship has provided important insights to the ways that the concept of choice has been integral to the marketing of privatization mechanisms such as charter schools and to the overt promotion of a consumer-oriented citizenship (see, for example, Ball & Youdell, 2008; Bartlett, Frederick, Gulbrandsen, & Murillo, 2002; Lipman & Hursh, 2007; Saltman, 2010).

Yet as we shall see, the historical trajectory of neoliberal restructuring in education dates back further than the 1980s, and can be understood as emerging in the post-*Brown* moment. Extending this timeline can help us see that neoliberal restructuring in the United States (1) does not only have racialized outcomes but, rather, is organized through race; and (2) is directly tied to the structure of individual rights within the capitalist state (and thus, not reliant upon privatization mechanisms alone).

I draw on critical race theorist Cheryl Harris's concept of *Whiteness as property*, which she articulates as the ways that U.S. histories of slavery and genocide are continually inscribed into "racially contingent forms of property and rights," and consistently animated by the right to exclude, thus preserving the formations of power that produce both private property rights and Whiteness as the baseline for citizenship (Harris, 1993). I join Harris's concept of Whiteness as property with Chandan Reddy's (2011) theorization of amendments as "frames [that] conserve and reactivate the force of their textual bodies, even while displacing the origins of that force and restructuring its appearance" to examine how choice became the amendment to state-sanctioned segregation (p. 15). That is, *Brown v. Board of Education* (1954) signified a moment when universal rights to education were won, thus indicating a different structure of citizenship than Jim Crow. Yet *how universal rights were structured (as individual choices) becomes critical to understanding how the continuity of a tiered citizenship was both guaranteed and embedded within the state*. In the paragraphs that follow, I provide a critical genealogy of choice policies and legislation in the post-*Brown* period to examine how choice—as amendment to Jim Crow—anticipated the right to exclude and also became central to rationalizing the inequality that results from exclusion as the necessary outcome of democratic freedom, thus reinvigorating the story of American exceptionalism.

Whiteness as Property and the Racial State: Universal Rights as Individual Choices

As is well known, in 1954 the U.S. Supreme Court determined that separate but equal schools could never be equal. Yet after *Brown v. Board of Education* (1954), the question still remained as to how and when desegregation would be carried out. The following year, the Supreme Court addressed this question in *Brown v. Board of Education II* (1955). As such, *Brown* signaled the possibility of two paths. The first required the state to redistribute resources. The second allowed for freedom to be reconciled otherwise. As it happened, the Court failed to provide any clear guidance about how desegregation should take place, and states and municipalities were granted the freedom to develop their own implementation plans at their own pace, and "with all deliberate speed."

In 1955, the same year as *Brown II*, Milton Friedman put forth a vision for the restructuring of public education. Central to his plan of how schools should be organized was an argument that choice, rights, and freedom are inextricably linked. The timing of Friedman's prescription for public education was not by chance. Rather, Friedman framed his plan as a response to *Brown*, which, he argued, presented the problem of reconciling desegregation with a conceptual framework of freedom as individual liberties (such as the freedom of expression or freedom of speech). When it came to educating one's child, Friedman argued, the practice of individual liberties and freedom was likely to overlap with exclusionary practices. And so, he reasoned, while state-sanctioned segregation was morally wrong, equally questionable was state-enforced desegregation as it impeded upon an individual's right to choose the most appropriate means of educating their child.[2] This conundrum could be fixed, he argued, by the principle of choice. Choice, or rights with *flexibility*, Friedman argued, could preserve democratic process by ensuring that parents who were unhappy with a particular school would have the freedom to withdraw their child and reinvest in a range of options—private, public, religious, or even segregated—that better suited their needs. Guaranteeing rights with flexibility would provide what Friedman called a "third alternative" to forced segregation or forced desegregation.

It is worthwhile to note that choice also has, at different historical moments, represented a progressive demand that signified desegregation and educational justice. Indeed, as Michael Fabricant and Michelle Fine (2012) and James Forman Jr. (2005) have documented, more than a mechanism of oppression alone, the concept of choice has been a contested terrain that has represented decidedly different visions from different blocs historically. However, it is using Friedman's theory of choice as a "third alternative" to state-enforced desegregation—that was based on preserving the co-constitutive relationship between individual freedom and capitalism that grounds the United States' liberal democracy—that I trace a particular genealogy of choice that emerged post-*Brown* that came to animate a range of policy reforms that were critical to the continued structuring of Whiteness as property.

Post-Brown *South: Freedom of Choice Plans*

In the years following *Brown II*, several states (including, for example, Virginia, South Carolina, Arkansas, Alabama, Mississippi, Georgia, North Carolina, and Louisiana) developed what came to be known as Freedom of Choice plans. These plans utilized a variety of means and mechanisms that ranged from local student assignment plans, the development of publically funded all-White schools, to the development of voucher systems that funded private all-White schools. Yet diverse as their tactics were, the unifying element of these plans was that they were animated by Friedman's vision of choice as a third alternative and supported by the state. This support included funding as well as legal/policy mechanisms (see, for example, Alexander & Alexander, 2004; Gordon, 1994; Turner, 2004). As Helen Hershkoff and Adam S. Cohen (1992) observe, in the case of Choctaw County, Alabama, where private school enrollment rose from 25,000 to 535,000 within just 6 years (1966–1972), "many governmental entities throughout the South provided buildings, donated educational supplies... The movement's rhetorical commitment was to individual freedom in choosing public or private schooling" (p. 3). Likewise, in the well-known case of Prince Edward County, Virginia, a series of state laws cut off funds to the local school board, thus forcing all public schools to close for five years between 1959 and 1964. The schools that developed in the wake these closings were voucher supported and all White. The state-sponsored use of Freedom of Choice plans to create private schools for White students has come to be aptly termed "segregation academies" (Champagne, 1973; Ladson-Billings, 2004; Walder & Cleveland, 1971).

And in Prince Edward County, as was the case elsewhere, the consequences of segregation academies extended beyond that of education. Indeed, as Black families were forced to determine if and how their children would go to school, many children went without schooling; many siblings were separated from one another; some children were sent to live with relatives in nearby counties or far away; and some children attended separate schools that their families and others tried to construct in context of necessity. As Kara Miles Turner (2004) documents, the impacts on Black children of this era—who have come to be termed as the "lost generation"—ranged in scale and scope and included intergenerational social, emotional, and physical health.

It took nearly 10 years for the Supreme Court to determine that such voucher-driven segregation academies were unconstitutional. Yet despite the Court's findings in *Griffin v. County School Board* (1964), which declared, "there has been entirely too much deliberation and not enough speed in enforcing the constitutional rights which we held in *Brown v. Board of Education*," various state and municipal governments were able to reconstitute choice-based plans to preserve segregated education through separate schools (Turner, 2004, p. 1689).

In the case of New Kent, Virginia, for example, the county devised a plan that included two public schools: one White and one Black. As Klint Alexander and Kern Alexander (2004) observe, the plan was defended by the local school board that contended that it had fulfilled its obligation mandated by *Brown II* by adopting a plan in which every student, regardless of race, could "freely choose the school he or she would attend" (p. 1139). Like the argument for rights made by Friedman, the school board of New Kent claimed it could not be held culpable for the fact that individual choices resulted in separate schools. The infrastructure of all-White schools was thus maintained by using tactics that ranged from the school-based "counseling out" (of Black students) to other forms of community pressure against integration (Gordon, 1994). When the case of *Green v. County School Board of New Kent County* was brought before the Supreme Court in 1968, the Court determined that the so-called neutrality of choice that guided Freedom of Choice plans was no longer satisfactory. Although the Court did not prohibit such plans, it mandated that other methods of desegregation—that were both speedier and more effective—should be first considered and devised. Yet in the absence of strict guidance, the Court's discouragement of Freedom of Choice plans lacked any teeth. And so, the separation of students by race continued as voucher systems were reinvigorated and resulted in the rapid development of state-subsidized private schools.

Post-Brown *North: De facto or State-Sanctioned Segregation?*

If the aftermath of *Brown* in the South was characterized by new tactics developed by those with power to preserve the structures of Jim Crow, the North was also characterized by its own brand of continuity. Throughout Northern cities, Black and Latino/a communities worked to dismantle the state-engineered (and thus not quite de facto) segregation that they confronted. In New York City, the movement for decent and desegregated schooling had been steadily mounting and was marked by moments such as 1958, the year that nine Black mothers went to jail (Back, 2003). The group of women, who later became known as the Harlem Nine, refused to send their children to public schools that they believed would harm them. Ironically perhaps, the mothers' campaign for desegregated school was called "Freedom of Choice for Junior High Schools," and resulted in what is recognized as the first court decision that recognized the structured character of de facto segregation (Back, 2003). The struggle waged by these mothers became a precursor for the movement for community control of schools, a movement that 10 years later was able to galvanize working-class parents of Color across New York City to keep their children home from school as part of the movement for Community Control of Schools.

Likewise, Black mothers in Boston, propelled by the comparable conditions as the Harlem Nine, engaged in a similar fight. Indeed, the groundwork laid by Black mothers such as Ruth Balson and Ellen Jackson as well as the Black Student Union and other formations was critical to the 1974 federal ruling that the structures of segregation in Boston's public schools needed to be undone (Theoharis, 2003). The decision, which called for a mandatory busing plan, was met with massive White resistance. As the nation watched, violence shook Boston as White communities defended their right to freedom, their right to exclude (Theoharis, 2003). Forty years later, the violence of these years is still remembered and referenced in discussions about desegregation. The consequences of these joined struggles—in New York City and Boston—waged in the post-*Brown* North, are critical to understanding the trajectory of national education reform policies in the years that followed.

From Milliken *to Magnets: The State, Capitalism, and the Limitations of Rights*

1974 was also the year that the Supreme Court issued the *Milliken v. Bradley* decision in which the Court determined that municipal governments could not be required to desegregate their schools unless segregation was explicitly outlined as an intentional and affirmative policy. As Harris observes, in *Milliken*, the Court interpreted the capitalist state as neutral (and free), thus ensuring the continued structures and capacities of Whiteness as property to exclude (Harris, 1993).

Subsequent to *Milliken v. Bradley* (1974), and in the wake of violence that erupted from the Boston busing plan, and in response to increased White flight from urban areas, the creation of the Federal Magnet Program provided yet another iteration of choice-based policies. Magnet schools were first developed in the 1960s and 1970s but were widely implemented throughout the 1980s and 1990s (Beal & Hendry, 2012). The goals of magnet schools/programs are two-fold: (1) to "magnetize" or make attractive—through the development of curriculum, resources, and learning themes—schools that might otherwise not be chosen; and (2) thereby encourage students and their families to "choose" a school that lies outside of their neighborhood (West, 1994). Both goals are supposed to result in desegregation outcomes, or more specifically, the reduction of racial isolation. As such, magnet schools rely on a market-driven framework of choice, one that places the onus for desegregation on families (and the choices they make) rather than on school districts or municipal governments. More specifically, magnet schools have consistently been targeted for implementation in urban areas where municipal governments have identified the need to make public schools more attractive to White parents *and* as a way to circumvent mandatory student assignment plans (Carl, 1994). As has been widely documented, magnet schools and programs have been limited in their stated goals of reducing racial isolation. Further, several scholars have demonstrated that while some magnets have contributed to desegregation efforts, others have been ineffectual in reducing segregation, and still others have exacerbated segregation (Beal & Hendry, 2012; Carl, 1994; West, 1994).

Freedom by Choice Revisited: Vouchers to No Child Left Behind

In 1990 another experiment in school choice—the Milwaukee Parental Choice Program—which revisited the mechanism of voucher programs, gained national attention. The program had strong state-based support from Governor Tommy Thompson (who also became widely known in the 1990s for his welfare-to-work—or workfare—program); federal support (from the Bush Administration); and private backing (from the Bradley and Heritage Foundations, two conservative policy organizations that were, at the time, entrenched in lobbying for voucher programs nationally). Further, as Pedroni and Apple (2005) and Dougherty (2004) document, the voucher program was also undergirded by an unlikely alliance between these primarily White and conservative forces, and some sectors of the Black community who called for the creation of a separate Black school district (a call that grew out of an assessment that integrated education had not, and would not, advance the needs and well-being of Black families). When it began, the voucher program in Milwaukee provided low-income students with a $2,446 voucher that was redeemable as full tuition at a state-approved private school. Five years later, by 1995, Republicans had gained control of the Wisconsin state legislature and raised the voucher amount to $4,600 while also expanding the range of schools included in the program (which would come to include religious schools). As the voucher program continued to expand (by 2003 it served more than 11,000 children), the majority of participants in the program were almost exclusively Black and Latino/a, thus raising critiques that the voucher program worked to increase segregation (Alexander & Alexander, 2004). Moreover, Walter C. Farrell and Jackolyn E. Mathews (2006) find that in addition to increasing segregation, voucher participants were often subjected to inferior schools with fewer resources and poorer facilities and made "no consistently significant improvement in academic achievement" (p. 527).

In 2001 the No Child Left Behind Act (NCLB) joined freedom of choice with calls for increased accountability. Like the voucher movement in Milwaukee, NCLB advocates made particular reference to the ways that public education has historically abandoned low-income communities of Color. In particular, the Bush Administration promised that NCLB would close the *achievement gap* for low-income students and students of Color by increasing accountability, opportunity, and choice through guidelines that allowed for local governments to penalize schools, teachers, parents, and students for poor academic outcomes. NCLB also required that the data used to determine student achievement be disaggregated and as such, a common sound bite of the Bush Administration was that NCLB would bring an end to the "soft bigotry of low expectations" (Bush, 2004). According to Bush, race *did* matter, and NCLB was going to address this reality head-on. Vouchers were initially written into NCLB, but were later removed as the legislation worked its way through various committees. The concept of choice, however, remained: Students at schools that failed to demonstrate Adequate Yearly Progress (through the measure of high-stakes tests) for two consecutive years were structurally empowered to choose to transfer to a better performing public school in their district.[3] Thus, the framework of market competition proposed by Friedman became embedded within the state. Yet as Monty Neill (2003) and Roslyn Arlin Mickelson and Stephanie Southworth (2005) note, the transfer option simply did not work and was not a feasible plan that could be sustained with the infrastructure of many school systems. In most cases the seats were not available and so, the right to choose did not work for poor families. Further, there was no move for the state to reinvest in "failing" public schools. Rather, the abandonment that had historically organized such schools became only further entrenched. As such, the right to choose under NCLB was not more than a hollowed-out statutory right for most. Those with political and economic power already benefitted from the right to choose; those to whom Bush claimed this right was extended experienced little change in accessing a better education for their child. And so, while NCLB did not bring greater choice (or resources) to communities who, since *Brown*, have continued to be historically underserved by public education, the legislation did solidify a new freedom: one for markets of private enterprise within the public.[4]

Despite more than 60 years of reforms that failed to undo separate and unequal education, the logic of choice as the panacea to inequality and preserver of freedom persists. On one hand, as one District 3 elected official who I interviewed put it, the freedom of individualism is as "American as apple pie." Yet joined to this particular definition of freedom is what could be argued to be just as American: the right to exclude. Friedman appears to have understood this twinned nature of choice within capitalism and was keenly prescriptive about the structuring of private, or individual, choices as rights *within* the realm of the public and within the structure of citizenship well before the 1980s and long before the current iteration of charter management corporations. Indeed, while *Brown I* indicated the end of state-enforced segregation and the end of separate but equal schooling, *Brown II* ensured that the same ends, the structuring of Whiteness as property embedded within the state, would be achieved through different means—through choice.

American Exceptionalism and a History of Overcoming

This chapter began with a vignette from a Head Start center and a conversation among a group of three low-income mothers trying to gain access to decent schools for their children within the most segregated and unequal district in the nation's largest school system. Nicole is an immigrant from Ghana who migrated to the United States six years ago. Edith is from the Dominican Republic and has spent longer in the United States than Nicole, but is also a relatively recent immigrant. Tasha, who is African American, questioned: *What's new?* The historical particularity of Tasha's location as a U.S.-born Black woman coupled with her location as a mother of limited economic means informed her understanding that exclusion in the supposedly post-racial and post–civil rights United States was nothing new but, perhaps an indication of the changing same, or what Reddy might term an amendment.

Despite the epistemological and historical critique of rights that Tasha's insights point to, every May, as the occasion of the anniversary of *Brown v. Board of Education* (1954) approaches, media outlets across the nation flood with news reports that disclose findings about how our schools continue to be segregated and unequal. These reports are attached to a number of prescriptions about what should be done to fix inequality. On one hand, these prescriptions point to an understanding of *Brown* as turning point in U.S. history, one where the wrongs of exclusion were made right. On the other hand, the diagnoses embedded within these assessments often imply that the problems of inequality could be ameliorated if parents and students only made the proper use of their rights by making the right choices. According to these assessments, inequality in education post-*Brown* has continued *despite* choice, and is attributable to the ways that parents and students are unevenly equipped with information, the differences in their social networks and access to social capital, and how their "savvy-ness" or know-how is contoured by race and income (Ball & Vincent, 1998; Beal & Hendry, 2012). As such, inequality in education is understood as the consequence of "bad" or uninformed yet "fair" and democratic choices.

As I examine elsewhere, this trajectory of thought is indicative of the ideological infrastructure of choice that accompanied the post-*Brown* policies and legislation outlined above, and was established by the Moynihan (1965) and the Coleman (1966) Reports (Aggarwal, 2013). Taken together, these reports spawned decades of policy reforms and initiatives that are consistently joined by their ability to repress political and economic questions and foreground an isolated, bounded, homogeneous, and racialized concept of culture, understood as values, behaviors, and attitudes. Such policies have only further entrenched state abandonment by leaving the structures that produce inequality decidedly intact. More insidious perhaps, by rendering invisible the material structures of inequality, and foregrounding a particular concept of culture as the site of intervention and "reform," these policies have also narrated the problem of social reproduction in the post-*Brown* era as attributable to the character of parental care or the capacities of parents to make the right choices for their children.

In this section, I briefly discuss how this ideological infrastructure is intimately tied to a particular telling of *Brown,* and how this telling is much more than a story about education but rather is a story about America. As we will see, this story, which narrates inclusion, the overcoming of persecution, and freedom as a project already won, locates the continued production of a tiered citizenship as resulting from the attitudes, care, values, behaviors, and choices of poor and working-class people of Color.

Brown: *A Story of America*

According to Gloria Ladson-Billings (2004), *Brown v. Board of Education* is the most common Supreme Court case listed in state school curricula, and there is also a general consensus among high school teachers, judges, and law professors that *Brown* is one of the most important cases that students should be required to learn about throughout school. Asking us to think critically about the pedagogical investment in *Brown*, Ladson-Billings asserts that the reification of *Brown* within the United States has been critical to the production of a national narrative:

> *Brown* has taken on a mythic quality that distorts the way many Americans have come to understand its genesis and function in society. Our tendency is to view *Brown* as a "natural" occurrence in the nation's steady march toward race relations and progress (Crenshaw, 1988). This notion of progress is coupled with a view of America as a nation endowed with inherent "goodness" and "exceptionality." (p. 3)

Understood as such, *Brown* is indicative of the founding stories that Nikhil Pal Singh (2005) notes that American exceptionalism relies upon: stories that centralize the overcoming of persecution through democratic tolerance and universalism achieved by racial and ethnic inclusion. As Singh contends, the continued inscription of racial exclusion becomes obscured and rationalized through these critical narratives. As a result, a contradictory universalism provides a scaffolding of exclusions within the liberal democracy of the United States.

Undergirded by stories like *Brown*, which depict overcoming and racial transcendence, education is one of the major arteries that have, in the second half of the 20th century, consistently pumped new life into this contradictory universalism, the character of which is well illustrated by the excerpt below. Taken from President Obama's speech (July 17, 2009) delivered at the 100th anniversary celebration of the National Association of the Advancement of Colored People (NAACP), the excerpt, while lengthy, is demonstrative of a particular story of rights and racial democracy on one hand and a recognition of the continuance of inequality structured by race, on the other.

> There's a reason the story of the civil rights movement was written in our schools. There's a reason Thurgood Marshall took up the cause of Linda Brown. There's a reason why the Little Rock Nine defied a governor and a mob. It's because there is no stronger weapon against inequality and no better path to opportunity than an education that can unlock a child's God-given potential. And yet, more than half a century after *Brown v. Board,* the dream of a world-class education is still being deferred all across the country. African American students are lagging behind white classmates in reading and math—an achievement gap that is growing in states that once led the way in the civil rights movement. Over half of all African American students are dropping out of school in some places. There are overcrowded classrooms, and crumbling schools, and corridors of shame in America filled with poor children—not just black children, brown and white children as well...
>
> ... We've got to say to our children, yes, if you're African American, the odds of growing up amid crime and gangs are higher. Yes, if you live in a poor neighborhood, you will face challenges that somebody in a wealthy suburb does not have to face. But that's not a reason to get bad grades—that's not a reason to cut class—that's not a reason to give up on your education and drop out of school. No one has written your destiny for you. Your destiny is in your hands—you cannot forget that. That's what we have to teach all of our children. No excuses. No excuses. (Politico Staff, 2009)

Obama's articulation of education as a site that is at once equal and yet not equal, the guarantor of the freedom to make one's own future as well as the institution through which futures are differentially prescribed, is not new. Rather, it points to how, since 1954, the structuring of universal rights as individual choices in education has allowed for inequality in education to be explained as a byproduct for which no actors (state or otherwise) are culpable, but rather as the historical residue of the aberration of state-sanctioned apartheid *and* as a necessary consequence of liberal freedom (understood as individual liberty).

As critical race theorist Derrick Bell (2004) reminds us, "*Brown*... served to reinforce the fiction that, by the decision's rejection of racial barriers posed by segregation, the path of progress would be clear. Everyone can and should make it through their individual ability and effort" (p. 7). Thus, as Obama outlines above, the problem of structural racism—understood as the likelihood of poorer learning conditions, and as in correlation to life expectancy—must be overcome by the post-racial bootstraps of personal responsibility, hard work, perseverance, and the ability to dream big: *"No one has written your destiny for you. Your destiny is in your hands—you cannot forget that."*

Public education thus becomes reified as the node through which the Civil Rights Movement articulated its vision and demands for justice, even as within such popular narrations, the radical critique offered by Black freedom struggles is simultaneously obfuscated (Alonso, Anderson, Su, & Theoharis, 2009). And the burden of freedom, given the equal structuring of rights, rests upon the individual family: the capacities of care, the types of choices made by parents, and the ability of parents and students to dream big and aim high. And so it happens that at present, even as students' schools like ACP and Edon continue to be separated based on race and income, they read the official narrative of the Civil Rights Movement as told through U.S. history books—one that explains that theirs is not a structured violence, but simply the residue of histories that have already been made and rights that have already been won.

Conclusion: A Not-New but Renewed Fight

Still, despite the ways that the story of *Brown* is narrated, the structuring of universal rights as individual choices has not precluded cracks in the contradictory universalism that grounds American exceptionalism; and there are moments when these cracks are made more visible.

The winter of 2011 brought such a moment, when two Black mothers—Kelley Williams-Bolar of Akron, Ohio and Tanya McDowell of Bridgeport, Connecticut—were arrested within months of one another. Both women were charged with felonies of fraud and grand theft for "stealing" the educations of their children. The women did what countless middle- and upper-middle-class parents I encountered in the course of my research attested to doing every day: make use of an address where they do not reside full-time to access a public school that they deem to be desirable. Despite being a commonly acknowledged practice, in the cases of both Williams-Bolar and McDowell, the local school districts spent months, along with thousands of public tax dollars, investigating the two mothers to prove their criminality. And, in both cases, city officials tallied the per pupil yearly cost to estimate a $15,000 price tag, per child, of "stolen" goods. According to officials, the rationale for the extensive investigations and prosecutions was simple and urgent: It was necessary to make a public example out of the wrongdoing to deter others from doing the same; and in response to the controversies raised by the media coverage that both cases received, the mayor of Norwalk, Richard Moccia, attempted to qualify the charges brought against McDowell, "This is not a poor, picked-upon homeless person. This is an ex-con... She has a checkered past at best... This woman is not a victim" (Leonard, 2011).

Yet these attempts to shape public sentiment against the two women did not hold, and could not do the ideological work intended. Something broke or perhaps was brought into sharper focus: the unfinished promise of *Brown*, of public education in relationship to citizenship, equality, and democracy in the United States—a relationship that was supposed to be rectified in 1954. For Tasha, Edith, and Nicole, the stories of McDowell and Williams-Bolar resonated with their own and others they knew. For these mothers, it was not uncommon to have your five-year-old child asked by school officials where they slept at night, nor was it uncommon for school social workers to pay a "random" visit to one's home to verify an address. Indeed, to return to Nicole's description: The schools *are* racism and discrimination.

But every day, Tasha, Nicole, and Edith (and countless others) struggle, to secure what is not guaranteed and often not gotten: a decent education for their child. Informing their labors is a particular knowing that is inculcated as a result of inhabiting the cracks of a contradictory universalism, one that a recent study from the Robert Woods Johnson Foundation affirmed—that premature death is significantly determined by access to education, which is stratified by race and class (Tavernise, 2012). These findings also verify Ruth Wilson Gilmore's (2007) definition of racism as "the state-sanctioned or extralegal production and exploitation of group-differentiated vulnerability to premature death" (p. 28). In such a formulation, education becomes representative of life while unequal, or segregated, education becomes representative of differentially valued life.

To be sure, Tasha, Nicole, Edith, and other mothers from the Head Start center who have joined them to organize for the desegregation of their schools are involved in a not new but renewed fight. It is a fight for the same things that the Harlem Nine engaged in nearly 60 years ago. These joined struggles point to the contemporary echoes of the Black radical tradition, which can be found in the everyday practices of care work carried out by low-income mothers of Color. Indeed, as these mothers (and others) work to fasten the futures of their children within the structured legacies of organized abandonment, embedded in their struggles is a fight for life, for freedom of a different kind: one that requires transformation rather than amendments, and necessarily requires the undoing of Whiteness as property.

References

Aggarwal, U. (2013). *Public education in the United States: The production of a normative cultural logic of inequality through choice*. Doctoral dissertation, Graduate Center of The City University of New York.

Alexander, K., & Alexander, K. (2004). Vouchers and the privatization of American education: Justifying racial segregation from *Brown* to *Zelman*. *University of Illinois Law Review*. 1131.

Alonso, G., Anderson, N. S., Su, C., & Theoharis, J. (2009). *Our schools suck: Students talk back to a segregated nation on the failures of urban education*. New York: New York University Press.

Arendt, H. (1959). Reflections on little rock. *Dissent, 6*(1), 45–56.

Back, A. (2003). Exposing the "whole segregation myth": The Harlem Nine and New York City's school desegregation battles." In J. Theoharis & K. Woodard (Eds.), *Freedom north: Black freedom struggles outside the South, 1940–1980*. New York: Palgrave Macmillan.

Ball, S. J., & Vincent, C. (1998). "I heard it on the grapevine": "Hot" knowledge and school choice. *British Journal of Sociology of Education, 19*(3), 377–400.

Ball, S. J., & Youdell, D. (2008). *Hidden privatisation in public education*. Brussels: Education International.

Bartlett, L., Frederick, M., Gulbrandsen, T., & Murillo, E. (2002). The marketization of education: Public schools for private ends. *Anthropology & Education Quarterly, 33*(1), 5–29.

Beal, H. K. O., & Hendry, P. M. (2012). The ironies of school choice: Empowering parents and reconceptualizing public education. *American Journal of Education, 118*(4), 521–550.

Bell, D. (2004). *Silent covenants:* Brown v. Board of Education *and the unfulfilled hopes for racial reform*. Oxford: Oxford University Press.

Brown v. Board of Education, 347 U.S. 483, 74 S. Ct. 686, 98 L. Ed. 873 (1954).

Brown v. Board of Education, 349 U.S. 294, 75 S. Ct. 753, 99 L. Ed. 1083 (1955).

Bush, G.W. (2004). President's Remarks in Minneapolis. Retrieved from: http://www.whitehouse.gov/news/releases/2004/10/20041030-8.html

Carl, J. (1994). Choice as national policy in England and the United States. *Comparative Education Review, 38*, 294–322.

Center for Immigrant Families. (2004). *Segregated and unequal: The public elementary schools of District 3 in New York City*. New York: Author.

Champagne, A. (1973). The segregation academy and the law. *The Journal of Negro Education, 42*(1), 58–66.

Coleman, J. S., Campbell, E. Q., Hobson, C. J., McPartland, J., Mood, A. M., Weinfeld, F. D., & York, R. (1966). *Equality of educational opportunity*. Washington, DC: U.S. Department of Health, Education, and Welfare. Office of Education. 1066–5684.

Dougherty, J. (2004). *More than one struggle: The evolution of Black school reform in Milwaukee*. Chapel Hill: University of North Carolina Press.

Fabricant, M., & Fine, M. (2012). *Charter schools and the corporate makeover of public education: What's at stake?* New York: Teachers College Press.

Farrell, W. C., Jr., & Mathews, J. (2006). The Milwaukee School Voucher Initiative: Impact on Black Students. *The Journal of Negro Education, 75*(3), 519–531.

Forman, J., Jr. (2005). Fifty years after *Bolling v. Sharpe*: The secret history of school choice: How progressives got there first. *Georgetown Law Journal, 93,* 1287–2095.

Friedman, M. (1955). The role of government in education. In R. A. Solo (Ed.), *Economics and the public interest*. New Brunswick, NJ: Rutgers University Press.

Gardner, D. P. (1983). *A nation at risk: The imperative for educational reform*. Washington DC: U.S. Department of Education.

Gilmore, R. W. (2007). *Golden gulag: Prisons, surplus, crisis, and opposition in globalizing California*. Berkeley: University of California Press.

Gordon, W. M. (1994). The implementation of desegregation plans since *Brown. Journal of Negro Education*, 310–322.

Green v. County School Board, 391 U.S. 430, 88 S. Ct. 1689, 20 L. Ed. 2d 716 (1968).

Harris, C. I. (1993). Whiteness as property. *Harvard Law Review*, 1707–1791.

Hershkoff, H., & Cohen, A. S. (1992). School choice and the lessons of Choctaw County. *Yale Law & Policy Review*, 1–29.

Kucsera, J., & Orfield, G. (2014). New York State's extreme school segregation: Inequality, inaction, and a damaged future. Los Angeles: UCLA, The Civil Rights Project / Proyecto Derechos Civiles.

Ladson-Billings, G. (2004). Landing on the wrong note: The price we paid for *Brown. Educational Researcher*, 3–13.

Leonard, D. (2012, March). NO WAY OUT: Mother jailed for "stealing" child's education. *Ebony*. Retrieved from http://www.ebony.com/news-views/no-way-out-mother-jailed-for-stealing-childs-education#axzz3ABXCnwWM

Lipman, P. (2011). *The new political economy of urban education: Neoliberalism, race, and the right to the city*. New York: Taylor & Francis.

Lipman, P., & Hursh, D. (2007). Renaissance 2010: The reassertion of ruling-class power through neoliberal policies in Chicago. *Policy Futures in Education, 5*(2), 160–178.

Matter of Skipwith, 14 Misc. 2d 325, 180 N.Y.S.2d 852, 180 N.Y.2d 852 (Dom. Rel. Ct. 1958).

Melago, C. (2008, February 3). Left in dark over No Child Left Behind. *New York Daily News*. Retrieved from http://www.nydailynews.com/new-york/education/left-dark-child-left-behind-article-1.306014

Mickelson, R. A., & Southworth, S. (2005). When opting out is not a choice: Implications for NCLB's transfer option from Charlotte, North Carolina. *Equity & Excellence in Education, 38*(3), 249–263.

Milliken v. Bradley, 418 U.S. 717, 94 S. Ct. 3112, 41 L. Ed. 2d 1069 (1974).

Neill, M. (2003, Fall). Making lemonade from NCLB lemons. *Rethinking Schools.*

Pedroni, T., & Apple, M. (2005). Conservative alliance building and African American support of vouchers: The end of *Brown*'s promise or a new beginning? *The Teachers College Record, 107*(9), 2068–2105.

Politico Staff. (2009, July 16). Obama's remarks at NAACP centennial. Retrieved from http://www.politico.com/news/stories/0709/25053.html

Reddy, C. (2011). *Freedom with violence: Race, sexuality, and the US state.* Durham, NC: Duke University Press.

Saltman, K. J. (Ed.). (2010). *Schooling and the politics of disaster.* New York: Routledge.

Singh, N. P. (2005). *Black is a country: Race and the unfinished struggle for democracy.* Cambridge, MA: Harvard University Press.

Tavernise, S. (2012, April 3). Longevity up in U.S., but education creates disparity, study says. *The New York Times.*

Theoharis, J. (2003). "I'd rather go to school in the South": How Boston's school desegregation complicates the civil rights paradigm. In J. Theoharis & K. Woodard (Eds.), *Freedom North: Black freedom struggles outside the South, 1940–1980.* New York: Palgrave Macmillan.

Turner, K. M. (2004). Both victors and victims: Prince Edward County, Virginia, the NAACP, and "Brown." *Virginia Law Review,* 1667–1691.

Walder, J. C., & Cleveland, A. D. (1971). The South's new segregation academies. *Phi Delta Kappan,* 234–239.

West, K. C. (1994). A desegregation tool that backfired: Magnet schools and classroom segregation. *Yale Law Journal,* 2567–2592.

Notes

1. I have provided pseudonyms for all schools, people, and references (such as street names).
2. Hannah Arendt made a similar argument in "Reflections on Little Rock."
3. In 2012 at least 33 states were granted NCLB waivers, which many cite as an indication of the legislation's failure.
4. In New York City, for example, findings indicate that the combination of a lack of infrastructure and confusing bureaucracy made the transfer provision ineffective at best while in many cases, it actually exacerbated problems. According to a 2008 *New York Daily News* article, of the 181,000 students eligible to transfer to better schools, less than 2% did (Melago, 2008).

6. Charter Schools: Demystifying Whiteness in a Market of "No Excuses" Corporate-Styled Charter Schools

TERRENDA WHITE

The proliferation of charter schools across urban communities of Color is often celebrated as an equity measure that provides more educational choices for students and families. However, the kinds of choices represented, and the actors who structure them, challenge fundamental claims of a "diverse" market of options. Indeed, researchers warn that charter schools increasingly represent a franchised industry of replicated schools subsidized by a small but powerful bloc of largely White venture philanthropists and private foundation leaders (Scott, 2008, 2009). Frankly, when children and families of Color seek alternative choices outside of district schools, they will likely encounter charter schools that are privately coordinated and hierarchically organized by regional and national management organizations that offer a branded "package" of practices (White, 2014). In this chapter, I focus on what these practices are, the beliefs of educators and school leaders who structure them, and the relations of power they signify. In doing so, I argue that assumptions about the equitable nature of charter schools must confront the troubling patterns of White privilege they have rendered, including social and cultural dimensions of racial inequality that maintain barriers to culturally inclusive and responsive teaching inside schools.

While the basic legal definition of a "charter" has not changed over the years—they are legislative contracts granted by public authorizers at state and district levels that permit autonomy from district rules in exchange for accountability—the forces mobilizing for charter schools have shifted dramatically. In its early years, charter school advocates consisted of a diverse set of actors with varied ideas about the purposes these schools would serve.

For some supporters, charter schools offered needed autonomy for teachers to develop inclusive pedagogy that could better serve children marginalized in district schools. For other supporters, charter schools were an answer to the inertia of large bureaucratic school systems and offered community-based models of schooling more responsive to families and the varied needs of their children. But for others still, charter schools were an opportunity to enact market-based visions of schooling based on choice and competition, modeled specifically on schools in the private sector, and thus a first step toward deregulating and dismantling public schools altogether. But while charter schools were a heterogeneous group in the 1990s, the decades that followed have witnessed homogenizing trends related to the dominance of a market-oriented vision, which includes less and less the pedagogical vision of teachers or the inclusive vision of community groups at the local level.

Despite significant shifts in who structures charter schools and for what purposes, leaders at the national, state, and city levels have courted these schools as an expressed equity measure, supporting their rapid growth in cities such as Detroit, Chicago, New Orleans, New York City, Washington, D.C., and Newark. Indeed, over the past 25 years, the number of charter schools has grown to nearly 6,000 schools across 42 states, serving approximately 2 million children (CRPE, 2013). And while these schools serve a small portion of the nation's total students, approximately 6% of total public school enrollment, their concentration in urban communities means they have a much higher enrollment of children, ranging from nearly a quarter of students in Harlem, New York, to nearly one-half of students in Washington, D.C., to a full 100% of students in New Orleans (Dreilinger, 2013; NYCSC, 2012; Rich, 2014). Schools that report large waiting lists, moreover, are referred to as oversubscribed charter schools and are highlighted by leaders as evidence of parent demand (NAPCS, 2013). However, waiting lists are largely misleading (Welner & Miron, 2014), and the larger context shaping choices of parents and families includes mass closings of district schools, marketing campaigns by some charter schools, and significant differences in resources between privately subsidized charter schools and local district schools (Miron, Urschel, & Saxton, 2011).

What remains obscure to parents and families, however, are the social and cultural dimensions of race and power that have structured the charter sector and have shaped approaches to teaching and learning. To explore this question, I engaged in a qualitative research study situated in four charter schools in New York City, which also included interviews with regional directors, school leaders, and teachers. My findings illustrate the inertia of school practices when norms are predicated on Whiteness, even as schools are marketed as diverse and innovative choices for children and families of Color. In particular, I focused on charter schools referred to in education research as "No Excuses" (NE) charter schools because of their distinct practices, which are grounded in a framework that emphasizes behavior, explicit teaching of middle-class values and norms, and a technocratic focus on data and test score production (Thernstrom & Thernstrom, 2004). Oftentimes, these schools belong to a distinct management structure, referred to in research as a "franchised" or "corporate-style" of organization (Scott & DiMartino, 2010). Franchising involves a central agency that supports the set-up of individual charter schools, while a corporate style involves a central agency with direct control over each school site, including direct oversight of school operations of each new school (Scott & DiMartino, 2010).

As we'll see in the sections to follow, my findings show that senior agents in a corporate-style charter school in New York City exerted considerable influence over curriculum and daily instruction. Despite the good intentions of school actors, which included White, Black, and Latino/a educators, their practices were often in response to the expressed interests of predominantly White senior agents whose focus rested primarily on test score production and organizational expansion. The focus on production and expansion, unfortunately, did little to address the racialized cultural differences between largely Black and Latino/a students and predominantly White leaders whose normative ideas about schooling were predicated explicitly on the practices of middle-class White communities.

To explore the meaning of these processes, the sections to follow are organized to accomplish four main goals. First, I review theories of Whiteness as an ideology that works to legitimate private expansion and restructuring efforts in urban cities by framing these efforts as benign and beneficent for communities of Color. Second, I illustrate some of the normative and detrimental ways that Whiteness shaped everyday practices inside a privately managed charter school in a predominantly Black community. Third, I consider the structural dimensions of Whiteness that work, in a contradictory way, to promote the proliferation of charter schools that teach middle-class norms yet maintain structural segregation of low-income Black and Latino/a children from middle-class schools and neighborhoods. Lastly, I draw implications for how critical studies in Whiteness can reframe discussions about charter school outcomes, by considering problematic patterns of high student suspension and attrition as institutional forms of racialized cultural marginalization and exclusion. An analysis of this nature helps to articulate the importance of early (and currently minoritized) visions of charter schools that framed equity more broadly, were inclusive of teachers and local communities, and were thus better able to support the development of schools with inclusive practices for culturally and linguistically diverse students in a multiracial and multicultural nation.

Charter Schools and Urban Restructuring: The Duality and Utility of Whiteness

W. E. B. Du Bois mapped an early framework of Whiteness that included both its structural roots and its cultural limbs. In "The Souls of White Folk," Du Bois (1920/2003) argued that Whiteness was deeply intertwined with imperialist endeavors involving Western expansion, which worked to legitimate the spatial, economic, and cultural appropriation of lands, resources, and materials of darker peoples across Africa, Asia, and the Americas. While noted nearly a century ago, Du Bois' observations provide an important framework for understanding the duality and utility of Whiteness in contemporary moments of massive local and global restructuring.

Specifically, Du Bois warned that ideologies of race and culture can both mask and fuel capitalist interests involving commerce, such as the amassing of capital and the accumulation of profit. For instance, the imagery of "noble-minded men" sailing into foreign lands to uplift people of Color was described as both masking and facilitating commercial interests (Du Bois, 1920/2003, p. 63). While this imagery framed darker peoples as an existential Other whose "problem" constituted a "darker mind" and a "misguided character" (pp. 66–67), it framed commercial endeavors as beneficent assimilationist projects on the part of those who possessed Whiteness. These observations highlight both the utility of racial ideology as a tool for White capitalist expansion, as well as the cultural and structural duality of Whiteness that frames expansion efforts as both *benign* and *beneficent* to those marked un-White.

Using Du Bois' framework, one ought to consider the cultural and structural dimensions of Whiteness today, and gauge its utility amid contemporary forms of private expansion via local and global restructuring of urban cities and urban schools. Indeed the changing realities of local schools in urban cities are part and parcel of the changing realities of urban space in a global market (Lipman, 2011; Lipman & Saltman, 2007). Contemporary efforts to "revitalize" urban cities and to spur economic growth rely on market-based formulas that promote deregulation and privatization of public housing and other facilities and services in urban communities (Hyra, 2008). In a similar vein, restructuring efforts in education rely on implementing markets of privately managed public charter schools to revitalize public education and troubled urban schools in particular. However, market-based restructuring efforts in urban cities have proven untenable for local businesses and for low-income and working-class Black and Latino/a residents who have been displaced by commercial businesses and the influx of White and Black middle-class residents (Hyra, 2008; Pattillo, 2007). In education, leaders have yet to address similar consequences for parents, families, teachers, and community groups whose participation at the local level has clashed with the interests of powerful investors and private groups (Buras, 2007; Buras, Randels, & Salaam, 2010; Lipman, 2011; Lipman & Saltman, 2007).

A Du Bois-ian critical framework of Whiteness, however, demands attention to the changing-same contradictions between endeavors to reform (and uplift) people of Color and the simultaneous appropriation and exploitation of people of Color and their institutions. The political and pedagogical value of community-based charter schools, for example, is morphed by the disproportionate influence of private sector elites who help to drive both the expansion and the character of the charter sector via the proliferation of privately managed charter schools (Fabricant & Fine, 2012; Scott, 2008, 2009). And as the expansion of charter schools reflects the expansion of private sector elites, these efforts are simultaneously intertwined with 19th-century imagery of noble-minded, largely White, and male benefactors whose interests are framed as beneficent projects to improve public schools and in particular the academic outcomes of urban school students. My observations of practices inside urban charter schools, however, show that many such schools go beyond efforts to restructure the organizational features of public schools (i.e., school hours, calendar days, and curriculum). These schools also endorse practices that target Black and Latino/a children themselves, whose cultural norms, languages, and traditions are viewed not only as impediments to market competition but also as sources of racial disparity in academic outcomes, and are thus targets of restructuring as well.

Du Bois' critical framework ought to apply here, as the structural roots of private expansion are yet again intertwined with dominant beliefs about race, beliefs that are stubbornly tethered to constructions of people of Color as having "misguided character" and "darker minds" for which contemporary forms of assimilationist projects are legitimate. In this sense, the structural and cultural dimensions of Whiteness work not only to facilitate the private restructuring of public schools in urban communities, but legitimates proliferation of particular *kinds* of charter schools focused on behavior management and rigid adherence to dominant cultural norms and expectations. Using Du Bois' framework, therefore, one must cast a critical look at the ways in which current reforms have recreated old patterns of dispossession for communities of Color (i.e., of local control of public institutions) in the service of private expansion and White capital accumulation. In this vein, Du Bois' warnings radiate well into the 20th and 21st centuries, in that Whiteness constitutes a cultural and structural duality, and a utility for contemporary local and global restructuring processes.

Charter Schools and the Contemporary Politics of Race in a Post–Civil Rights Era

While it is not the expressed intent of White leaders or managers of charter schools to enact racist practices or policies, the impact of these forces are nonetheless problematic and in many ways represent contemporary forms of racism. Indeed I argue that particular frames of Whiteness work to structure the political appeal and proliferation of particular kinds of charter schools over others. For example, charter school advocates who emphasize choice and competition as sufficient forms of equity, over and above critical interrogation and eradication of structural inequality, often build on frameworks that are central to contemporary racial ideology. These frames include *abstract liberalism* and *cultural racism*, which promote what researchers call "color-blind racism" (Bonilla-Silva, 2006). These frames work together to forsake attention to more systemic reforms and, through its emphasis on the individual, mystify the perpetuation of group-based discrimination and White racial accumulation (Leonardo, 2009). As acts of mystification, abstract liberalism and cultural racism allow White Americans to hold carefully to "fables of the past" (Du Bois, 1920/2003, p. 64) about the historic causes of group inequality and at the same time deploy "strategic blindness" and "epistemologies of ignorance" (Mills, 2008, p. 18) about current forms of White racial domination and privilege. In education, contemporary elements of Whiteness, and the frames upon which it hinges, shape the structural expansion of market-driven charter schools and the normative practices inside them.

Abstract Liberalism

Abstract liberalism is the appeal to liberal values on one hand, such as equal opportunity and freedom of markets through choice and competition, while on the other hand simultaneously denying the ways in which those values fall short for people of Color in the legal, political, and economic institutional life of the country (e.g., voting, jobs, neighborhoods, schools, and universities). Historically, while liberal values in the United States include ideals of freedom and equal opportunity, these values did not extend to groups who were constructed as Other in 18th- and 19th-century America. For this reason, Charles Mills (1997) describes the early and inherent Whiteness of American liberal theory as a "racial contract" (p. 3) that fails to address racial injustices, such as the degradation of Native Americans, the transatlantic slave trade and the persistent subjugation of Black Americans, as well as America's participation in imperialism and colonization abroad.

By mid-20th century, liberalism was extended to greater masses of Americans, due largely to the abolitionist and women's movement in the 19th century, the upheaval of working classes urging for labor rights in the early 20th century, and the push for racial equality in the form of civil rights in the mid-20th century. Together, these eras yielded what has been regarded as a social-reform liberalism (Bonilla-Silva, 2006). For more than three decades, however, a re-articulation of classical forms of liberalism have dominated, with a renewed emphasis on individual choice, competition, and free markets, largely on behalf of business owners and corporate leaders. While commerce and free markets have always played a role in capitalist America, neo-liberal efforts have worked to detach from liberalism the expansions and protections secured in previous eras, epitomized, for example, in the New Deal, the Great Society, and the Civil Rights eras. In this vein, neoliberal policies also represent what theorist David Harvey (2005) calls "dis-embedded" liberalism, whereby entrepreneurial freedoms are not only dis-embedded from social and political regulations but are also *hostile* to such concerns and are thus a deliberate retreat from protections in the form of labor rights, social welfare provisions, and race-conscious policies (p. 11).

In light of this history, abstract liberalism is a useful interpretive frame to understand entrepreneurial mobilization and support for market-oriented visions of charter schools. The heightened emphasis on choice, which casts working-class and low-income Black and Latino/a families as individual rational actors, also minimizes structural factors shaping racially segregated and disparately funded schools and the systemic reforms needed to redress the collective experiences of discrimination and barriers of opportunity facing these communities. Choice and competition, moreover, justifies and exacerbates institutional forms of discrimination inside schools, such as punitive treatment of low-scoring students, under-enrollment and exclusion of students with special needs, or racial disparities in suspension and expulsion rates, as well as high student attrition rates. In a deregulated system of choice, each of these trends is more easily cast as results of students' and families' individual actions and decisions in an otherwise fair and open market of choices. Moreover, because liberalism involves ideas of individual merit and achievement, low-performing students on standardized tests (and their teachers) are framed as individual failures due to lack of individual effort, poor character, or bad behavior. In this light, students' individual actions are framed as inoculated from the broader context circumscribing group privilege and disadvantage. Lastly, while abstract liberalism emphasizes the individual choices of children and families, it masks the disproportionate and collective power of private sector elites, such as business leaders, corporate executives, and investment bankers, whose "education entrepreneur networks" (Kretchmar, Sondel, & Ferrare, 2014, p. 2) exert considerable force in the political support for the expansion of charter schools.

Cultural Racism

As Americans de-emphasize structural factors shaping Black-White dispar-ities and often make appeals to liberal values of individual choice, surveys show that Americans attribute pathological cultural traits to disadvantaged groups (Wilson, 2010). Although racism in prior centuries involved ideolo-gies that constructed people of Color as biologically inferior, contemporary racism involves beliefs in cultural deficiency of disadvantaged groups (Bobo, Kluegel, & Smith, 1997). Racial ideologies rooted in biogenetic beliefs have declined in recent decades, yet the persistence of racial disparities is often rationalized on the basis of culture. In education, an example of cultural racism includes statements such as "'Mexicans do not put much emphasis on education'" or "'Black students are not personally motivated'" (Bonilla-Silva, 2006, p. 28). Consequently, cultural racism works to "explain the social position [of Whites] as a group and their collective accomplishments" while rationalizing the treatment of members in non-White groups and prescribing the way that these groups should behave (Wilson, 2010).

In this vein, contemporary theorists of race refer to culture-based racism as "color-blind" racism or "laissez-faire racism," which constitutes a percep-tion that Blacks (for example) are responsible for their own economic predic-ament and are therefore undeserving of special government support (Bobo et al., 1997). Because "laissez-faire racism" is a similar framework to cultural racism within in a post–Civil Rights era, I use both terms interchangeably. In education, laissez-faire racism is reflected in the ways in which low-scoring children of Color are vulnerable to punitive treatment and exclusion by school leaders in a choice-based system, and whereby high-stakes testing increas-ingly positions low scorers as a liability to an organization's "brand" and are thus "un-deserving" of inclusion. Culture-based prescriptions of behav-ior, moreover, are manifested in No Excuses models of schooling, which de-emphasize critical forms of pedagogy and culturally inclusive practices in favor of a rule-driven, character-based, behavioral model of teaching and learning (explored further in the following sections).

Deconstructing Charter Schools Through Abstract Liberalism and Cultural Racism

The charter sector today is undoubtedly gripped by both the abstract liberalism that dominates 21st-century color-blind discourse, as well as cultural forms of racism that shape rigid school practices and deficit beliefs about low-income communities of Color. As the former (liberalism) frames individual choice, competition, and free trade as forms of equity, the latter (cultural racism) emphasizes lack of personal responsibility on the part of poor families and children of Color, as well as improper character and behavior as primary sources impeding social mobility. While these frames shape discourse about choice and competition, they mystify the ways in which all schools and communities are increasingly dis-embedded from race-conscious remedies and broader social and political reforms. Indeed, these frames deploy the duality and utility necessary for the perpetuation of Whiteness, in that they work simultaneously to cloak the expansion of choice and competition (embodied in the dominant framing of charter schools) in a discourse of equity while also promoting a retreat from group-based equity goals that challenge White privilege and racial segregation, including goals for more equitable school funding, desegregation initiatives, as well as broader social goals such as redistributive tax policies, labor rights (e.g., full employment, living wages, collective bargaining), and social welfare programs for the poor. Hence, while quasi-education markets extend choices in education to communities of Color, the celebration of these choices ignores the ways in which the most important choices for social mobility are perpetually limited to these groups, due to racial discrimination in housing markets, labor markets, and in finance and mortgage lending (Denton, 1994). Indeed the choice of where to live in America has been circumscribed by discrimination and racial segregation in housing for nearly a century, and which serves as the bedrock of wealth and social mobility in America and fuels school segregation and funding disparities between schools and districts.

At the micro-level of schools and classrooms, abstract liberalism and cultural racism bring hyper-focus to the students' individual choices, behaviors, and academic outcomes, yet minimizes needed attention to "intangible" forms of equity, such as equal respect for, and incorporation of, students' culture as resources for meaningful and engaging learning experiences (Carter, 2003, 2005, 2013). In this sense, as students are encouraged to rely primarily on individual values of agency and hard work, this emphasis is implemented in the absence of recognition and inclusion of important forms of "Black" cultural capital (Carter, 2003), as well as "community cultural wealth" (Yosso, 2006), such as resilience and aspirational capital exhibited in communities of Color. Heavy emphasis on individual behavior and character values also comes in the absence of critical pedagogical traditions that engage students in both the de-construction and confrontation of structural inequalities shaping their lives and the schools in which they learn.

Inside a No Excuses Corporate-Style Charter School: Cultural Dimensions of Whiteness

To understand the various ways in which Whiteness operates in a market-driven charter sector, both culturally and structurally, I engaged in a two-year qualitative research study in which I observed and interviewed school managers, leaders, and teachers in one urban community in New York City. Before I began observations inside schools, however, I analyzed state-level data from charter authorizers to understand longitudinal trends in the number of charter schools in the neighborhood, beginning in the late 1990s when charter schools were first established in the community. Structurally, I learned that not only was there a steady increase in the number of charter schools in the community, over a 15-year period, but there was also a marked shift in the types of entities that were granted charters. Indeed, while community organizations and youth development groups founded the earliest charter schools in the neighborhood, these kinds of charter schools were later outpaced by the rise in charter schools founded by nonprofit charter management organizations (CMOs). By 2012 there were more than 40 charter schools concentrated in the neighborhood, yet two-thirds of these schools were managed by CMOs, and three CMOs alone managed one-half of all charter schools in the community (White, 2014). Extended observations inside one CMO-affiliated charter school revealed that central agents for the school's CMO (e.g., regional managers and directors) not only managed school operations, but exerted direct control over curriculum and the flow of everyday classroom teaching and learning. While school leaders and educators included White, Black, and Latino/a individuals, the most senior agents (i.e., board members, investors, and executives) for the school's CMO were largely White; the majority of whom were leaders in investment banking, equity funds, asset management firms, and private schools.

More important, however, were the cultural norms and assumptions shaping school practices and approaches to learning. Indeed constructions of "normality" and standards for behavior were explicitly predicated on the perceived norms of middle-class children, even as these norms were presented as universal standards of right and wrong, or good and bad, in terms of speech, language and communication, clothing style, dress, and presentation. Less explicit, however, were the ways in which class expectations signaled racialized cultural beliefs that marked local residents in the predominantly Black community in which the school existed as "awkward" and deficient. One teacher, Mr. Charles, who was an African American male and an instructional coordinator for his school's CMO, noted with ease: "[Our organization] is trying to produce somebody who can be competitive and transition into the middle class... So our [CMO] asks 'What does a middle class family provide for their child?'" Ironically, while middle-class status was an ideal goal for school leaders, the structure of charter school enrollment in the city perpetuated extreme segregation from middle-class communities and children (Kucsera & Orfield, 2014). Nonetheless, efforts to provide tangible resources similar to middle-class families was well intentioned and included provided access to tutors, after-school and summer enrichment programs, and even expensive trips and monetary rewards (for students with good grades).

However, Mr. Charles expressed concern with the racialized cultural dimensions of his organization's focus on middle-class attainment and middle-class standards of behavior, noting in particular the CMO's lack of recognition for the cultural strengths and traditions of the children and families in the local neighborhood: "Educators are not supposed to make students feel as though historically their people don't function on the level as another group of people within the same nation. You shouldn't make some groups feel inferior... but I think kids in this [local neighborhood] are in just that sort of predicament." Indeed, observations in charter schools similar to Mr. Charles's school revealed cultural dimensions of Whiteness that shaped implicit norms and expectations. While these norms were expressed as "best practices" and celebrated as "No Excuses" approaches that emphasized the importance of behavior and data-tracking—approaches with intentions to promote academic achievement and college-readiness—these practices were nonetheless constructed in direct response to the interests of largely White senior managers, and predicated on the norms of children in White middle-class communities. By examining beliefs about race and culture among school actors, it is possible to demystify the ways in which Whiteness framed Black and Latino/a children as "problems," and for whom academic activities were accompanied by assimilationist projects involving race and culture.

"Like Scarsdale": Whiteness as Invisible and Normal. Among senior managers and regional directors of a charter school in New York City, the invisibility and normality of Whiteness was expressed on several occasions. In a meeting among leaders of charter schools—schools that were each connected to the same regional franchise and managed by the same CMO—cultural dimensions of Whiteness served as an invisible referent for how Black and Latino/a children should speak. Among the 10 to 12 leaders in the room, the most senior member engaged the group in a discussion about the "awkward" speech patterns of students in the local community, particularly when compared to the more "precise" speech patterns of children in a nearby suburban White community, known as Scarsdale.

Scarsdale served as an important referent for the organization's marketing team, which often celebrated its ability to outperform children in Scarsdale on state tests. In an effort to outperform children in Scarsdale, however, the schools' leaders often used the suburban community as a cultural referent for how to articulate and organize expectations for students in their schools. In this sense, proper ways of speaking, behaving, and presenting oneself in dress and attire were justified using references to children in Scarsdale. The local speech patterns of children in the community, in contrast, were deemed abnormal in light of the comparative and hierarchical referent of White children elsewhere.

School leaders decided, therefore, that success for children in the local community partly hinged on their ability to speak more precisely in their everyday conversations with adults and teachers. In tandem were training manuals for newly hired teachers that emphasized precision as a social and cultural value, as well as a specific expectation for speech among children across the organization's schools. As one manual stated, "We must live and breathe *precision!* In doing so, we are helping to dramatically improve our students' life odds!" Students who failed to demonstrate precision in classroom activities, however, including in question-and-answer interactions with teachers, were verbally reprimanded and often lost turns to speak during class discussions. Generally, the exaggerated power attributed to precision on the part of school leaders was an example of abstract liberalism, primarily because its symbolic value masked the structural conditions of White middle-class children who indeed had much better material odds and life chances.

Research by critical multicultural educators, in contrast, interprets speech patterns of students in more nuanced ways and thus recognizes the importance for integrating knowledge of local and historic practices of racially diverse communities into school curriculum and pedagogy (Delpit, 2002). In this perspective, multicultural educators would challenge the "awkward" and seemingly less precise depictions of speech described by charter school leaders in New York, and consider instead the ways in which language practices are rooted in a variety of cultural traditions, particularly among African American groups, such as African American Vernacular English (AAVE) (Rickford, 1999). Indeed researchers in teacher education, particularly teachers of English, have acknowledged that "The child who speaks in AAVE is not making language errors; instead, she or he is speaking correctly in the language of the home discourse community" (Wheeler & Swords, 2004, p. 471). Indeed the pedagogical value and use of AAVE is substantiated by researchers who have established that learning outcomes improve when teachers help students compare and contrast the structure of AAVE with the structure of Standard English (SE) (Rickford, 1999).

Unfortunately, these traditions were neither acknowledged by leaders in a New York City charter school nor were they explored in teacher-training sessions with educators. Instead, leaders and educators presented ideas of precision as *the* way to speak (i.e., the right way to speak), and in doing so allowed the structural position and cultural norms of White children in Scarsdale to shape the everyday experiences and school opportunities of children in a less privileged Black community. The invisibility of Whiteness, therefore, worked to legitimate and regulate standards of speaking, against which many children were labeled as either normal or deviant and subsequently reprimanded. In this sense, school practices predicated on Whiteness not only prevented the inclusion of more culturally and linguistically diverse traditions, but the exclusion of these traditions reproduced institutional environments that lacked cultural flexibility (Carter, 2013) and cultural equality (Carter & Reardon, 2014), and thus hindered potential for more positive academic outcomes (Rickford, 1999).

"I don't know what they are like": Cultural Asymmetry of School Practices. Ms. Simmons, a White teacher in a privately managed charter school, expressed openly in an interview that she lacked social and cultural knowledge about the predominantly Black and Latino/a students she taught, including practices embedded in the social life of her students' family and community members. Her self-identified deficits in cultural knowledge compelled her to question her school's focus on individualized test-based forms of equity and competition. While Ms. Simmons was proud of her school's high test scores, she pondered the fact that several students and families had exited the school over the years, leaving the school and the organization with an acutely high student attrition rate. Ms. Simmons questioned whether the time devoted to test preparation compromised her focus on building sustainable relationships with students, including knowledge of students' lives outside of school, and the community in which they lived. "When I first entered the classroom it was all about data and instruction and the achievement gap... but I wish I knew more about the community I am teaching in."

The limited attention to building knowledge about students and their lives at Ms. Simmons's school, in an effort to deepen instruction and relationships with students, contrasted significantly to the time devoted to enforcement of rigid behavior management policies. "Since there are a lot of gaps between the time my students leave school, go home, and come back, I wonder how different they are outside of school and whether they really need to always sit up straight with their hands folded on their laps and say 'yes ma'am' to me all day." In light of both her own and her school's lack of knowledge about the social practices and cultural repertoires of students, Ms. Simmons questioned the asymmetrical nature and premise of her school's No Excuses character values: "You know, [my] charter school has certain character values [that we teach students]. But I'm interested to know what those values are based on. Does the community have *any* input on these things? Or are *we* [charter school actors] just sort of saying it *to* them?" By recognizing the one-sided nature her own and her institution's cultural knowledge and values that shaped non-academic expectations in her school, Ms. Simmons illustrated the denial of recognition and visibility of communities of Color in the construction of everyday practices in schools. The one-sidedness, and particularity of Whiteness upon which school practices and character values were framed, represented a failure to see (and value) the community context in which the school operated. This failure prevented the inclusion of various forms of cultural wealth and character values operating in the community already.

From Underserved to Un-deserving: Low-Scoring Students as Culturally Deviant. In additional interviews and observations inside a similar charter school that adopted No Excuses approaches to teaching, respondents noted a hyper-focus on student behavior, character, and individual hard work as the best way promote to high test scores, high school completion, and future college admission. While seemingly benign, teachers and leaders relied on cultural and behavioral explanations to explain the struggles of low-scoring students (often referred to as "1s" and "2s" because of their score numbers on standardized tests). In several instances, the outcomes of low-scoring students were rationalized as results of behavioral and cultural deviance, which constructed these students as "un-deserving" of material rewards and thus warranted punishment and exclusion from symbolic forms of status and school privilege.

In these processes, Whiteness was perpetuated as both a form of abstract liberalism and cultural racism. The former (liberalism) emphasized the hard work and effort of high-scoring students yet devolved rather quickly into the latter form (cultural racism) when school actors explained the struggles of low-scoring children as tied to group-based stereotypes about low-income communities. As an example, most school actors articulated with ease a culture-based rationale for mobility and achievement. "Many of our kids are coming from poor families and so have poor models of language, behavior, ethics, principles, and character," stated one school leader. These beliefs worked later on to justify the punitive nature of school practices that framed poor children, particularly those with low scores. For example, Mr. Charles noted, "We do trips around the world, for kids who score a '4' on the test, because we feel that the kids from middle class and upper class families get to travel and take vacations around the world with their families. So we try to even the playing [field] in that way." When asked what children with lower scores receive, such as those marked as 1s (below basic) or 2s (basic), Mr. Charles replied, "Well, if you're a 1 or 2, you don't get anything." Hence, Mr. Charles explained that not only were school rewards meant to resemble the kinds of rewards accessible to middle-class children, rewards for test scores also conveyed symbols of merit and thus deservingness. In doing so, Mr. Charles articulated an abstract liberalism that explicitly inscribed and distributed middle-class resources as rewards for individual hard work while marking low-scoring students, consequently, as undeserving due to individual failure and symbolically justified denial of middle-class status.

Consequently, liberal rationales about individual achievement devolve easily into forms of "cultural racism," whereby cultural explanations about the outcomes of poor children are associated with ideas about poor character. These assumptions hearken back to Du Bois' observations about the framing of people of Color as having a "misguided character," frames that historically served to legitimate capitalist expansion and hierarchical relations of power in the form of White privilege. While social practices in the charter school were not constructed in a malicious way, the liberal norms and cultural assumptions about achievement worked nonetheless to legitimate punitive treatment and exclusion of disadvantaged students from material resources and school privileges, while also masking the structural advantages shaping success for middle-class children. These norms also limited the capacity of school actors to develop culturally relevant forms of teaching aimed at affirming the cultural practices and social identities of students (Ladson-Billings, 1995) and creating more culturally equitable school curriculum and pedagogy (Carter & Reardon, 2014).

The Proliferation of Corporate-Style Charter Schools: Structural Dimensions of Whiteness

Structurally, the closing of public schools and the proliferation of privately managed charter schools represents the material dispossession of public space in communities of Color and the private accumulation of these spaces for private groups with bottom-line interests. As early as 2000, data from the U.S. Department of Education showed that approximately 927 charter schools across 27 states were more likely to enroll Black and Latino/a students than White students (RPP International, 2000). By the mid-2000s, charter schools continued to enroll Black students at twice the rate of traditional public schools (Nelson, Rosenberg, & Van Meter, 2004). And in 2013, a study by the Center for Research on Education Outcomes (CREDO) showed that the 5,274 charter schools across 42 states enrolled a much larger proportion of Black students (29%) than in all public schools (17%) (CREDO, 2013c). Conversely, though half of all public school students are White, their enrollment in charter schools is smaller (36%) (NCES, 2014; CREDO, 2013c). The enrollment of White students in charter schools has steadily declined since 1999 from a high of 51% of charter enrollment (Henig, 2013). In terms of class, moreover, trends have showed a rising percentage of charter schools serving high-poverty populations (from 13% to 33%) between 1999–2009, while the percentage of charters with more affluent enrollments have decreased sharply from 37% to 19% (Henig, 2013).

To some degree, these trends are related to state regulations about where charter schools can locate. In some states, charter schools can choose where to locate, while in other states charter schools are permitted to open only in areas of "greatest educational need" such as in failing school districts or to replace failing schools (CREDO, 2013c). For some researchers and charter school advocates, these current trends are a good thing, since the proliferation of these schools in low-income Black communities could reflect support for disadvantaged children, as well as demand on the part of parents who are dissatisfied with the poor conditions of district schools in their communities. In this sense, the rising number of charter schools could be seen as finally giving parents in disadvantaged neighborhoods more quality choices and alternatives. These trends, moreover, are an important contradiction to early critics of charter schools who feared that these schools would proliferate in suburban White communities, and thus provide middle-class families with more choices and a cost-effective means to exit public schools and subsidize a "private-like" education for their children (Henig, 2013). In this regard, the concentration of charter schools in low-income communities expands access.

However, as researcher Jeffrey Henig (2013) notes, "*not* targeting the elite is not the same as fully embracing the highly disadvantaged" (p. 13, italics added). Studies show that on average charter schools continue to have lower enrollments of high-needs students compared to district schools and the local "feeder" schools, which are local schools from which charter schools draw their students. Lower enrollment of high-needs students includes students with disabilities, special education students, or non-English-speaking students (CREDO, 2013c; Henig, 2013; Miron et al., 2011). Charter schools that typically serve these students are smaller, independent charter schools (Henig, 2013; Henig, Holyoke, Brown, & Lacireno-Paquet, 2005). However, as charter schools morph into networks and "super networks" (CREDO, 2013a) of three or more replicated schools under management of for-profit and nonprofit entities, stand-alone charter schools will represent a shrinking portion of the total number of charter schools in many inner cities. These trends have consequences for whether all students will find support in the charter sector. Indeed, in 2013 while feeder schools enrolled 13% of English language learners and 11% of special needs students, charter schools across 27 states enrolled 9% and 8%, respectively (CREDO, 2013c). In cities like New York, disparities in enrollment of high-needs students are starker. By some estimates as high as 18% of students in New York City were classified as special needs in 2014, while charter schools enrolled approximately 9% (IBO, 2014). In other studies, the proportion of special needs students in the city's district schools was 17% while charter schools enrolled 12% (CREDO, 2013b). Likewise, approximately 16% of students in the city's local district schools were classified as English language learners in 2012, but charter schools enrolled less than half of that with 5% of ELL students (CREDO, 2013b). Hence, while charter schools are increasingly concentrated in low-income communities of Color and do not enroll high numbers of affluent children (referred to as "creaming the top"), researchers suggest that these schools do nonetheless "crop off" service to students with special needs in disadvantaged communities (Lacireno-Paquet, Holyoke, Moser, & Henig, 2002).

Regardless, these trends focus on the location and demographic enrollment of charter schools and not the *kinds* of charter schools, and charter school practices, created in different communities. In states like Arizona, researchers have noted qualitative differences between charter schools in minority communities and a subset of schools catering to non-Hispanic Whites. Researchers studying charter high schools in Phoenix, and in several rural towns in Arizona, found that schools that were predominantly Hispanic focused on vocational education while charter schools that were predominantly White were more often focused on college preparation (Cobb & Glass, 1999).

Researcher Janelle Scott (2008, 2009), moreover, finds that the kinds of charter schools proliferating in cities are distinct in that they are managed, funded, and structured in important ways. Scott finds, for example, that charter schools in most cities are primarily managed by charter management organizations (CMOs), the growth of which is funded by a network of corporate-affiliated foundations and "venture philanthropists." Similar to venture capitalists who seek companies in which to invest and subsequently reap profit, Scott describes venture philanthropists as those who seek out educational reforms perceived as innovative and push for their growth by investing significant financial support. These investors measure returns not by profit, but by growth in student achievement such as test scores (Scott, 2009; Scott & DiMartino, 2010).

As an example, the Walton Family Foundation is a philanthropic group governed by the prominent family that founded Walmart. The foundation was spotlighted as having "subsidized an entire charter school system" in Washington, D.C. (Rich, 2014). Having granted more than $165 million in direct grants in 2013 alone, as well as $335 million over time, the Walton Family Foundation has helped fuel enrollment growth in charter schools in cities like Washington, D.C., where charters enroll close to half of all public school students. Philanthropic foundations like the Walton Family are responsible for nearly one in every four charter school start-ups in the country (Rich, 2014). Several more philanthropic foundations similar to Walton have also shaped the proliferation of charter schools in cities, including Bill and Melinda Gates of Microsoft; Eli Broad, a Los Angeles insurance billionaire; and Susan and Michael Dell, who are leaders in computer technology and retail. These groups have many overlapping interests, but analysts often describe them as following a distinct ideological path (Rich, 2014).

For example, philanthropic foundations, like the Walton foundation, typically fund corporate-style charter organizations that endorse No Excuses frameworks, in addition to schools with longer school days, longer calendar years, more discipline and structure, and more rigorous testing (Zinmeister, 2014). Specifically, No Excuses approaches have been described as creating "a disciplined, orderly and demanding counterculture in which to inculcate middle-class values" (Brooks, 2009). Indeed, expounding on these approaches, *New York Times* columnist David Brooks noted, "The basic theory is that middle-class kids enter adolescence with certain working models in their heads... Many kids from poorer, disorganized homes don't have these internalized models" (2009).

Ironically, philanthropic support for schools that deploy stern attempts to train low-income children in the ways of middle-class norms ignores the fact that these schools are structured in ways that maintain and exacerbate the segregation of these children from middle-class communities. Research on the impact of charter schools on segregation has documented that the enrollment patterns of charter schools works not only to reproduce racial and economic segregation across schools, but in many ways is the driving force of school segregation in many urban communities (Kucsera & Orfield, 2014; Miron et al., 2011). In this way, No Excuses corporate-sponsored charter schools promote social and cultural conformity to middle-class norms, while structurally maintaining "containment" in the form of racial and economic segregation (Scott & DiMartino, 2009). Moreover, the material resources of corporate elites to shape the kinds of school choices available to urban residents, particularly in gentrifying urban cities, is in stark contrast to the vulnerable social and material standing of Black and Latino/a residents facing displacement and dispossession of public properties and public schools (Buras, 2011).

Conclusion: The Consequences of Whiteness in a Market-Driven Charter Sector

Race, as noted throughout this book, is a fundamental driver shaping neoliberal school reforms of late, and charter schools are no different. In this chapter, I argued that particular dimensions of Whiteness have structured the kinds of charter schools (and subsequent school practices) replicating across low-income communities of Color in particular. In the service of children and families, research must continue to take a qualitative look at practices inside these schools, as well as the beliefs about race, culture, and achievement among actors who work in these spaces. In this way, reformers can better understand how racial disparities and changing-same patterns of White privilege, via capitalist accumulation amid material and cultural marginalization of communities of Color, have emerged in the charter sector.

The consequences of cultural and structural dimensions of Whiteness are evident in the troubling racial disparities that have emerged in the charter sector. While charter schools have improved their less than stellar impact on student learning in recent years (CREDO, 2009a, 2013b), particularly for disadvantaged students in urban communities, these improvements come with red flags, including the disproportionately high suspension and expulsion rates of charter schools in many cities, the substantially high levels of student attrition of often celebrated charter schools (e.g., a nearly 15% attrition rate each year in Knowledge Is Power Program [KIPP] charter schools and as high as 30% in the middle school grades, reflecting predominantly African American students), as well as the chronically lower rates of enrollment of students with special needs and limited English (CREDO, 2013a; Miron et al., 2011; Zubrzycki, Cavanagh, & McNeil, 2013). In light of these trends, the focus on raised test score outcomes, particularly among celebrated schools, is often a pyrrhic victory, whereby schools lauded for high outcomes have also failed to extend access to all students or have "lost" high numbers of the students they have enrolled. Hence, researchers must make clear the ways in which these losses perpetuate existing racial disparities in opportunity and outcomes, and represent challenges to notions of equity that rest narrowly on increasing the number of school choices instead of the quality and inclusiveness of these choices. Indeed I argue that despite the ways in which such school attrition is framed, as choices on the part of families to leave these schools in light of other market options, these trends likely represent issues of race and cultural conflict, and are experienced acutely by students who are "cultural non-conformers" (Carter, 2005). These are students who believe in education, and whose families have sought additional options in a market of school choices, but may nonetheless interpret rigid cultural expectations as institutional discrimination and rejection of their social and cultural identities. Institutional practices that push students toward conformity, therefore, work to further marginalize disadvantaged students and perpetuate pervasive norms of Whiteness that render schools culturally inflexible and unequal for culturally and linguistically diverse children (Carter, 2005; Carter & Reardon, 2014).

Hence, and in light of the structural and cultural dimensions of Whiteness that have shaped the direction and expansion of charter schools in the past decade, research must identify and illustrate cautionary trends that must be resolved if charter schools are to represent the hope that its advocates claim. There is much to learn in this sense from the broader scholarship on Whiteness, which has taken seriously the need to demystify it, primarily highlighting its cultural dimensions. In this way, some scholars have focused on making Whiteness visible *to* Whites, who often fail to see the particularity of their cultural experiences, which are taken for granted as universal (Dyer, 2005).

Critical social theorists of race and education, moreover, express concern that normative examinations of Whiteness focus too heavily on the experiences of Whites, to the exclusion of the structural forces shaping inequalities between racialized groups. According to Zeus Leonardo (2009), for example, efforts to make Whites more cognizant of their own racialization, and the privileges it accrues, help White audiences map the psychological and social advantages of Whiteness, but do not deconstruct ongoing processes of racial domination that make cultural dominance possible. In this sense, culture-based studies on Whiteness may overlook important processes of material domination enacted in relationship to people of Color. A more critical analysis of Whiteness, therefore, demands that scholars not only make visible the hegemonic norms of White privilege in everyday life, but to take up Du Bois' courage to name the bottom-line interests historically rooted in Whiteness, such as White capital accumulation and material dispossession of peoples of Color.

In this chapter, therefore, I aimed to make visible the dimensions of Whiteness shaping charter school expansion and charter school practices, particularly by focusing on the duality and utility of Whiteness in a moment of massive restructuring. Cultural dimensions of Whiteness are visible in many No Excuses practices, which go beyond benign instructions for improving character values and behaviors of young pupils, and indeed convey racialized cultural biases about right and wrong social norms. These biases—represented as universal standards of human behavior when in actuality are particular forms of life conditioned by vastly different and disparate social contexts—regularly deny recognition of diverse socio-linguistic and cultural practices, many of which are part and parcel of the cultural wealth in communities of Color. The structural dimensions of Whiteness, moreover, are also evident in the changing structure of charter school management and private sector expansion. In light of these forces, researchers must critically interrogate how the bottom-line production goals of largely White private investors intersect with low-income predominantly Black and Latino/a communities whose structural realities and cultural relations of power inside and across schools are largely unchanged.

References

Bobo, L., Kluegel, J. R., & Smith, R. A. (1997). Laissez faire racism: The crystallization of a kinder, gentler, anti-Black ideology. In S. Tuch & J. Martin (Eds.), *Racial attitudes in the 1990s*. Westport, CT: Praeger.

Bonilla-Silva, E. (2006). *Racism without racists: Color-blind racism and the persistence of racial inequality in the United States* (2nd ed.). Lanham, MD: Rowman & Littlefield.

Brooks, D. (2009). The Harlem Miracle. *The New York Times, 7*.

Buras, K. (2007). Benign neglect? Drowning yellow buses, racism, and disinvestment in the city that Bush forgot. In K. J. Saltman (Ed.), *Schooling and the politics of disaster* (pp. 103–122). New York: Taylor & Francis.

Buras, K. (2011). Race, charter schools, and conscious capitalism: On the spatial politics of Whiteness as property (and the unconscionable assault on Black New Orleans). *Harvard Educational Review, 81*(2), 296–387.

Buras, K., Randels, J., Salaam, K. Y., & Students at the Center. (2010). *Pedagogy, policy, and the privatized city: Stories of dispossession and defiance from New Orleans.* New York: Teachers College Press, Columbia University.

Carter, P. L. (2003). "Black" cultural capital, status positioning, and schooling conflicts for low-income African American youth. *Social Problems, 50*, 136–155.

Carter, P. L. (2005). *Keepin' it real: School success beyond Black and White.* New York: Oxford University Press.

Carter, P. L. (2010). Race and cultural flexibility among students in different multiracial schools. *Teachers College Record, 112*(6), 1529.

Carter, P. L. (2013). Student and school cultures and the opportunity gap: Paying attention to academic engagement and achievement. In P. L. Carter & K. Welner (Eds.), *Closing the achievement opportunity gap: What America must do to give every child an even chance.* New York: Oxford University Press.

Carter, P. L., & Reardon, S. F. (2014). Inequality matters. William T. Grant Foundation. Retrieved from http://wtgrantfoundation.org

Center for Research on Education Outcomes. (2009a). Charter school performance in New York City. Retrieved from https://credo.stanford.edu/research-reports.html

Center for Research on Education Outcomes. (2009b). Multiple choice: Charter school performance in 16 states. Retrieved from https://credo.stanford.edu/research-reports.html

Center for Research on Education Outcomes. (2013a). Charter school growth and replication. Retrieved from https://credo.stanford.edu/research-reports.html

Center for Research on Education Outcomes. (2013b). Charter school performance in New York City. Retrieved from https://credo.stanford.edu/research-reports.html

Center for Research on Education Outcomes. (2013c). National charter school study. Stanford, CA: Stanford University. Retrieved from http://credo.stanford.edu

Center on Reinventing Public Education. (2013). Hopes, fears, and reality: A balanced look at American charter schools in 2012. In R. J. Lake (Ed.), *Hopes, fears, and reality: A balanced look at American charter schools.* Center on Reinventing Public Education. Retrieved from http://www.crpe.org

Cobb, C. D., & Glass, G. V. (1999). Ethnic segregation in Arizona charter schools. *Education Policy Analysis Archives, 7*(1), 1–36.

Delpit, L. (2002). *The skin that we speak: Thoughts on language and culture in the classroom.* New York: New Press.

Denton, N. (1994). Challenge to White America. *Journal of Intergroup Relations, 21*(2), p. 19.

Dreilinger, D. (2013, December 19). Recovery School District will be country's first all-charter district in September 2014. *The Times-Picayune.* Retrieved from http://www.nola.com/education

Du Bois, W. E. B. (1920/2003). *Darkwater: Voices from within the veil.* New York: Humanity Books.

Dyer, R. (2005). The matter of Whiteness. In P. S. Rothenberg (Ed.), *White privilege: Essential readings on the other side of racism* (2nd ed.). New York: Worth Publishers.

Fabricant, M., & Fine, M. (2012). *Charter schools and the corporate makeover of public education: What's at stake?* New York: Teachers College, Columbia University.

Harvey, D. (2005). *A brief history of neoliberalism.* New York: Oxford University Press.

Henig, J. R. (2013). Charter inroads in affluent communities: Hype or turning point? In R. J. Lake (Ed.), *Hopes, fears, & reality: A balanced look at American charter schools in 2012* (pp. 9–30). Center on Reinventing Public Education & University of Washington Bothell. Retrieved from http://www.crpe.org

Henig, J. R., Holyoke, T. T., Brown, H., & Lacireno-Paquet, N. (2005). The influence of founder type on charter school structures and operations. *American Education Journal, 111*(4), 487–522.

Hyra, D. S. (2008). *The new urban renewal: The economic transformation of Harlem and Bronzeville.* Chicago: University of Chicago Press.

Independent Budget Office, New York City. (2014). New York City public school indicators: Demographics, resources, outcomes. Retrieved from http://www.ibo.nyc.ny.us

Kretchmar, K., Sondel, B., & Ferrare, J. (2014). Mapping the terrain: Teach for America, charter school reform, and corporate sponsorship. *Journal of Education Policy, 29*(6), 742–759.

Kucsera, J., & Orfield, G. (2014). New York State's extreme school segregation: Inequality, inaction, and a damaged future. The Civil Rights Project/Proyecto Derechos Civiles. Retrieved from http://civilrightsproject.ucla.edu

Lacireno-Paquet, N., Holyoke, T. T., Moser, M., & Henig, J. R. (2002). Creaming versus cropping: Charter school enrollment practices in response to market incentives. *Educational Evaluation and Policy Analysis, 24*(2), 145–158.

Ladson-Billings, G. (1995). Toward a theory of culturally relevant pedagogy. American educational research journal, 32(3), 465–491

Leonardo, Z. (2009). *Race, Whiteness, and education.* New York: Taylor and Francis.

Lipman, P. (2011). *The new political economy of urban education: Neoliberalism, race, and the right to the city.* New York: Taylor & Francis.

Lipman, P., & Saltman, K. (2007). Feasting on disaster: Urban school policy, globalization, and the politics of disaster. In K. J. Saltman (Ed.), *Schooling and the politics of disaster* (pp. 83–103). New York: Taylor & Francis.

Lubienski, C. (1999). *Diversification and duplication in charter schools and grant-maintained schools: An exploration in the political economy of school choice.* Paper presented at the Annual Conference of the Comparative and International Education Society, Toronto, Canada. April 14–18.

Lubienski, C., Scott, J., & DeBray, E. (2011). The rise of intermediary organizations in knowledge production, advocacy, and educational policy. *Teachers College Record.*

McIntosh, P. (2005). White privilege: Unpacking the invisible knapsack. In P. S. Rothenberg (Ed.), *White privilege: Essential readings on the other side of racism*. New York: Worth Publishers.

Mills, C. W. (1997). *The racial contract*. Ithaca: Cornell University Press.

Mills, C. W. (2008). White ignorance. In R. Proctor & L. Schieinger (Eds.), *Agnotology: The cultural production of ignorance*. Stanford, CA: Stanford University Press.

Miron, G., Urschel, J. L., Mathis, W. J., & Tornquist, E. (2010). Schools without diversity: Education management organizations, charter schools, and the demographic stratification of the American school system. Boulder and Tempe: Education and the Public Interest Center and Education Policy Research Unit. Retrieved from http://epicpolicy.org/publication/schools-without-diversity

Miron, G., Urschel, J. L., & Saxton, N. (2011). What makes KIPP work? A study of student characteristics, attrition, and school finance. Western Michigan University: National Center for the Study of Privatization in Education, Teachers College, University, and Study Group on Educational Management Organizations.

National Alliance for Public Charter Schools. (2013, June 27). National charter school waitlist numbers approach one million. Washington, D.C. Retrieved from www.publiccharters.org

National Center for Education Statistics. (2014, April). Charter school enrollment, 1999–2000 to 2011–2012. Washington, DC: U.S. Department of Education, Institute of Education Sciences, National center for Education Statistics. Retrieved from http://nces.ed.gov/programs/coe/indicator_cgb.asp

Nelson, F. H., Rosenberg, B., & Van Meter, N. (2004). Charter school achievement on the 2003 National Assessment of Educational Progress. Washington, DC: American Federation of Teachers.

New York City Charter School Center. (2012). The state of the NYC charter school sector: 2012. New York City Charter School Center. Retrieved from http://www.nyc-charterschools.org/

Pattillo, M. (2007). *Black on the block: The politics of race and class in the city*. Chicago: University of Chicago Press.

Rich, M. (2014, April 25). A Walmart fortune, spreading charter schools. *New York Times*. Retrieved from www.nytimes.com

Rickford, J. R. (1999). The Ebonics controversy in my backyard: A sociolinguist's experiences and reflections. *Journal of Sociolinguistics, 3*(2), 267.

Rickford, J. R. (2004). What is Ebonics (African American Vernacular English)? *Linguistic Society of America*. Retrieved from http://www.linguisticsociety.org

RPP International. (2000, January). The state of charter schools 2000: National study of charter schools fourth-year report. Washington, DC: U.S. Department of Education, Office of Educational Research and Improvement.

Scott, J. (2008). Managers of choice: Race, gender, and the philosophies of the new urban school leadership. In C. Lubienski & P. C. Weitzel (Eds.), *School choice policies and outcomes* (pp. 149–176). New York: SUNY Press.

Scott, J. (2009). The politics of venture philanthropy in charter school policy and advocacy. *Educational Policy, 23*(1), 106–136.

Scott, J., & DiMartino, C. (2009). Public education under new management: A typology of educational privatization applied to New York City's restructuring. *Peabody Journal of Education, 84*, 432–452.

Scott, J., & DiMartino, C. (2010). Hybridized, franchised, duplicated, and replicated: Charter schools and management organizations. In C. Lubienski & P. C. Weitzel (Eds.), *The charter school experiment: Expectations, evidence, and implications.* Cambridge, MA: Harvard University Press.

Thernstrom, A., & Thernstrom, S. (2004). *No excuses: Closing the racial in learning gap.* New York: Simon & Schuster.

Welner, K. G., & Miron, G. (2014). Wait, wait. Don't mislead me! Nine reasons to be skeptical about charter waitlist numbers. Boulder: National Education Policy Center. Retrieved from http://nepc.colorado.edu

Wheeler, R. S., & Swords, R. (2004). Codeswitching: Tools of language and culture transform the dialectically diverse classroom. *Language Arts, 81*(6), 470–480.

White, T. (2014). Culture, power, & pedagogy(s) in market-driven times: Embedded case studies of instructional approaches across four charter schools in Harlem, NY. Doctoral dissertation, Teachers College, Columbia University.

Wilson, W. J. (2010). Why both social structure and culture matter in a holistic analysis of inner-city poverty. *The ANNALS of the American Academy of Political and Social Science, 629*, 200–219.

Yosso, T. J. (2006). Whose culture has capital? A critical race theory discussion of community cultural wealth. *Race, Ethnicity, and Education, 8*(1), 69–91.

Zinmeister, K. (2014, March 28). The charter school performance breakout. *Wall Street Journal.* Retrieved from www.wsj.com

Zubrzycki, J., Cavanagh, S., & McNeil, M. (2013). Charter schools' discipline policies. *Education Week, 32*(21), 1, 16–17, 19–20.

7. Philanthrocapitalism: Race, Political Spectacle, and the Marketplace of Beneficence[1] in a New York City School

AMY BROWN

> The problem of our age is the proper administration of wealth, so that the ties of brotherhood may still bind together the rich and the poor in harmonious relationship.
> —Andrew Carnegie (1889) in *The Gospel of Wealth*

> I can conceive of no greater mistake, more disastrous in the end to religion if not to society, than that of trying to make charity do the work of justice.
> —William Jewett Tucker, liberal theologian in response to Carnegie[2]

Introduction

In a meeting held in June 2013, the head of the United Negro College Fund (UNCF) reported that the organization would be updating its slogan from "A Mind Is a Terrible Thing to Waste" to "A Mind Is a Terrible Thing to Waste but a Wonderful Thing to Invest In" (Demby, 2013). Each ad would include the new tagline, "Invest in Better Futures." Several undergraduates spoke at the meeting, each ending their story with the phrase, "I am your dividend." The journalist who wrote the story points out that the change represents a clear shift from language grounded in community activism to one situated in markets, investment, and economic value creation. What are the implications of profiling Black students as "dividends" that are needy and deserving of charity only if they are able to demonstrate the ability to become entrepreneurs within a neoliberal and profit-oriented context? In other words, as economies of need become economies of profit in education, how does the categorization of Black students as representative of fiscal

potential in an "affect economy" (Adams, 2012) intersect with the maintenance of inequality and White supremacy? In this chapter, I demonstrate that
this discursive shift toward profit, strategic investment, and empowerment
of the private sector in shaping educational philosophy and policy is evident,
not only in philanthropic organizations like the UNCF, but also increasingly
in public educational institutions, such as the College Preparatory Academy
(College Prep), a small, traditional public school in New York City, where I
conducted two years of ethnographic teacher research.

While many scholars have focused on the insidious ways that philanthropists can influence the formation of public policy in education (Baltodano,
2012; Ravitch, 2010; Saltman, 2010), in this chapter, I qualitatively document the ways in which the lived experience of privatization in urban
education rearticulates race, class, and gender inequalities (Lipman, 2011;
Shiller, 2011). My findings at College Prep demonstrate a clear relation
between philanthrocapitalism, White supremacy, and economic inequity, and
I argue here for critical awareness of and resistance to this problematic trend.
While adding to much of the literature on philanthropy and race (Richey &
Ponte, 2011; Zhang, Gajjala, & Watkins, 2012), and on philanthropy and
education, I use political scientist Murray Edelman's theories of how a political spectacle of educational crisis serves to mask a structural crisis (Edelman,
1988; M. Smith, Kahn, Heinecke, & Jarvis, 2004). I trace a brief history of
what Ealy (2014) calls the "problem industrial complex" and connect this to
a racialized political economy of education in New York City under former
Mayor Michael Bloomberg. Through describing College Prep, and then analyzing its relationship to funders, I demonstrate how the problem industrial
complex intersects with the experience of College Prep teachers and students.
I conclude with possibilities for resistance.

Philanthropy, Race, and Education: A Brief History

The ways in which we understand social problems—and their remedies—are
influenced by structures of power. According to Edelman (1988), political
developments are always creations of the publics concerned with them. He
argues that political media uses various tactics to entertain, distort, or shock a
largely nonvoting public. These tactics are what he calls a "political spectacle."
Explanations of problems, he argues, are always constructions that are likely
to reinforce dominant ideology. "The spectacle," he writes, "carries no meaning in itself. It is always a gloss on the phenomenal worlds of individuals and
groups" (Edelman, 1988, p. 93). In addition to political media, philanthropists in education—and, as I show, those who must cater to them—construct

a political spectacle of social justice that maintains White hegemony, both in the past and through the present.

White, wealthy men have historically had a role in constructing and solving educational problems (and furthering educational inequities). In fact, in the late 19th century, industrialists such as Andrew Carnegie, John D. Rockefeller, and Julius Rosenwald invested in primary and secondary schooling as well as college education to ensure that semi-skilled, and, often, African American, workers were well trained (Gasman, 2012). Anderson (1988) notes that these philanthropists laid the groundwork for the development of Black education in the United States: By and large, corporate philanthropic foundations favored industrial training and the maintenance of racial inequality. Watkins (2001) argues that the philanthropic architects of many educational institutions were faced with the same dilemma that many philanthropists are faced with today: how to ideologically reconcile great wealth with social altruism (p. 181). The way that they did this was through a financial and political project of accommodationist education, teaching the values of conformity, obedience, sobriety, piety, and enterprise for Black people, thus combining constitutional ideals of freedom with social subservience (Watkins, 2001, p. 182). In other words, after the Civil War, states Watkins (2001), "America's apartheid had to be made workable. It needed to appear natural and ordained. Beyond that, Blacks needed to be convinced that their lot was improving" (p. 182). According to Edelman (1988), "ideology and material conditions are part of the same transaction" (p. 3). White philanthropists had to create an ideology—a political spectacle—that could justify their privilege in the context of racialized material conditions of great inequity. They did this through systematic construction of benevolence and charity that continues through the present.

While the Carnegies and the Rockefellers of their day were known for their level of philanthropic giving, Hay (2013) argues that today, we appear to be entering a new "golden age of philanthropy" because of philanthropists' power in shaping public policy and because of unprecedented emphasis on "impact" and "measurable goals." Ealy (2014) marks the beginning of today's "big philanthropy" as the late 1960s with the publication of Cornuelle's *Reclaiming the American Dream (1965)*, and the subsequent publication of *Healing America* (1983), both of which asserted that it was not up to "big government" to solve social problems; rather, this should be the "task of philanthropy to support anew the 'vast, idle capacities of individuals and institutions to act freely and directly on public problems'" (p. 89). Others trace the beginning of this "golden age" to a 2009 meeting between a select group of the super wealthy dubbed the "Good Club" (Rogers, 2011).

Predominantly White men,[3] the attendees included Bill Gates, Warren Buffett, David Rockefeller, Ted Turner, Michael Bloomberg, and George Soros. At that meeting, the Good Club chose global population growth as the problem to target. As Rogers (2011) aptly states, "this is not a choice of a group concerned with public opinion. It veers into the murky waters of women's reproductive rights and religious, cultural and ethnic politics and not least, eugenics" (p. 376). A year later, in 2010, Bill and Melinda Gates and Warren Buffett announced the "Giving Pledge," that 40 million American billionaires had pledged to give at least half of their wealth to charity either during their lifetime or after their death (Rogers, 2011, p. 376). Philanthropists such as the Gates family began to take on other "challenges," for example, "extreme poverty and poor health in developing countries, and the failures of the American education system" (Gates & Gates, 2014). While the intentions of Gates, Buffett, Bloomberg, and others may be framed as benevolent, it is also important to point out that in addition to increased political power and influence, the philanthropic sector enjoys a financial reward: tax-exempt status and sometimes charitable deductions for donors (Ealy, 2014). In fact, as Saltman (2011) points out,

> Although roughly half of wealth given to foundations comes in the form of small donations, the real financial benefits principally go to the big givers at the top of the economy who are able to significantly reduce their tax burdens. For every ten dollars given by the Gates Foundation, four dollars is lost from the public wealth in taxes. The philanthropist would otherwise give his money to the public in the form of taxes. (p. 8)

In this way, the construction of social problems and the political spectacle involved in solving them reinforces the class privilege of the elite.

Today's big philanthropists are popularly known as "philanthrocapitalists." *Philanthrocapitalism* is a more advanced version of venture philanthropy. It is loosely based on the practices of venture capital investing and is often focused on achieving measurable results. It is often characterized by a high degree of involvement by donors with grantees (Jenkins, 2011). Philanthrocapitalism, then, is a form of wealth transfer, often from a wealthy individual through a foundation or to an organization, so as to affect some kind of "social justice" (Lorenzi & Hilton, 2011). It rests upon an ethic of neoliberalism, that is, an adherence to classic liberal economic values of deregulation, competition, free markets, and the entrepreneurial self (Friedman, 1962). Neoliberalism is more than just the laissez-faire capitalism espoused by Adam Smith (1776). Rather, according to Baltodano (2012), neoliberalism as a political rationale implies active political intervention and the manipulation of social institutions, including the media, the law, universities, and the state. It is a form of state-enabled capitalism that seeks to intensify the alliances between corporations and cultural institutions. As Baltodano (2012) explains, neoliberal economics become a political rationale because the needs of government are subsumed—and often support—the needs of the market. This occurs through a political spectacle of justice as choice and innovation through market competition. As I demonstrate in this chapter, in education, students and teachers are often aware that they are used as "props" to uphold this performance.

Philanthrocapitalists do not only enjoy a financial benefit. They also enjoy political benefit. This is especially evident through what Rogers (2011) has named "philanthropolicymaking," as philanthrocapitalists such as Bill and Melinda Gates, Sam Walton, and Eli Broad demonstrate a plutocratic (and often experimental) influence over the formation of public policy. Some scholars critique "philanthropolicymaking" (Rogers, 2011; Williamson, 2012) and warn against the strong alliances between philanthrocapitalists and the state (Keohane, 2013). Others advocate for critiquing the movement in general (Edwards, 2011; Husock, 2011). Even some who seem to be in favor of schools raising supplementary funds through partnerships with nonprofits or corporations admit that it is systemically problematic (Green, 2012) and that philanthropy may serve to justify extreme inequality (Thorup, 2013).

Major philanthrocaptialists are involved in public schools (Ravitch, 2010), but as Saltman (2011) argues, their involvement is both racially and class coded:

> The neoliberal declaration of a "failed system"… is not leveled explicitly against rich, predominantly White communities and public schools for whom high levels of historical investment and the benefits of cultural capital have resulted in high achievement, traditionally defined. Rather, the declaration of "system failure" is leveled against working-class and poor, predominantly non-White communities and schools. (p. 5)

He explains that this tends to place blame on the public (rather than the private sector) for educational inequalities. While educational funding is linked to wealth through property taxes and local funding, he explains, the private sector has continually played a role in creating and continuing inequality (Saltman, 2011, pp. 5–6). Connecting failure to poor and working-class, non-White communities, and subsequently entrusting the private sector for solutions, is a process that serves to insulate White middle-class and elite privilege. "Failing" schools, often Black and Brown schools, compete for finite resources that are allocated by the private sector, while those schools deemed as "succeeding," often White, continue to benefit from longstanding social and historical privilege. While it may seem as if "failing" students and schools need funders to "save" them, in a racialized political economy, funders depend on students to construct their own privileged identities. This is one facet of "racial philanthrocapitalism" (Brown, 2012). Resources continue to be unevenly distributed, furthering problematic and pervasive narratives that connect success to Whiteness. Thus, systemic inequity does not change.

As Shiller (2012) points out, the experimental and plutocratic influence of philanthrocapitalists was especially evident in New York City when the Gates Foundation advocated in the early 2000s for moving to a system of small schools to foster competition and choice for parents. As a result, Shiller writes, today, New York City has more than 300 small schools, which were originally supposed to be based around innovative and unique themes, but were also still held accountable for improving their test scores. Despite Gates's wholehearted embrace of small themed schools in New York City, in 2008, their foundation announced that it planned to shift the focus of its education grant making from the creation of small schools toward an effort to double the amount of low-income people who complete a college degree or certificate by age 26 (Jenkins, 2011, p. 45; Naylor, 2011). The Gates Foundation seems to make somewhat arbitrary and experimental decisions about when to invest—and when to abandon—its policy experiments, often with little or limited data. In the context of White supremacy, these decisions are actually far from arbitrary. Despite discourse that masks the furthering of race and class inequality with the language of reform, increasing privatization and corporatization of public education has racial, political, and economic consequences (Fabricant & Fine, 2012, 2013; Mora & Christianakis, 2011).

While there have been some philanthropic initiatives to combat structural racism (HoSang, n.d.), race is often avoided in philanthropic conversations (Venkatesh, 2002), which tend to focus on short-term deliverables and returns as well as simply reporting current disparities (HoSang, n.d.). More importantly, benevolent philanthropic discourses in the United States and globally function as "cultural scripts" that maintain and perpetuate power differentials, rearticulating Whiteness as associated with "progress, technology and civilization, while situating Blackness (and other marginalized identities) within the discourse of nature, primitivism and pre-modernity" (Richey & Ponte, 2011; Zhang et al., 2012, p. 205). For example, as Richey and Ponte (2011) point out, advertising for Bono's "Product Red" constructs a certain kind of AIDS victim (heterosexual, Black, African women and children) as a racialized and gendered primitive "other" that consumers can help "save" through their purchases. Although they function at the policy or marketing level, and are often lived at a local level, these neocolonial and cultural scripts are attributable to the hegemonic influence of an ostensibly well-meaning private sector. In what follows, I focus on the ways in which the political spectacle of justice through charity and philanthropy was contested and maintained at College Prep.

College Prep

In New York City, philanthrocapitalists' investment—and disinvestment—in educational experiments occurs in a context of a public school system of just over one million students where just over 40% are Hispanic, about 28% are Black, 16% Asian, and 15% White (NYCIBO, 2013). Importantly, White students are more highly represented in the lower grades, and Black students in the higher grades. While 17% of New York City's public school students were born outside of the United States, more than 42% of them do not speak English at home, and students overwhelmingly come from low-income households: More than 79% qualify for free or reduced-price school meals (NYCIBO, 2013, p. 7). In this context, philanthropists construct problems and solutions, then construct a different problem and solution that obscures the previous. This is political spectacle in action.

College Prep opened as a part of former New York City Mayor Michael Bloomberg's New Century Schools Initiative (NCSI), which began as a result of the shift in New York City's schools to mayoral control in 2002. As mentioned earlier, Bloomberg and former Chancellor Joel Klein advocated (with great financial and political influence from the Gates Foundation, as well as the Carnegie and Soros Foundations) for opening hundreds of small themed schools of choice in poor urban communities in New York City (Shiller, 2011). Based on a competitive, market model, these schools were supposed to increase choice for parents and foster competition in the name of quality. Behind a political spectacle of reform and improvement, however, Shiller found that these reforms actually made schools "accountable to funders rather than families" and "put decision making in the hands of school reformers rather than sharing it with parents and community members" (Shiller, 2011, p. 55). These reforms did not explicitly engage social structures of White supremacy and race inequality, nor did they enable democracy.

The school opened in 2004, and in 2008 created its own, in-house non-profit foundation, which I call "the Foundation" to solicit funds from the private sector. College Prep's website thanks five foundations, seven elected officials, 34 companies and organizations for their charitable donations, and also thanks more than 300 individuals who have each donated $5,000 or more to the Foundation. At the time I conducted my research, from 2008 to 2010, of the 458 students enrolled in the school, grades 9 through 12, 81% identified as Black, 17% as Hispanic, 1% as Asian/Pacific Islander, and fewer than 1% as White or American Indian (nysed.gov, 2008–2009). Funders included a corporate firm ("the Firm") that was also a primary founder of the school, as well as the Robin Hood Foundation, an organization of venture philanthropists who are ostensibly committed to fighting poverty in New York City (robinhood.org, 2014), as well as the Bill and Melinda Gates Foundation.

When it first opened as a small, traditional public school, College Prep shared a building with an elementary school and was located next to a large public housing project in a Brooklyn neighborhood with little commerce and difficult access to subways. When I walked through the neighborhood to interview at the school in the spring of 2008, I passed bodegas, take-out Chinese restaurants, and liquor stores, most of which separated customers from cash registers by bulletproof glass. I was hired to teach English at the school the following fall.

When I began teaching and research at College Prep, the school had created the Foundation, its own, in-house, nonprofit organization. Staff members at the Foundation worked to solicit grants and resources from outside organizations. A main contributor to the Foundation was the corporate Firm that had also helped to found the school, although there were several other organizations and individuals who contributed to the Foundation. The school had moved into a newly refurbished building in a different neighborhood that was close to several subway lines and was located next to many stores, restaurants, hotels, and a college campus. Parents who visited commented on the building's "corporate" feel. The two years I conducted research at College Prep were my fourth and fifth as a New York City teacher; I had taught English in two other schools previously. As a teacher new to College Prep, I was astounded by the wealth of resources that were available to me as compared to the two other public schools where I had previously worked. At those schools, it had been a struggle to procure photocopies, paper, or to have access to working computers for students, but at College Prep, I had access to unlimited copies and paper, I had an LCD projector and interactive whiteboard in my classroom, and there was both a standing and mobile computer lab for students. Students had access to a college advising office and myriad extracurricular after-school and summer opportunities. This was due largely to funding accrued through the Foundation.

College Prep's Racialized Relationship to Funders

In terms of its resources, College Prep was a fabulous environment in which to teach, but I experienced, along with many of my colleagues and students, the tension that recipients of grants often feel (Lawrence, 2002). While we were grateful, we were uncomfortable with our racialized relationship to funders. In other words, access to resources meant that funders and some teachers were constructed as the "good White saviors," while students were constructed as the "needy, Black or Brown other." A 12th-grade student wrote on a schoolwide student questionnaire that I disseminated in the spring of 2010 that asked about school life, home life, aspirations, and literacy practices, "College Prep is not what it seems. College Prep is a very slick mixed-up school. A lot of lies are put into promoting this school." This student seems to be referring to the tension between the racialized spectacle or performance required to acquire resources, and then the "real," everyday local occurrences beyond the spectacle.

The school's 93% graduation rate and 97% college acceptance rate for seniors stood out as compared to other New York City schools, where the graduation rate in 2010 was 62.7% (schools.nyc.gov, 2010). Yet many teachers complained about grade inflation. One White, male teacher went so far as to say in a meeting, "We mold situations here in an inauthentic way because we so badly want a final product... we never let kids fail, and they are not accountable. If you don't have a pen, I give you one, and if you don't have a printer, I print it out for you." Students, on the questionnaire, echoed him, saying, in response to a question that read: "How does your experience at College Prep compare with the experiences of your friends/siblings who don't go to College Prep?"

> Academic wise it's great, the teachers teach you in a way that you can't fail. But the kids take advantage of that.
>
> College Prep is a good place, but sometimes babies the students too much, and doesn't know exactly how or when to let us fly away.
>
> College Prep is more academic but the students are babied.

In the quotes above, students and staff members demonstrate their awareness of the necessity of furthering an image of impact for funders. Funders feel they are "making a difference" by contributing to a school whose data stand out from the rest, a school that shows Black and Brown urban students doing what they are not supposed to do, that is, being academically successful and college bound. Staff members work hard to convince funders that they have an impact. Part of what makes this so attractive to—and comfortable for—funders, however, is that it seems to be a unique exception to the rule. Instead of investing in the kind of social change that demonstrates the potential to effect systemic change and perhaps lead to racial, economic, and educational equity across the board, funders insulate their privilege by upholding the current system of inequity and competition.

The inauthentic "molding of situations" to further race and class narratives that would make funders comfortable was especially apparent to me when I attended a benefit for the Foundation at the Firm during the spring of 2010. The benefit, held in the evening, in one of the Firm's banquet rooms, featured music, several buffets of hors d'oeuvres, an open bar, and a keynote speaker. Attendees paid for tickets and were encouraged to contribute more money to the Foundation once they arrived. I watched as predominantly Black and Latino/a students and predominantly White staff members were carefully selected and invited to the benefit to represent the College Prep image for what Sebastian Thomas, the head of the Foundation, said, were "100–150 of the school's most generous supporters." From my observation, these supporters were elite, predominantly White men who worked in the corporate sector. Teachers seemed young, energetic, and ready to put the time in to "save" those whom they taught, while students seemed appropriately "articulate," needy, "at-risk," and deserving of funders' charity. Indeed, when Mr. Thomas asked teachers for their suggestions of which students to invite, there were a few that Mr. Thomas found to be "too volatile" to represent the school: The benefit was not a time to take a chance on a student who might not uphold the right image for funders. Mr. Thomas coached us in a series of meetings beforehand to dress modestly ("like teachers"), not to partake in any alcohol at the open bar, not to eat much (since we were concentrating on talking up the school and on getting donations), and not to walk around the room in groups larger than two. Students and teachers at the event played their part. Funders contributed 34% of the Foundation's annual budget through checks they dropped into a box as they left (and were, according to Mr. Thomas, our second highest source of funding behind the Robin Hood Foundation).

Funders, staff members, and students all played important roles at the benefit as well as, when needed, in a school context to ensure that College Prep looked on paper like a success story. Sociohistorical and economic narratives of privilege and oppression seemed to dictate the spectacle that informed all of our actions. While race was never explicitly mentioned at the benefit, we enacted and furthered clearly raced and classed demarcations between funders, staff, and students. As teachers and students articulated above, a similar pattern rang true when it came to assessments, and thus, graduation and college matriculation rates. College Prep, technically no different from any other traditional public school, had to compete in an unequal marketplace for resources and opportunities that, in an ideal world, should be available to every student and teacher, in and beyond College Prep. In addition to the benefit, College Prep staff used other strategies to insulate its marketability. In the next section, I detail another aspect of College Prep's political spectacle: a film used to advertise the school to potential funders.

The College Prep Movie

On the first Wednesday of each month at College Prep, the bell rang to dismiss students at 1:48 p.m., and staff stayed in the building for a series of meetings. In addition to a weekly grade team meeting that lasted until 3:30, we had a full staff meeting that began at 3:45 and ended around 5:00. First Wednesdays were long for teachers, and so on meeting days lunch was catered, compliments of the Firm. Platters of wraps and sandwiches, snack bags of chips and pretzels, cookies, water and soft drinks are a familiar sight in the guidance suite during fourth and fifth periods, a preemptive reward for the hours we would spend collaborating later. This Wednesday, in the spring of 2010, was especially remarkable because we were told that we would be viewing the "College Prep movie," a promotional film created by two filmmakers who were hired pro bono by the Foundation to funnel in private donations.

As teachers entered, we noticed that there were two celebratory sheet cakes on a table at the side of the room, and that there were wooden chairs set up facing a screen and a podium. We took our seats and listened as Sebastian Thomas, dressed in tie and blazer, shared how thrilled he was about the outcome of the film we were about to watch. He congratulated the filmmakers, two young White women who were sitting in the back. They smiled and waved.

Sarah Maxwell and Michelle MacLeod, two of College Prep's enrichment coordinators, and Angela Moore, a ninth-grade special education teacher, had been asked by Mr. Thomas to give us a short introduction to the film, and they approached the podium. Staff became quiet, our clipboards on our laps, waiting to see what was in store.

Ms. Maxwell, the young, White ninth-grade enrichment coordinator, filled us in on how the film would be used as a tool for eighth-grade recruitment. "Students are the best ones to sell the school," she emphasized. Ms. McLeod, the tenth-grade enrichment coordinator, told us that "the film captures the community around each child," and that "it shows what enrichment at College Prep really is." New York City–native Ms. Moore, the only teacher and the only African American at the podium, said that the film "captures the passion, energy and relentless work ethic that makes College Prep set the standard for excellence." She emphasized, "The film captures the most important parts of the school." We recruit, she said, the best and brightest of New York City teachers, the strongest teachers, those who know what it takes to move students from the bottom to the top. This all comes through, she said, in this short movie.

Mr. Thomas stepped back up to the podium and added that the film would also, of course, be shown to prospective funders, such as Time Warner or other corporate philanthropists. "Without further ado," he announced, "we give you the first College Prep movie!" Someone in the back of the room dimmed the lights and the film began. We saw Principal McCarren and Mr. Thomas on the screen first. They painted a portrait of the school as an unscreened public school, one that is academically rigorous as well as focused on critical thinking. The face of a young, Black male student flashed onto the screen. "Without education," the student said, "you don't have anything." Other student perspectives were highlighted. One student said, "If things start getting shaky at home, someone at school will get me back on track." Another student warned, "Be prepared to have faculty on your back." Another expressed, "Especially coming from the environment that I grew up in, it helps me to know that I don't have to go down the wrong path."

The camera cut to an interview with La'Trice Williams, one of my closest personal friends at College Prep since we shared a classroom the previous school year. In the film, she said that she was from South Central Los Angeles, and that "if it weren't for the educators in my life, I wouldn't be here. Working at College Prep gives me the opportunity to give back to my community." I snuck a look at her, seated down the aisle from me. Her face was expressionless as she stared straight ahead at the screen. Months before, she reluctantly agreed to be interviewed for the film. After the interview took place, I remember that she returned to the classroom we shared, pulled me aside, and told me that the experience had been somewhat strange.

We had already talked at great length about her feeling frequently tokenized by White staff and administrators as one of only a few African American teachers at the school, and as one of the only teachers at the school who grew up in circumstances that were similar to many students. Of the interview, she said that "it was obvious why they wanted me to be there, and it was obvious what they wanted me to say. I had to play my role in order to sell College Prep to the White liberals who throw money at us to save these 'poor Black and

Brown kids.'" She shook the experience off, but her resentment was obvious, and through the two years that we worked at the school, her patience and tolerance for how she was treated by some White staff members wore thin.

The narrator continued: "We offer students as many opportunities as possible to interact with the adult professional world." The film then cut to Howard Jackson, an African American 12th-grade English teacher. "Here," he said, "students can re-imagine their possibility." We saw Mr. Thomas again, who stated, "This school is transformative and life-changing for its students." This was juxtaposed by a statement by an African American male student: "This school set the foundation for helping me to be what I want to be when I want to be it, whether it's president, senator, or lawyer." On this meritocratic note, the film ended. The lights came up in the library to a chorus of applause. Mr. Thomas told us to help ourselves to cake, and said that the filmmakers would walk around, eager to answer any questions, and to get our reactions to the film.

In the film, the school was portrayed so favorably that the gravest threat to students' education and college matriculation seemed to be their own challenging backgrounds and circumstances. Parents and older community members were absent, serving to reinforce the College Prep narrative of urban teachers and students working together (with funders' help), against all odds, to pull students up by their bootstraps, and help them to graduate securely on the road to achievement in the real world—in this case, synonymous with college readiness and a secure place in the middle class.

Ms. Moore, Ms. MacLeod, and Ms. Maxwell were right: The film presents an image of College Prep that showcases the hard work of both teachers and students. It demonstrates how many enrichment opportunities and resources exist for those students who are deemed "worthy." It is expertly produced and will certainly aid in bringing in more donations to the Foundation, which will translate into more enrichment opportunities for students and more resources for students and teachers. Just as with the benefit, as well as teachers' and students' comments regarding grade inflation, the College Prep movie highlights the school as a good investment choice for funders who have the luxury of deciding where and how resources should be allocated without engaging the roots of social and economic privilege and oppression. Patricia Burch (2006, 2009) examines the trend that she names the "new educational privatization" in the United States: in other words, the ways in which funds are transferred from government and public institutions to private companies and organizations, and the close linkages between those who hold power in private markets and the formation of public policy. The need to cater to unsackable "modern day royals" like Walton and Gates inhibits us from critically analyzing the ways in which experimental altruism on a market of beneficence (Ealy, 2011), often enacted through the political spectacle of "social justice," furthers racism and inequity.

Beyond College Prep

I spoke with Ms. Williams about her experience watching the College Prep movie in a follow-up interview during the summer of 2012. When we talked, she was no longer at College Prep; she was working as the deputy director of an organization that runs advocacy training and mobilization programs for parents of students who are in charter schools. She had recently accompanied her boss to a fundraiser for KIPP charter schools in Newark, New Jersey. Arianna Huffington was the keynote speaker. The evening started with a cocktail hour where an elementary school choir performed, followed by a middle school drumline. Then, the founder spoke about the organization's growth and potential funders watched films about the school. "I was right back at College Prep," Ms. Williams said,

> And then it was time to raise the money. And you can now text your pledge, so they put up a screen and you text your pledge and you can see the screen. The starting pledge was $25,000 for their new elementary school. And they said, "we need six new classrooms," and just like that, texts went up. And they raised, I think over half a million dollars that night... the idea that I am sitting next to people who can text to pledge $25,000—it's crazy to me. So that part of the program is over, so you go out, more cocktails, and you come back in and it's time for dinner. And they put a teacher and a student at each table. The teacher— White woman, from Northern Michigan. The student—Black kid from Newark. And all over again, I'm remembering College Prep, but now I'm on the other side. Now this teacher thinks I am someone who can text to pledge $25,000. And so she's like trying to sell to me why she does this work and why she loves it so much. It makes my blood boil!

Ms. Williams experienced dissonance because of her dual positionality in this situation: As a Black woman, and a former teacher, she saw through the hype, recognizing the spectacle that the market of beneficence requires. Not only was she disgusted by the assumption that donations from a predominantly White, elite class would "save" poor black students from Newark, she was disgusted at the role that the teacher, the student, the funder, and she played in perpetuating race and class inequities.

Cory Booker was the next speaker, and Ms. Williams remembered him saying to the room full of mostly White funders that it was their generosity that made the evening possible. "Your generosity," Ms. Williams repeated to me, shaking her head, "your generosity, your generosity." She continued:

And then I remembered being a high school kid and sitting in a room and hearing everyone talk about me like I wasn't there. And hearing everyone talk about how messed up my life was. And how I needed them to save me. And I looked across the table at this girl who is in the eighth grade and I was like, "I remember being you, and I still feel like you in these moments." And every single kid in that room was checked out. They were totally checked out. They were either on their phones, or talking to each other, or trying to go to the bathroom together... because any part of the presentation that talked about the need to save them from Newark talked about them in a way that made them feel uncomfortable in middle school. And they gotta sit through those things because they are chosen over and over again. They choose the same kids, over and over again. They've gotta sit through those presentations over and over again, and all they keep hearing is, it's not their hard work that makes a difference, it's not their parents that makes the difference. It's these White folks who are giving them $25,000 a pop who make their lives possible.

Like other teachers whom I spoke with in follow-up interviews, Ms. Williams is pained by the implications of students' and teachers' involvement in selling a story to enforce funders' self-aggrandizing narratives of generosity and by the inequities that this political spectacle depends on. From her perspective and experience as a former student, as a former teacher and as someone who was committed to moving toward racial and educational equity, she was frustrated by the ways in which, at every level, from student to teacher to funder, philanthrocapitalism in education depends on a racialized narrative that operates under the guise of neutrality.

Conclusion

Philanthropists and the publics that currently compete for their gifts must recognize that "political understanding does not spring from designating one interpretation as fact, truth or scientific finding" (Edelman, 1988, p. 123). Rather, political understanding comes from interrogating the range of meanings that one can attach to any political phenomenon. Political understanding has the potential to generate change in actions or beliefs.

In this "golden age of philanthropy," those who participate in philanthropic relationships must work to push ambivalence about the political spectacles in which they participate to the point of strategic counter-discourses that "challenge hegemony by undermining its presuppositions and offering alternatives" (Edelman, 1988, p. 129). In other words, as nonprofits take on the responsibility for citizens that the state has shirked, it may be instructive to remember that the purpose of the work is to "gain liberation, not to work for the organization's longevity" (Gilmore, 2009, p. 51). Eikenberry (2009) suggests ways that voluntary and nonprofit organizations can create and apply a democratic counter-discourse in seeking grants and private funding. Funding may not have to dictate norms—there may be ways in which, given the reality of the current system, schools can partner with nonprofits and/or philanthropists to accept resources, but resist furthering problematic narratives about students and their communities (Gilmore, 2009).

Much philanthropy in public education, under the guise of "measurable impact," purports to be neutral (O'Connor, 2002). Edelman (1988) writes, "a spectacle... seems to have a self-evident meaning" (p. 125). Political spectacle, in this case, in the form of philanthropic narratives, presents itself as fact, but obscures other possible meanings, interpretations, and problems; at College Prep, and in the fundraiser that Ms. Williams mentioned, a spectacle of benevolence, charity, and altruism not only obscures but also furthers the raced and classed power imbalance present in U.S. public education when, as the epigraph for this chapter states, charity does the work of justice. Social equity cannot be attained only through the generosity of those who are in positions of power and privilege. Rather, we will move toward justice by restructuring a system that currently insulates the privilege of the White and wealthy under the guise of generosity and neutrality. Whether this means shifting the ways we pay taxes, creating a means for universally affordable and available food and health care, creating universally available childhood education, or ending cycles of environmental destruction, social change cannot come from dependence on inequity, charity, or selective investment.

Teachers and students, such as those at College Prep, are aware of the contradictions behind the spectacle, and they realize that they are props in a problematic narrative: Gifts often come with strings attached (Hay, 2013; Saltman, 2011). Although the data I gathered at College Prep demonstrate what I would characterize as ambivalence as opposed to resistance, teachers, students, and families continue to carve out a space for critique, for caring, and for teaching and learning. While this form of resilience may not be counterhegemonic, it might represent a moment of recognition in the face of racial capitalist oppression (Katz, 2004). In a market of beneficence, in the name of acquiring needed resources, Black and Latino urban students and their predominantly White teachers critique their roles in upholding the power and privilege of those who can afford to give, while they themselves remain in a position of subservience. As Mr. Matthews, a Black faculty member, put it in our 2012 follow-up interview:

> We as a school expect that once a child graduates and they go to college the family and the student is forever indebted to the school in terms of "look what we did for your child," as opposed to "look what your child did for himself or herself"... [when I was in high school], it was like, my parents always congratulated

me, it was always intrinsic, you know, that I was motivated and I wanted to do this, and I never felt indebted to my school. And I think it was maybe just my understanding of public education is that everybody deserves it. This is my right... everybody should get this regardless.

Mr. Matthews clearly sees the problems inherent in philanthropic investment in the public sector. In his view, students should not have to depend on charity for their right to a free public education.

Saltman (2011) echoes this sentiment as he argues that those who want to donate to charitable or philanthropic causes might contribute to a public fund, as opposed to strategically investing in the competitive market of the "problem industrial complex." In addition to teachers, students, and communities who maintain their resilience and perhaps move toward reworking or resisting their problematic categorization, philanthrocapitalists must be more open to public critique or debate (Hess, 2012) so that the super wealthy might contribute in ways that strengthen civil society (Jenkins, 2011). If their intentions are truly good, donors must also start a more open dialogue with those involved in social movements (Ramdas, 2011) and move toward models of greater transparency to change entrenched social structures of White supremacy, patriarchy, and economic inequality. Teachers, students, philanthropic organizations, and funders need to collaborate in questioning the ways in which a market of beneficence furthers privilege and oppression by depending on problematic narratives of need and deservedness to exist, then strive to enact more radical modes of generosity that value, above all, equity and liberation.

References

Adams, V. (2012). The other road to serfdom: Recovery by the market and the affect economy in New Orleans. *Public Culture, 24*(1), 185–216.

Anderson, J. (1988). *The education of Blacks in the south: 1860–1935.* Chapel Hill: University of North Carolina Press.

Baltodano, M. (2012). Neoliberalism and the demise of public education: The corporatization of schools of education. *International Journal of Qualitative Studies in Education, 25*(4), 487–507.

Bosworth, D. (2011). The cultural contradictions of philanthrocapitalism. *Society, 48*, 382–388.

Brown, A. (2012). A good invesment? Race, philanthrocapitalism and professionalism in a New York City small school of choice. *International Journal of Qualitative Studies in Education, 25*(4), 375–396.

Burch, P. (2006). The new educational privatization: Educational contracting and high stakes accountability. *Teachers College Record, 108*(12), 2582–2610.

Burch, P. (2009). *Hidden markets: The new education privatization.* New York: Routledge.

Cohen, R. (2002). Making philanthropy accountable. *Souls: A Critical Journal of Black Politics, Culture and Society, 4*(1), 63–68.

Cornuelle, R. (1965). *Reclaiming the American dream: The role of private individuals and voluntary associations.* New Brunswick, NJ: Transaction Publishers.

Cornuelle, R. (1983). *Healing America.* New York: Putnam.

Demby, G. (2013). New ads still warn a mind is a terrible thing to waste. *Code Switch: Fronteirs of Race, Culture and Ethnicity.* Retrieved from http://www.npr.org/blogs/codeswitch/2013/06/14/191796469/a-mind-is-a-terrible-thing-to

Ealy, L. (2011). Justice, beneficence and the modern age. *Society, 48,* 403–406.

Ealy, L. (2014). The intellectual crisis in philanthropy. *Society, 51*(1), 87–96.

Edelman, M. (1988). *Constructing the political spectacle.* Chicago: University of Chicago Press.

Edwards, M. (2011). Impact, accountabilty and philanthrocapitalism. *Society, 48,* 389–390.

Eikenberry, A. (2009). Refusing the market: A democratic discourse for voluntary and nonprofit organizations. *Nonprofit and Voluntary Sector Quarterly, 38*(4), 582–596.

Fabricant, M., & Fine, M. (2012). *Charter schools and the corporate makeover of public education: What's at stake?* New York: Teachers College Press.

Fabricant, M., & Fine, M. (2013). *The changing politics of education: Privatization and the lives left behind.* Boulder: Paradigm.

Foley, D. (1997). Deficit thinking models based on culture: The anthropological protest. In R. Valencia (Ed.), *The evolution of deficit thinking: Educational thought and practice* (pp. 113–131). London: Falmer.

Friedman, M. (1962). *Capitalism and freedom.* Chicago: University of Chicago Press.

Gasman, M. (2012). What's new is old? *Phi Delta Kappan, 93,* 8–11.

Gates, B., & Gates, M. (2014, August 6). Letter from Bill and Melinda Gates. Retrieved from http://www.gatesfoundation.org/Who-We-Are/General-Information/Letter-from-Bill-and-Melinda-Gates

Gilmore, R. W. (2007). In the shadow of the shadow state. In Incite! Women Of Color Against Violence (Eds.), *The revolution will not be funded: Beyond the non-profit industrial complex* (pp. 41–52). Cambridge, MA: South End Press.

Good, J. G., & Eames, E. (1996). An anthropological critique of the culture of poverty. In G. Gmelch & W. Zenner (Eds.), *Urban life: Readings in urban anthropology.* Prospect Heights, IL: Waveland.

Green, D. (2012). Investing in high school. *Phi Delta Kappan, 93,* 28–33.

Hay, I. (2013). Questioning generosity in the golden age of philanthropy. *Progress in Human Geography,* 1–19.

Hess, F. (2012). Philanthropy gets in the ring. *Phi Delta Kappan, 93,* 17–21.

HoSang, D. (n.d.). The structural racism concept and its impact on philanthropy. Retrieved from http://racialequity.org/docs/CIF5The%20Structural%20Racism%20Concept%20.pdf

Husock, H. (2011). Disaggregating public purposes. *Society, 48*, 391–392.

Jenkins, G. (2011). Who's afraid of philanthrocapitalism? *Case Western Reserve Law Review, 61*(3), 1–69.

Kailin, J. (1999). How White teachers perceive the problem of racism in their schools: A case study in "liberal" Lakeview. *Teachers College Record, 100*(4), 724–750.

Katz, C. (2004). *Growing up global: Economic restructuring and children's everyday lives.* Minneapolis: University of Minnesota Press.

Keohane, G. L. (2013). *Social entrepreneurship: How innovative change-makers are testing new solutions to entrenched social, economic and environmental problems.* New York: McGraw Hill Financial Global Institute.

Lawrence, K. (2002). Reconsidering community building: Philanthropy through a structural racism lens. *Souls: A Critical Journal of Black Politics, Culture and Society, 4*(1), 45–53.

Lewis, O. (1959). *Five families: Mexican case studies in the culture of poverty.* New York: Basic Books.

Lipman, P. (2011). *The new political economy of urban education: Neoliberalism, race and the right to the city.* New York: Routledge.

Lorenzi, P., & Hilton, F. (2011). Optimizing philanthrocapitalism. *Society, 48*, 397–402.

Mora, R., & Christianakis, M. (2011). Charter schools, market capitalism and Obama's neoliberal agenda. *Journal of Inquiry & Action in Education, 4*(1), 93–111.

Moynihan, D. P. (1965). *The Negro family: The case for national action.* U.S. Department of Labor.

Nasaw, D. (2006). Introduction. In D. Nasaw (Ed.), *Andrew Carnegie: The "gospel of wealth" essays and other writings* (pp. vii–xiii). New York: Penguin Classics.

Naylor, C. (2011). The dearth (or is it the death?) of discourse in the United States: What does Diane Ravitch say about educational change, and why is there so little response? *BCTF Information Handbook* (Vol. BCTF Research Report, pp. 1–15). Vancouver, BC: BC Teachers' Federation.

NYCIBO. (2013). New York City public school indicators: Demographics, resources, outcomes. New York: New York City Independent Budget Office.

Nysed.gov. (2008–2009). The New York State School Report Card, 2010. Retrieved from www.nystart.gov/publicweb

O'Connor, A. (2002). Foundations, research and the construction of "race neutrality." *Souls: A Critical Journal of Black Politics, Culture and Society, 4*(1), 54–62.

Powell, J. (2002). Proposal for a transformative, racially just philanthropy. *Souls: A Critical Journal of Black Politics, Culture and Society, 4*(1), 41–44.

Ramdas, K. (2011). Philanthrocapitalism: Reflections on politics and policy making. *Society, 48*, 393–396.

Ravitch, D. (2010). *The death and life of the great American school system.* New York: Basic Books.

Richey, L., & Ponte, S. (2011). *Brand aid: Shopping well to save the world.* Minneapolis: University of Minnesota Press.

Robinhood.org. (2014). Robin Hood, 2014. Retrieved from https://www.robinhood.org/

Rogers, R. (2011). Why philanthro-policymaking matters. *Society, 48,* 376–381.

Saltman, K. (2010). *The gift of education: Public education and venture philanthropy.* New York: Palgrave Macmillan.

Saltman, K. (2011). From Carnegie to Gates: The Bill and Melinda Gates Foundation and the venture philanthropy agenda for public education. In P. Kovacs (Ed.), *The Gates Foundation and the future of U.S. "public" schools* (pp. 1–20). New York: Taylor & Francis.

Sanjek, R. (1991). The Ethnographic Present. *Man, 26*(4).

schools.nyc.gov. (2010). New York City Department of Education.

Shiller, J. (2011). Marketing new schools for a new century: An examination of neoliberal school reform in New York City. In P. Kovacs (Ed.), *The Gates Foundation and the future of U.S. "public" schools.* New York: Taylor & Francis.

Shiller, J. (2012). Venture philanthropy's market strategies fail urban kids. *Phi Delta Kappan, 93,* 12–16.

Smith, A. (1776). *The wealth of nations.* New York: Simon and Brown.

Smith, M., Kahn, L.-M., Heinecke, W., & Jarvis, P. (2004). *Political spectacle and the fate of American schools.* New York: RoutledgeFalmer.

Thorup, M. (2013). Pro bono? On philanthrocapitalism as ideological answer to inequality. *ephemera: theory & politics in organization, 13*(3), 555–576.

Valencia, R. (2010). *Dismantling contemporary deficit thinking: Educational thought and practice.* New York: Routledge.

Venkatesh, S. (2002). Race and philanthropy: An introduction. *Souls: A Critical Journal of Black Politics, Culture and Society, 4*(1), 32–34.

Viederman, S. (2002). The future of philanthropy. *Souls: A Critical Journal of Black Politics, Culture and Society, 4*(1), 35–40.

Watkins, W. (2001). *The White architects of Black education: Ideology and power in America, 1865–1954.* New York: Teachers College Press.

Williamson, B. (2012). *Mediators and mobilizers of curriculum reform: Education policy experts of the third sector.* Stirling, Scotland: School of Education, University of Stirling.

Zhang, Y., Gajjala, R., & Watkins, S. (2012). Home of hope: Voicings, whiteness and the technological gaze. *Journal of Communication Inquiry, 36*(3), 202–221.

Notes

1. I credit Ealy (2011) for the use of this term.
2. Quoted in Nasaw (2006).
3. In fact, Rogers (2011) notes that only 20 of the approximately 1,011 billionaires in the world are women, about 2%. Approximately half are American (p. 376).

8. edTPA: Doubling Down on Whiteness in Teacher Education

BARBARA MADELONI

As a system of privilege emerging within a sociopolitical historical context, Whiteness is marked by denial of its hegemony and the inability to engage across difference with deep understanding and respect. In this chapter I argue that the edTPA, a newly mandated teacher candidate assessment, reproduces Whiteness and, thus, is an instrument of White supremacy. That is, as a standard, corporate instrument the edTPA reproduces the dominant narrative of teaching, learning, and knowledge, and silences and excludes others voices and possibilities. Its demands for obedience, the hierarchies that allow it to be imposed, and its presumption of objectivity all work to reproduce the Whiteness institutionalized in our schools and practices.

As an instrument of neoliberal logic, the edTPA is the teacher education equivalent of Common Core State Standards, high-stakes testing, and value-added teacher evaluations. Each of these imposes a narrowly quantitative narrative of teaching and learning on schools, students, and teachers. Each eliminates understandings of teaching and learning that acknowledge the social-political context in which education takes place and the rich messy complexity of schools. The narrative of Whiteness is reinforced at the macro and micro levels through many policies, tools, and practices. This chapter focuses on the edTPA as one such tool. I write from inside my lived experience as a teacher educator whose work and purpose was disrupted by the edTPA and who came to understand it as one more manifestation of Whiteness. Those of us committed to educational justice have a duty to name these tools of Whiteness and how they work to undermine education for liberation, and then refuse them.

The edTPA: What Is It? Where Did It Come From?

The edTPA is a performance assessment of student teaching designed to assess that "A new teacher is ready for practice when he or she can help each student in the classroom understand and improve their learning from Day One on the job" (American Association of Colleges of Teacher Education, 2014). Student teachers create a digital portfolio in response to prompts about planning, instruction, and assessment. In its current form, the instrument consists of a series of essay questions and requires that student teachers video record their classroom practice, answer questions about their video, and submit the video and what can be a 50-page document to Pearson, Inc. for scoring by a "calibrated" scorer. Scorers are hired on a contractual basis and paid per edTPA scored, after undergoing training and calibration in the use of the edTPA rubrics (Pearson, 2014). The rubrics include items for assessing the teacher's effectiveness teaching "academic language."

The edTPA was developed under the leadership of Linda Darling-Hammond and the Stanford Center for Assessment Learning and Equity (SCALE) with the goal of creating a national assessment of student teaching readiness. To address the issues of scale that accompany a nationwide assessment, SCALE entered into a contract with Pearson, Inc. to oversee delivery and scoring (SCALE, 2014). Initially piloted in 22 states, it is now required in some form in five states and must be completed for certification in New York State since May 2014 (SCALE, 2014).[1] A writing intensive exercise, some suggest it is more a measure of writing than of teaching (Berlak, 2010). Faculty users of the edTPA are required to sign a nondisclosure agreement, limiting the possibilities for teacher educators to analyze and discuss the instrument both with colleagues and students.

Standardization and the Performance of Whiteness

The edTPA is an instrument of standardization that seeks to define teaching and learning in a relatively narrow, predictable, and measureable frame. To appreciate how the standardization of teaching through the edTPA operates as a tool of Whiteness, it is important to explore how standardization itself operates to reproduce White supremacy.

Standardization in education, as in the setting of normative curriculum and assessments, reproduces the dominant ideology (Weilbacher, 2012). It negates uncertainty and, in so doing, narrows the possibilities for what can be seen and known. The act of standardization requires acceptance that there is a norm, which requires erasure of difference. In contexts in which power is denied, such as occurs within Whiteness, the standard as norm reflects the dominant voices. This tends to go unrecognized in conversation about education policy where there is a ready acceptance that we "need standards." To examine how Whiteness works, we must ask how something becomes "standard" and what the implications are for those ideas and practices that fall outside of or "below" the standard.

As promulgated by "reformers," standards are said to develop outside of culture and context; they express an ostensibly agreed upon knowledge base (Darling-Hammond, 2012). To accept this possibility, we have to assume that there exist uncontested spaces where present and historical issues of power and voice hold no sway. Just as Whiteness assumes itself as the norm, standardization defines the limits of what it means to teach and learn; of how we encounter and grow knowledge; of how we know ourselves as learners and what constitutes learning; and of the kinds of communities we grow through education. Just as the performance of Whiteness emerges within the context of exclusion, standards exclude other possibilities. Even if their developers espouse inclusivity and attend to difference in the development of standards, standardization itself is homogenizing and neutralizing (Delandshere & Petrosky, 2004). Though educators, as individuals and within communities, have ideals, critical knowledge, and a sense of purpose, to not reify those of the dominant culture these must always be on the edge of being undone. "Excellence must be valued, but standards cannot be absolute or fixed" (hooks, 1994, p. 157).

Forgotten in the current obsessive focus on standards and standardization is knowledge educators share from lived experience: Teaching is uncertain work (Freidrich, 2014; Taubman, 2009). It is intimate and relational and emerges within the complicated reality of students and teachers together in the community of a classroom and the world as it enters the classroom (hooks, 1994). It is deeply contextual, both at the micro and macro levels. Learning to teach means learning to encounter yourself and the other within the web of history and society with openness and uncertainty. This means learning to see, name, and interrogate the Whiteness at the center of public education (Cochran-Smith, 2000; Gay, 2010; Ladson-Billings, 2000; Lea & Griggs, 2005); Parker & Stovall, 2004; Picower, 2009; Sleeter, 2001). The performance of Whiteness emerges within structures of power that support particular ways of knowing ourselves and each other. These ways of knowing/being ourselves are not immutable. "Identities are not inside individuals but in the space between interacting individuals" (Diversi & Moreira, 2009, p. 20).

To examine Whiteness in education is to disrupt taken-for-granted assumptions about knowledge, access, and language. Our identities are subject to interrogation and disruption, to new performances that challenge the dominant narratives and open space for other ways of teaching and learning. In my own practice, I reach to develop "engaged critical intellectuals, future and past teachers, who will be able to develop an embodied reflexivity of lived experience as a specific cultural site for struggle, resistance, and transformation" (Diversi & Moreira, 2009, p. 190). This examination and interrogation of Whiteness and identity cannot be standardized. It emerges within relationships that challenge, grow trust, and reach toward love (hooks, 1994). The examination of Whiteness is not something to be measured, limited, contained, or owned. We can only keep entering the uncertainty of interpersonal encounters as authentically, as answerably, as possible.

edTPA and the Performance of Whiteness

The edTPA comes to teacher education as an instrument of standardization and Whiteness. Teacher education in the United States is already steeped in Whiteness (Cross, 2005; Hayes & Juarez, 2012; Ladson-Billings, 2000, 2006; Sleeter, 2004). Teacher educators meet the demands of the state through the certification process, demands that embody the dominant power structures (Lea, 2011). Teaching is more and more the work of White women, who account for 85% of the teacher workforce (Feistritzer, 2011). As a critical pedagogue, I hoped to expose Whiteness institutionalized in our schools and buried in our consciousness, and to support new teachers to see and name racism and grow practices for liberation.

Naming racism and Whiteness, and creating new knowledge of self and other, is embodied work, which grows within relationships of trust, conflict, and openness to uncertainty, vulnerability, and new knowledge. When we understand teaching to be embodied work, we "enter the classroom 'whole' and not as 'disembodied' spirit" (hooks, 1994, p. 193). But the edTPA, as an "objective" standardized instrument, marginalizes embodied knowledge, just as Whiteness does.

In place of teaching as embodied, the edTPA calls for a standardization of the performance of teaching: a performance of the certainty and containment that is Whiteness in education. This performance presumes its authority and its objectivity through the conceit of rubrics scored with precision by calibrated scorers. Under the watchful eye of the unknown "calibrated" authority, edTPA calls forth a specific kind of performance from student teachers. It is a performance marked first by obedience. That the calibrated scorer must not know the student teacher or the specific context of the teaching further reinforces the epistemological underpinnings of the edTPA, which, emerging from a frame of White supremacy, denies knowledge as embodied. The scoring of the edTPA denies the larger sociopolitical context of knowledge and identity. It presents and demands teaching and learning as able to be fixed, calibrated, and reproduced to specific demands. As well, as an instrument that requires obedience, it calls forth acquiescence rather than critical naming of power structures.

In standardizing what is valued in teaching, the edTPA excludes teaching as uncertain, critical, relationship-based work of the arts and humanities. It insists on attention to the development of content knowledge as the core activity of the classroom, pretends at the central idea of disciplinary knowledge as knowable (Freidrich, 2014), and presumes a social scientific frame for understanding ourselves and our work (Taubman, 2009). Each of these attributes of the edTPA reproduces Whiteness, but the center of the knot is the degree in which edTPA is grounded in certainty. For example, the edTPA's rubrics are designed around lesson-plan-driven teaching, linear in its form and focused on standards, objectives, and outcomes (Pearson & SCALE, 2012).[2] These demands rest on an assumption that we can (and should) know with certainty both the objectives and outcomes of a given classroom experience, but these might remain uncertain in a classroom in which the students drive the curriculum.

Defenders will claim that edTPA is not certain, that it allows room for a range of practices and interpretations, but these defenders accept the pretense that how we structure an experience has nothing to do with the experience (Adkins, 2012). The same hidden curriculum that we want student teachers to be aware of in their classroom practice is not acknowledged in the mandates and procedures we impose on teacher education. Yet, in the certainty of edTPA—in its rubrics, its calibration—it communicates that teaching and learning are measurable, are knowable. In denying process, which is where power resides, edTPA denies power and critical analysis. As in Whiteness, "objectivity" becomes a kind of innocence or denial of the subjectivity and embodiment that is our lived experience. And all the while edTPA exerts a profound message that teaching is and can be certain, fixed, and reduced to a number. In this sense, edTPA is another manifestation of the "rationalistic womb" from which "Whiteness begins to establish itself as a norm that represents an authoritative, delimited, and hierarchical mode of thought" (Kincheloe, 1999, p. 163). As a social justice teacher educator, the acceptance of normative practices, objectivity, and standards undermines the questions I am asking of teacher candidates, of our educational institutions, and of our society—questions to which the answers are uncertain and multiple.

As an example of how the edTPA constructs the epistemology of teaching as Whiteness, we need only look at its demands for the teaching of academic language, which must be explicit enough to be observed by scorers. This expectation, measured in rubrics, invites a narrow, uncritical epistemology in the classroom and reinforces hierarchies of knowledge. While some have argued for the teaching of academic language as necessary for students to gain access to power structures (Janks, 2010), a rubric that demands evidence "of students' use of the language function, vocabulary, and additional language demand(s) in ways that develop content understandings" (Pearson & SCALE, 2012, p. 31) uncritically narrows the possibilities for how we understand language and its relationship to power. Teaching academic language to support content learning is quite different from teaching the language of power within the frame of education for liberation. That these measurements are being calibrated within an instrument that uses its own academic jargon as an instrument of power (for credentialing) invites a concrete, observable, and reproductive understanding of language for both the student teacher and his or her students, and it narrows the possibilities for our work as educators committed to social justice in education.

Corporatization and Power: Neoliberalism, Racism, and Elitism

The edTPA represents in teacher education the manifestation of Kincheloe's (1999) warning that the 21st century would see the global dominance of Whiteness in data collection, surveillance, and ownership.

> Once all the nations on earth are drawn into the white reason of the market economy, then all land can be subdivided into real estate, all human beings' worth can be monetarily calculated, values of abstract individualism and financial success can be embraced by every community in every country, and education can be reformulated around the cultivation of human capital... The Western ability to regulate diverse peoples through their inclusion in data banks filled with information about their credit histories, institutional affiliations, psychological "health," academic credentials, work experiences, and family backgrounds will reach unprecedented levels... This does not mean that supremacy ends, but that it has produced a hegemony so seamless that the need for further structural or ideological change becomes unnecessary. (p. 3)

The imposition of edTPA is an instrument of this hegemony focused specifically on teacher education. It has been imposed with a startling display of power and denial of that power and with breathtaking arrogance at the micro level and macro level. State education departments signed on to edTPA without asking teacher educators whether or not they wanted to participate.

In my context, contract faculty, whose job security was more tenuous, were told we had to be calibrated and were given the assignment to implement the edTPA for the field test. Pearson, Inc., which oversees the distribution of edTPA and hires and trains scorers hired on a piecework basis, is one of the largest education companies in the world with a portfolio that includes testing, curriculum, text and online books, and professional development from preK through college. Pearson's obligations, as a publically traded company, are to stockholders to maximize profit. The hiring of piecemeal workers with no benefits or protections to do the work previously done by faculty is consistent with the neoliberal economic structures being imposed on public entities (Harvey, 2005).

Those who promulgate edTPA, including the American Association of Colleges of Teacher Education (AACTE), deny that Pearson's involvement is at all relevant to the impact of edTPA on teacher education. It is, they insist, simply a matter of needing a company capable of allowing edTPA to be "scaled up" (Adkins, 2012). They protest that Pearson did not develop edTPA and that scorers are carefully selected and trained (AACTE, 2014). The power of Pearson, Inc. and of the promulgators of the edTPA is denied, and those of us who object to where the power is located are criticized as being angry and unreasonable (Gorlewski, 2013).

Pearson's involvement with edTPA shines a light on the commodification of life under neoliberalism, a commodification made more possible within a history of occupation, slavery, and oppression. The story of White America is the story of valuing some bodies more than others, of owning other human beings, of stealing land. That the acquisition of material comforts can happen on the backs of and at the expense of others, in particular darker skinned others, saturates our history and still constructs our economic life. The questions posed by those who resist Pearson's involvement in edTPA are questions that challenge capitalism, the commodification of knowledge, the assault on workers' rights and protections, and the ways that considerations of profit are contrary to communities of love and support. Just as the question of who can perform Whiteness exposes essential differences about the fight for equity or justice, Pearson's involvement exposes differences of understanding of the nature of capitalism and its impact on our lives.

The history of capitalism is tightly intertwined with that of slavery, racism, and White supremacy. Capitalism made Black bodies chattel. It requires the exploitation of labor. In its more recent neoliberal manifestation, it asserts without pretense that to be human is to be subject to and compete within the market (Harvey, 2005). Neoliberal ideology refuses to name racism and White supremacy both current and historical, and yet it thrives on the ongoing exploitation and colonization of Black and Brown bodies, of land and labor.

This denial of race while exploiting Black and Brown children hit home for me personally when I faced the outrage that accompanied my being quoted in a news article naming the "rich white men" who control corporate education reform for Black and Brown children (Jonas, 2014). While the politics of the achievement gap of Black and Brown children is permissible conversation, naming Whiteness as an operating factor in decision-making and power is not. We see this denial and exploitation in many aspects of the neoliberal project including the privatization of prisons filled with Black and Brown men and women (Alexander, 2012) and the land grabs undertaken in the name of school reform in cities such as Chicago (Lipman, 2011). Predatory education reform is simply one more arena in which to colonize the land, exploit labor, and commodify human life, especially the lives of Black and Brown children (Lipman, 2011). Pearson's involvement with edTPA invites the wolf of capitalism into teacher education.

Through edTPA, Pearson, Inc. takes ownership of the likenesses, work, and ideas of teacher educators and student teachers. It is nothing short of astonishing, at a moment when questions of privacy are so critical, that supporters of edTPA insist that there is no reason to be concerned about the fact that videos of students and student teachers and the scholarly work of student teachers will be sent to a private corporation and then owned by that corporation. This denial is entirely in keeping with the commodification of human experience that is central to the neoliberal regime. If we are capable of reducing experience to a score on a rubric, then we must allow ourselves to not see the full complexity of the human beings who we treat in this way. When we blind ourselves to the individual and his or her story, we also lose sight of the context of racism and Whiteness that is central to our social, economic, and historical realities. In my work with supervisors of student teachers, I would ask them to write narratives of their experience in the classroom where student teachers were practicing. Within narrative we reflect on ourselves as observers, shift focus and perspective, engage details that illuminate in varied, surprising, and potentially contested fashion; we make a space to know ourselves in the context of White supremacy. The silencing of our lived experience is one more step toward our dehumanization, toward doing what we will with a person's likeness and his or her body.

Through edTPA, Pearson outsources the current work of teacher educators to unprotected workers paid on a piecework basis. This exploitation of labor is part of a growing trend to undo worker protections and casualize the workforce, leaving us all more subject to the demands of the market

(Harvey, 2005; Hill, 2007). When supporters of edTPA deny the economic ramifications of its imposition, they are refusing to acknowledge the broader political-economic context in which these decisions are made, a context in which workers have fewer rights and are subject to uncertain employment status that leads to fear and compliance. The neoliberal project counts on those of us who are protected by Whiteness to deny its violent and dehumanizing processes. It relies, as Apple (2001) describes, on a managerial class that enables its technocratic policies in exchange for access to power and privilege. In a world in which college faculty are increasingly contingent labor, resources for public education are dwindling, teachers and other education workers are under attack (Clawson & Page, 2011), the supporters of edTPA scoring tell us not to worry. But history tells us that capitalism requires exploitation and dehumanization; that dehumanization leads to exploitation. When we attempt to elide this part of history, we do so from the position of those who have access, from the position of those who know themselves as able to perform Whiteness and who, within that, know protections.

Pedagogy, Epistemology, Plurality, and a Deep Democratic Process

Whether stated or implicit in its content and process, every educational practice rests on answers to these questions: How do we understand what it means to know and what is the purpose of education? Is knowledge absolute and public education the place we reproduce the world as we know it? Or is knowledge constantly under construction, plural and situated, and education a process of naming and creating our world? The edTPA imposes answers to these questions on teacher educators, answers reflective of the dominant power structures of Whiteness.

Much of the history of schooling in the United States has been with the purpose of creating conformity, obedience, and acceptance of the system as it is. From the kidnapping of indigenous children who were denied their language, history, and knowledge to the ubiquitous faculty model, designed to prepare compliant factory workers, to the locked-down, canned curriculum test prep schools we currently see in too many schools serving Black and Brown children, schools have been sites of silencing and oppression. Knowledge, in these contexts, is defined, certain, and held by those in authority to be given to students. My pedagogy grows from an understanding of education as a site for liberation. Within this practice, narratives of resistance are always possible, from individual classrooms, to liberation schools, and in teacher education programs that embrace critical multicultural pedagogy. In these contexts learning is about critical questioning, knowledge creation, and participation in creating the world.

But edTPA denies these practices. First, it imposes a single pedagogy on the classroom, a pedagogy that understands human experience in behavioral terms and that sees teaching as goal directed and linear. The description of the planning task in the 2012 English language arts edTPA handbook makes this demand for a linear behavioral narrative quite clear. Students must "identify a central focus" and to "Identify the language that students will be expected to use to engage in the learning task and your instructional supports" (Pearson & SCALE, 2012, p. 5). From the demand for lesson plans, to evidence of teaching "academic language," to alignment with the common core, the idea of teaching presented by the edTPA excludes teaching as art, learning as circular and uneven, and students' knowledge, experience, and language(s) as central to the endeavor.

Schooled as many of us are in the ways of White American classrooms, this might seem a ludicrous critique. Who can challenge the lesson plan and core academic knowledge? More reason to draw attention to what we cannot see, cannot even imagine because of the domination of one ideology about how and why we teach and learn. To look at teaching through the lens of a rubric is to assert that what we know is what we see and that what we see can be unequivocally understood. We always see from a position, and acknowledging positionality is part of the work of communicating and of growing knowledge and social justice education. Our task is never to allow certainty to solidify, even as choices are made. That is our existential task. As the late Maxine Greene reminded us, "There are no final words, only questions" (Suzuki, 2014).

At its core, edTPA denies us our embodied knowledge. In teaching and learning there is no space of objectivity. There is only the place where human beings in our bodies interact within socio-historical contexts and attempt to both name the context and create something new within it (hooks, 1994). The gaze of the objective observer, idealized in the edTPA scoring process, exists within a space of privilege, denial, and power. Some will argue that objectivity is how we undo the socio-historical context, that by removing the embodied person we remove history and culture, and get to some pure knowledge or understanding. But there is no such place; power manifests in all kinds of places. To address historical oppressions we have to name them in the spaces they occupy. We cannot elide power; we have to name and face it.

The gaze of the edTPA scorer, disciplined to adhere to the rubric, is singular, but teaching, learning, and knowledge are plural and diverse (Biesta, 2001). A seasoned supervisor has a deep appreciation for the many perspectives and experiences that constitute a classroom; a seasoned teacher knows this as well. Teaching and learning are acts of empathy, of attentive listening with the wholeness of ourselves. Knowledge is multiple, plural, and always to be contested. Classrooms are not spaces where one individual determines what will be, but are communities that everyone participates in creating, except when we are subject to the limiting possibilities of Whiteness, behaviorism, and reproduction.

edTPA denies me my voice. It denies student teachers imaginative perspectives. It denies that our knowledge and experiences are embodied and demands a singular performance by the student teacher and the teacher educator. It denies history, power, and the influence of capital. It is deeply undemocratic in its process and imposition. I can hear in some readers the certainty that this is too much, that edTPA has some fine qualities, that this is extreme. I suggest that it is the core of Whiteness to deny voices of outrage and defiance, to call for politeness and moderation, to deny voices that name power, especially the power of Whiteness. Only in listening to these voices can we step toward a participatory democracy. This is not about vetting an instrument imposed on us, but about asking and discussing deeper questions of purpose and possibility. A vibrant democracy does not silence, does not end with "the majority rules." A deep democracy engages in attentive listening, grows empathy, sees and seeks to undo marginalization, and reaches toward justice. It holds within the possibility for all of our liberation.

The Resistance: Asserting Our Goals of Economic and Racial Justice, Naming and Taking Power, Working in Alliances, Saying No

In the spring of 2012 I was told by administrators that the students in the program I coordinated were to participate in a Pearson-Stanford field test of the then-named Teacher Performance Assessment. Student teachers, who understood that corporate powers were infiltrating preK–12 education, and many of whom were experiencing the narrowing of curriculum due to high-stakes accountability measures in the schools where they were teaching, did not want to be a part of the ongoing incursion of corporate reform into public education. I fought for their right to choose to participate or not in this field test and, when that right was acknowledged, 67 student teachers at the University of Massachusetts Amherst refused to send their work to Pearson (Winerup, 2012). They took this stand not for themselves as much as for the students who would come after them (Madeloni & Hoogstraten, 2013). Their understanding of why this mattered grew within a classroom where public education as reproduction or liberation was an ongoing question, where they had been asked to examine assumptions about knowledge, race, class, democracy, and corporate reform. Students objected to TPA for a variety of reasons, but for each they understood that it mattered that their voices be heard. They understood that at its core teaching is something that happens within the context of relationships and that these relationships were being denied.

Throughout my life as an educator, I have been reaching toward a practice that illuminates oppressions and opens the door to students coming together to name and fight for racial and economic justice. This is a journey for me, as I understand the ways my Whiteness privileges and blinds me, as I find my way to courage and trusting in solidarity. In some ways, taking a stand against edTPA can seem trivial, given the violence and abuse that is racism. But I became an educator precisely because it seemed this was a space where we could both undo our oppressions and re-imagine ourselves.

In the imposition of the edTPA I saw two choices. One was an invitation to go along to get along, to accept the deepening norming of our work, but to convince myself that it was not really all that bad, because the standards were not that bad and teacher education does need to prove itself. This invitation was familiar to me as a woman: Be quiet, don't disrupt, don't be hysterical. It was accessible to me as a White person. Turning my eyes from injustice is accepted within Whiteness; it is rational and reasonable. The other choice was to allow myself to know, feel, and name what was happening to me, the student teachers, and the work I care for. The other choice was to abandon some of my protections and take a stand, and to act from my privilege for something beyond protecting myself.

To act, I needed to feel the danger of edTPA in my bones. I needed to attend to processes and understandings outside of the frame of my Whiteness, which always invites me to close my eyes to power as long as that power does not directly hurt me.

Organizers spend a lot of time puzzling over how to get people to move over the threshold toward action. In general, we act when the pain hits home. In many ways, this was true in my case. It was in acting that I then discovered the tremendous hope and joy of solidarity. Still, while I might flail at inspiring others to action, we need strategies to be successful. First, we have to name the problem, which is what I hope to do in this piece. It matters to frame the problems of edTPA as a problem of Whiteness because this frame challenges those of us who claim to educate for social justice to know ourselves in relationship to it. We must ask ourselves, as I asked myself, Do we turn away or do we stare into it, name it, and build alliances to resist?

In the time since the student teachers took their stand against the field test, others have joined them. In the spring of 2014 graduate students at University of Illinois Champaign boycotted an edTPA field test. Through the winter and spring of 2013–2014 I was part of six panels or presentations, organized by students and faculty, exposing the problems of edTPA and strategizing resistance. In New York State, students and teacher educators spoke out to legislators calling for a halt on its implementation and winning some small victories. Student groups, Web pages, and social media sites are popping up and connecting with each other, determined to bear witness to the ways edTPA is distorting teacher education and teaching.

These are important and powerful developments. If teacher educators claim ourselves as educating for racial and social justice, then we have to live those ideals in our work. It is more than teaching preK–12 teachers how to teach for justice in their classrooms. It is fighting for it ourselves in our institutions, within our professional organizations, with our students, their students, and the communities of which we are a part. I was recently on a panel where I was asked what, if anything, is good about edTPA. I really cannot say anything positive about the instrument, but maybe the fact of it is forcing some of us out of our White silence. Maybe it is teaching us about erasure, exploitation, and what it means to feel without power. Maybe if we stay in that long enough, talk across positions about it, name what is happening, we will find the courage together to enter the uncertainty and imaginative possibilities of liberatory education.

References

Adkins, A. (2012). The educator and the hard sell. Web blog discussion. Retrieved from http://academeblog.org/2012/09/14/the-hard-sell-and-the-educator/

Alexander, M. (2012). *The new Jim Crow: Mass incarceration in the age of colorblindness.* New York: New Press.

American Association of Colleges of Teacher Education. (2014). AACTE president clarifies facts following NAME position statement on EdTPA. Retrieved from http://aacte.org/news-room/press-releases/aacte-presidentceo-clarifies-facts-following-name-position-statement-on-edtpa.html

Apple, M. (2001). Markets, standards, teaching and teacher education. *Journal of Teacher Education, 52*(3), 182–196.

Berlak, A. (2010). Coming soon to a credentialing program near you. *Rethinking Schools, 24*(4), 41–45.

Biesta, G. (2001). How difficult should education be? *Educational Theory, 51*(4), 385–400.

Clawson, D., & Page, M. (2011). *The future of higher education.* New York: Routledge.

Cochran-Smith, M. (2000). Blind vision: Unlearning racism in teacher education. *Harvard Review, 70*(2), 157–190.

Cross, B. (2005). New racism, reformed teacher education, and the same 'ole oppression. *Educational Studies, 38*(3), 263–274.

Darling-Hammond, L. (2012). The right start: Creating a strong foundation for the teaching career. *Phi Delta Kappan, 94*(3), 8–13.

Darling-Hammond, L., & Hyler, M. (2013, Summer). The role of performance assessment in the development of teaching as a profession. *Rethinking Schools, 27*. Retrieved from: http://www.rethinkingschools.org/archive/27_04/27_04_darling-hammond_hyler.shtml

Delandshere, G., & Petrosky, A. (2004). Political rationales and ideological stances of the standards-based reform of teacher education in the US. *Teaching and Teacher Education, 20*, 1–15.

Diversi, M., & Moreira, C. (2009). *Betweener talk: Decolonizing knowledge production, pedagogy and praxis.* Walnut Creek, CA: Left Coast Press.

Feistritzer, C. E. (2011). *Profile of teachers in the United States in 2011.* National Center for Educational information. Retrieved from http://www.edweek.org/media/pot2011final-blog.pdf

Freidrich, D. (2014). We brought it on ourselves: University based teacher education and the emergence of boot-camp-style routes to teacher certification. *Education Policy Analysis Archives, Vol. 22.* Retrieved from http://epaa.asu.edu/ojs/article/view/1193#.UtNa4NngaR8.facebook

Freire, P. (2009). *Pedagogy of the oppressed: 30th anniversary edition.* New York: Continuum.

Gay, G. (2010). Acting on beliefs in teacher education for cultural diversity. *Journal of Teacher Education, 61*(1–2), 143–152.

Gorlewski, J. (2013). What is edTPA and why do critics dislike it? Diane Ravitch's blog. Retrieved from http://dianeravitch.net/2013/06/03/what-is-edtpa-and-why-do-critics-dislike-it/#comments

Gorlewski, J. (2014, February 19). Proceedings as part of a public forum. *Public Education Now: "Reform" and Resistance in New York State.* New Paltz, New York: State University of New York at New Paltz.

Harvey, D. (2005). *A brief history of neoliberalism.* New York: Oxford University Press.

Hayes, C., & Juarez, B. (2012). There is no culturally responsive teaching spoken here: A critical race perspective. *Democracy and Education, 20*(1), 1–14.

Hill, D. (2007). Critical teacher education, new labour, and the global project of neoliberal capital. *Policy Futures in Education, 5*(2), 204–225.

hooks, b. (1994). *Teaching to transgress: Education as the practice of freedom.* New York: Routledge.

Janks, H. (2010). *Literacy and power.* New York: Routledge.

Jonas, M. (2014, Summer). Change agent. Retrieved from http://www.commonwealth-magazine.org/Voices/Conversation/2014/Summer/002-Change-agent.aspx#.VGRL-NaMEdU

Kincheloe, J. L. (1999). The Struggle to Define and Reinvent Whiteness: A Pedagogical Analysis. *College Literature 26*(3), 162–194.

Kincheloe, J. (2004). The knowledge of teacher education: Developing a critical complex epistemology. *Teacher Education Quarterly, 31*(1), 49–66.

Ladson-Billings, G. (2000). Fighting for our lives: Preparing teachers to teach African-American students. *Journal of Teacher Education, 51*(30), 206–214.

Ladson-Billings, G. (2006). It is not the culture of poverty it is the poverty of culture: The problem with teacher education. *Anthropology and Education Quarterly, 37*(2), 104–109.

Lea, V. (2011). Concocting crisis to create consent. In P. Carr, & B. Porfilio (Eds.), *The phenomenon of Obama and the agenda for education: Can hope audaciously trump neo-liberalism?* (pp. 23–47). Charlotte: Information Age Press.

Lea, V., & Griggs, T. (2005). Behind the mask and beneath the story: Enabling students-teachers to reflect critically on the socially-constructed nature of their "normal" practice. *Teacher Education Quarterly, 32*(1), 93–114.

Lipman, P. (2011). *The new political economy of urban education: Neoliberalism, race and the right to the city.* New York: Routledge.

Madeloni, B., & Hoogstraten, R. (2013). The other side of fear. *Schools: Studies in Education, 10*(1), 1–14.

Parker, L., & Stovall, D. (2004). Actions following words: Critical race theory connects to critical pedagogy. *Educational Philosophy and Theory, 36*(2), 167–182.

Pearson, Inc. (2014). *About edTPA.* Retrieved from http://www.edtpa.com/PageView. aspx?f=GEN_AboutEdTPA.html

Pearson, Inc., & Stanford Center for Learning Assessment and Equity. (2013). edTPA English language arts assessment handbook. Retrieved from http://www.edtpa. com/PageView.aspx?f=HTML_FRAG/GENRB_AnnounceHandbookUpdate. html

Picower, B. (2009). The unexamined Whiteness of teaching: How white teachers maintain and enact dominant racial ideologies. *Race, Ethnicity and Education, 12*(2), 197–215.

Sleeter, C. (2001). Preparing teachers for culturally diverse schools: Research and the overwhelming presence of Whiteness. *Journal of Teacher Education, 52*(2), 94–106.

Stanford Center for Learning, Assessment and Equity. *edTPA.* Retrieved from http:// www.edtpa.com/PageView.aspx?f=GEN_AboutEdTPA.html

Suzuki, D. (2014). Maxine Greene: "There are no final words, only questions." Retrieved from http://daiyusuzuki.blogspot.com/2014/06/maxine-greene-there-are-no-final-words.html

Taubman, P. (2009). *Teaching by numbers: Deconstructing the discourse of standards and accountability in education.* New York: Routledge.

Weilbacher, G. (2012). Standardization and Whiteness: One and the same? *Democracy and Education, 20*(2), 1–6.

Winerup, M. (2012). On education: Move to outsource teacher licensing process draws protest. *New York Times*, May 6.

Notes

1. Push back from teacher educators, students, and community members led New York State to implement a "safety net" for students who failed the edTPA in the spring of 2014. Students who fail may take and submit a passing score on a traditional multiple-choice standardized test, the ATS-W.
2. I was able to access the 2012 version of edTPA for the purposes of this chapter. More recent versions require coded access.

Appendix: Artifacts of Resistance

We end the book with a set of *artifacts of resistance* to complement the examples of struggles and social movement that are discussed throughout the book. They are a collection of speeches and actions taken by the educators and youth doing this work every day. First there is a speech by activist **Asean Johnson given when he was nine years old**, from Chicago, Illinois. Asean has become a nationally prominent speaker against various aspects of racist neoliberal school reform in Chicago and beyond. His reprinted speech from a 2013 rally on school closings in Chicago makes clear the devastating effects of racial, neoliberal reform strategies on youth and their communities. The **Dreamyard Action Project** is a New York City–based youth organization, and their 10-point platform, modeled after the Black Panthers, was a critical response to the impact of mayoral control. The **Teacher Activist Group (TAG)** platform provides a national scale response to current school reform. TAG is a network of educator-activist groups from different parts of the country, of which NYCoRE is a member. The platform is an articulation of what these local organizations, collectively, believe to be the foundation for a just educational system for all youth, families, and educators. Finally, we have images and documents from the **Stand-Up-Opt-Out campaign** organized by the Prospect International High School in Brooklyn, New York. The teachers at the high school refused to administer state exams to their students who are all newly arrived immigrants and were set up to fail by this exam.

Artifact of Resistance 1: Asean Johnson Speaks at the Rally Against School Closures in Chicago

Asean Johnson
Courtesy of New York Collective of Radical Educators, photo by Nicholas Ortiz, http://www.flickr.com/ortiznick

Speech at the Rally Against School Closures in Chicago

By Asean Johnson
May 20, 2013

Good evening, or, good morning.
My name's Asean Johnson. I'm from Marcus Garvey School, located on 103rd and Morgan. I come to you today to talk about the school closings.

Rahm Emanuel thinks that we all are toys; he thinks he can just come into our schools and move all our kids all over they lines, and just say, "Oh, we can build a building right here. Let's just take this school out—we don't care about these kids." But it's kids in there. They need safety.

Rahm Emanuel is not caring about our schools; he is not caring about our safety. He only cares about his kids. He only care about what he needs. He do not care about nobody else but himself.

He let Barbara Byrd-Bennett, a woman that's from Detroit who don't even know the streets of Chicago where I'm from, come in and close these schools. She should not be closing these schools. They need safety and protection. You should be investing in these schools, not closing them. You should be supporting these schools, not closing them.

WE SHALL NOT BE MOVED TODAY!

We are going to City Hall, we're confronting Rahm Emanuel.
We are not toys.
We are not going, not without a fight.

Like Martin Luther King said, like—I forgot his name but—he said that it is 90% of school closings are African American. This is racism right here. This is racism.
We are black and we are proud!
We are white and we are proud!
No matter what the color is,
No matter if you're Asian, Chinese, it doesn't matter.
You should not be closing these schools without walking into them and see-ing what is happening in these schools!

EDUCATION IS OUR RIGHT, THAT IS WHY WE HAVE TO FIGHT!
EDUCATION IS OUR RIGHT, THAT IS WHY WE HAVE TO FIGHT!
EDUCATION IS OUR RIGHT, THAT IS WHY WE HAVE TO FIGHT!

Transcript via rapgenius: http://news.genius.com/Asean-johnson-chicago-school-closings-speech-transcript-annotated

Speech viewable here: http://youtu.be/oue9HIOM7xU

Artifact of Resistance 2: The Resistance, DreamYard A.C.T.I.O.N Project

Courtesy of DreamYard A.C.T.I.O.N Project

Mission

We are a group of young activists called The Resistance from a youth arts organization: The DreamYard A.C.T.I.O.N Project. We focus on the issues in our society and with art, activism and organizing we try to change them. Our current topic is Quality Education. We, students in the South Bronx, are being deprived of a Quality Education and we hope that you will join us in our fight for Quality Education.

The 10 Point Education Platform for NYC Public Schools: What We Demand!

By The Resistance by The A.C.T.I.O.N. Project
July, 2011

1. We demand free quality education as a right guaranteed by the U.S. Constitution.

2. We demand the dismantling of Bloomberg's Panel for Educational Policy. We demand a new 13 member community board to run our public

schools (comprised of parents, educators, education experts, community members, and a minimum of 5 student representatives).

3. We demand quality instruction. Teachers should ethnically, culturally, and racially reflect the student body. We demand experienced teachers who have a history of teaching students well. Teacher training should be intensive and include an apprenticeship with master teachers as well as experiences with the communities where the school is located.

4. We demand stronger extra-curricular activities to help stimulate and spark interest in students. Students should have options, opportunities, and choice in their education.

5. We demand a healthy, safe environment that does not expect our failure or anticipate our criminality. We demand a school culture that acknowledges our humanity (free of metal detectors, untrained and underpaid security guards, and abusive tactics).

6. We demand that all NYC public school communities foster structured and programmatic community building so that students, teachers, and staff learn in an environment that is respectful and safe for all.

7. We demand small classes. Class sizes should be humane and productive. We demand that the student to teacher ratio for a mainstream classroom should be no more than 15:1.

8. We demand student assessments and evaluations that reflect the variety of ways that we learn and think (portfolio assessments, thesis defenses, anecdotal evaluations, written exams). Student success should not depend solely on high stakes testing.

9. We demand a stop to the attack on our schools. If a school is deemed "failing," we demand a team of qualified and diverse experts to assess how such schools can improve and the resources to improve them.

10. We demand fiscal equity for NYC public schools: as stated in the Education Budget and Reform Act of 2007 by the NYS Legislature, NYC public schools have been inadequately and inequitably funded. We demand the legislatively mandated $7 billion dollars in increased annual state education aid to be delivered to our schools now!

Artifact of Resistance 3: TAG National Platform

Image, mission, and platform courtesy of the Network of Teacher Activist Groups

Our Mission

The Network of Teacher Activist Groups (TAG) is a national coalition of grassroots teacher organizing groups. Together, we engage in shared political education and relationship building in order to work for educational justice both nationally and in our local communities. TAG believes that education is essential to the preservation of civil and human rights and is a tool of human liberation. Every child has a right to a high quality, equitably funded, public education based on: participatory democratic principles, community empowerment and self-determination, a challenging, comprehensive and critical curriculum, respect for cultural diversity and a commitment to anti-racism, equipping all students to deeply understand the roots of inequality and oppression and preparing them to act to change the world.

TAG Platform

1. Democratic School Governance:
TAG supports efforts to strengthen schools and communities by ensuring and protecting local parent, educator, and student leadership of school governance at all levels. We believe in diverse, democratically elected local school boards and councils. We support the creation of structures that enable meaningful and informed inclusive participation.

2. School and Community-Based Solutions to School Transformation:
TAG believes that local communities and those affected by school reform should be looked to for the wisdom and knowledge to transform their local

schools. This process should be bottom-up, participatory, and highly democratic to engage schools and communities in school improvement and transformation. There should be mutual responsibility and accountability among educators, families, youth, and communities. This process must secure the voice, participation, and self-determination of communities and individuals who have been historically marginalized.

3. Free, Public, and Equitable Educational Opportunities for All Students:

TAG supports measures that ensure every student access to a fully funded, equitable public education that is not threatened by market-based reforms such as vouchers, charter schools, or turnarounds by entities that divert public funds to private enterprise. We demand increased funding to end inequities in the current segregated and unequal system that favors those with race or class privilege. We believe that resources should be distributed according to need, and particularly to those historically under-resourced by the impact of structural, racial, and economic discrimination and disinvestment. Public schools should be responsive to the community, not the marketplace.

4. Curricula and Pedagogies that Promote Creative, Critical, and Challenging Education:

TAG supports transformative curricula and pedagogies that promote critical thinking and creativity in our students. Curricular themes that are grounded in the lived experiences of students are built from and extend community cultural wealth and histories. We promote a pedagogy that leads to the development of people who can work collaboratively, solve problems creatively, and live as full participants in their communities. We promote a vision of education that counters the multiple forms of oppression, promotes democratic forms of participation (community activism) in our society and that generates spaces of love and hope.

5. Multiple, High-quality, Comprehensive Assessments:

TAG supports creation of assessments that identify school and student needs in order to strengthen, not punish, schools. We call for ending the reliance on standardized tests as the single measure of student and school progress and performance. Comprehensive assessment should include work sampling and performance-based assessment and should be an outgrowth of student-centered curriculum and instruction.

High stakes tests have historically perpetuated existing inequality; in contrast, fair assessments should be used to provide teachers with the information they need to meet the needs of all of their students. High-stakes tests should not be used to determine teacher and school performance. Instead, teacher evaluation should be an ongoing practice with the goal of improving teachers' pedagogical, content, and cultural knowledge and should be based on authentic standards for the teaching profession, not student test scores.

6. Teacher Professional Development that Serves the Collective Interests of Teachers, Students, and Communities:

TAG believes that teacher professional development must support teachers to become effective partners with students and parents, and to be responsive to community needs. The form and content should be determined by teachers themselves with advice from parents and students and should work to develop social justice teaching practices.

7. Protect the Right to Organize:

TAG believes teachers have the right to organize to protect their rights as professionals and workers. Unions should be a place where teachers have a voice in creating and protecting an educational system that is set up in the best interests of students, families, and teachers. We support truly democratic governance of teacher unions and believe that they should champion policies that ultimately serve their communities.

8. School Climate That Empowers and Liberates Students:

TAG believes in working for school discipline policies and a school climate where students and teachers can thrive. Schools must be institutions that support the holistic social and emotional needs of all students, help equip young people with empathy and conflict resolution skills, and work to interrupt and transform oppressive dynamics that threaten the safety of the whole school community.

We support ending the practice of and reliance on punitive discipline strategies that push students out of school and into the military or prisons. Schools should remove zero tolerance policies, institute restorative practices and restorative justice models, and create time in the curriculum for community-building practices and social/emotional supports.

Artifact of Resistance 4: Stand Up Opt Out Campaign

Image courtesy of David Marshall. Letter courtesy of Rosie Frascella.

High school teacher Rosie Frascella at #StandUpOptOut demonstration
Courtesy of Rosie Frascella

Stand Up Opt Out Teachers' Statement

April 28th, 2014
Dear Chancellor Carmen Fariña,

We are New York City public school teachers at the International High School @ Prospect Heights. Over 95% of our students have recently arrived to the United States and are learning to read, write, and speak English. **After** much deliberation and thoughtful discussion with fellow educators, students, and parents, we have decided to abstain from administering the New York City ELA Performance Assessment.

The New York City ELA Performance Assessment serves no educational purpose for English Language Learners or their teachers. The test was constructed and formatted without any thought for the 14% of New York City students for whom English is not their first language. The level of English used in the pre-test administered in the fall was so far above the language levels of our recent immigrant student population that it provided little or no information about their language or academic proficiencies. Despite their best efforts and determination, the vast majority of our students received zero points, even though their classwork demonstrates increasing mastery of both English and academics. Accordingly, the test is an inadequate measurement of both student learning and instructional effectiveness. What is the point of spending valuable class time on an assessment that does not inform instruction?

When we administered the test in the fall, the experience was traumatic for both students and teachers. Ultimately, the lessons our students learned were about discouragement and failure. Their first experience as high school students taking a standardized test set the stage for future anxiety and confusion in subsequent testing situations. Participating in this assessment has and will continue to negatively impact their learning experiences and their confidence in their own abilities to succeed. Our students believe in the education system in our country, and they deserve a fair chance. This test, like many standardized tests, teaches them that no matter how hard they work, they will fail.

Our Objections to the ELA Performance Assessment

- The ELA Performance Assessment actively ignores the need to make accommodations for students who are learning English, such as providing reading aloud and rephrasing instructions, providing translations, etc. Such accommodations for English Language Learners are routinely given in other testing situations.
- The ELA Performance Assessment is intended to measure growth for people who already know English. Our students' growth will not be measured in this test because the test was not designed for new English language speakers. It was designed for those already fluent in English.
- Our students need every minute of instructional time they can get, and we work hard to make that time productive. This test is simply not a good use of their time or ours.

- Finally, 50% of parents and guardians in our school community have opted their students out of the exam.

We understand our decision to abstain from administering the test may impact aspects of our evaluations. Despite the potentially negative consequences, our professional judgment dictates that we cannot participate in this assessment. We are not willing to sacrifice the trust of our students, their feelings of self worth, and our professional duty to do what is best for them.

In good conscience, as educators dedicated to the learning of our students and the welfare of our school communities, we are not administering this test.

We applaud your memo to principals instructing that they respect families' rights to opt their children out of tests, we appreciate the respect you have already shown to educators as professionals and look forward to the changes you will make regarding the use of high stakes testing in our schools. **We ask that you remove the New York ELA Performance Exam in favor of an assessment created by educators who best know the individual needs of their students and classrooms.**

References

Amazing 9 year old Asean Johnson brings the crowd to their feet at Chicago school closings rally. (2013). Retrieved from http://www.youtube.com/watch?v=oue9HIOM7xU&feature=youtube_gdata_player

DreamYard Project. (n.d.). DreamYard A.C.T.I.O.N project. Retrieved from http://dreamyard.com/programs/dreamyard-art-center/out-of-school-programs/#a-c-t-i-o-n

Network of Teacher Activist Groups. (n.d.). Retrieved from http://www.teacheractivistgroups.org/

Stand Up Opt Out. (2014). Retrieved from http://standupoptout.wordpress.com/

About the Editors

Bree Picower is an Assistant Professor at Montclair State University in the College of Education and Human Development. Her book, *Practice What You Teach: Social Justice Education in the Classroom and the Streets,* explores a developmental continuum toward teacher activism. She co-edits *Planning to Change the World: A Planbook for Social Justice Teachers* published by the New York Collective of Radical Educators (NYCoRE) and the Education for Liberation Network. Her recent scholarly articles have appeared in *Teachers College Record, Teacher Education Quarterly*, and *Race, Ethnicity and Education.* She has taught in public elementary schools in Oakland, California, and New York City. As a core leader of NYCoRE and founding member of the national Teacher Activist Groups network, Bree works to create spaces for educators to sharpen their political analysis and act for educational justice. Resources and publications affiliated with her work can be found at www.usingtheirwords.org and she can be reached at bree@nycore.org.

    Edwin Mayorga is an Assistant Professor at Swarthmore College in the Department of Educational Studies. His ongoing project, *Education in our Barrios #BarrioEdProj*, is a digital, critical participatory action research project (D+CPAR) based in Latino core communities in cities in the northeastern United States. Working with local youth co-researchers, #BarrioEdProj traces the discursive and material effects of racialized neoliberal urbanism on, in, and through these communities. His recent scholarly articles have appeared in *Journal of Interactive Technology, Pedagogy, Peace and Conflict: Journal of Peace Psychology,* and *Multicultural Perspectives.* He was an elementary public school teacher in New York City prior to pursuing his PhD. For the last 11 years, he was a core leader of New York Collective of Radical Educators (NYCoRE). He is a participant in the National Latino Education

Research & Policy Project (NLERAP) and on the community advisory board of the Participatory Action Research Center for Education Organizing (PARCEO). You can find him on Twitter @eimayorga and @barrioedproj.

About the Contributors

Ujju Aggarwal is a writer, activist, and teacher. Her research grows out of her long-time work as a community organizer and educator. She has taught at Hunter College, Sarah Lawrence College, SUNY Educational Opportunities Center, and The New School. She is currently a postdoctoral fellow at the Institute for Urban Policy and Research Analysis (UT Austin). She works with the Parent Leadership Project, INCITE!, and is on the Community Advisory Board of the Participatory Action Research Center for Education Organizing.

Wayne Au is an Associate Professor in the College of Educational Studies at the University of Washington Bothell, and he is an editor for the social justice education magazine and publisher, Rethinking Schools.

Amy Brown is an anthropologist and educator whose work focuses on race, gender, and the impacts of privatization on public institutions. She brings five years of experience as a teacher in New York City public secondary schools to her scholarship. Her book, *A Good Investment? Privatization and Professional Performance in an Urban Public School*, is currently under contract with the University of Minnesota Press. She is a faculty member in the Critical Writing Program at the University of Pennsylvania.

Brian Jones is a former New York City public school teacher pursuing a PhD in Urban Education at the City University of New York Graduate Center. He co-narrated the film *The Inconvenient Truth Behind Waiting for Superman* and contributed to the book *Education and Capitalism: Struggles for Learning and Liberation*. He is a member of the Movement of Rank and File Educators, a caucus of the United Federation of Teachers. In 2012 Brian received a Lannan Cultural Freedom Fellowship.

Pauline Lipman is Professor of Educational Policy Studies and Director of the Collaborative for Equity and Justice in Education (CEJE), University of Illinois at Chicago, and an education activist. Her interdisciplinary research focuses on race and class inequality, globalization, and political economy of urban education, particularly the relationship of education policy, urban restructuring, and the politics of race. Her newest book is *The New Political Economy of Urban Education: Neoliberalism, Race, and the Right to the City*.

Barbara Madeloni is the president of the 110,000 member Massachusetts Teacher Association. A high school English teacher and teacher educator, her classroom work, writing, and union and community organizing center economic and racial justice and growing broad based alliances. Her most recent publications include chapters in *Social Context Reform: A Pedagogy of Equity and Opportunity* and *More Than a Score: The New Uprising Against High-Stakes Testing*.

David Stovall is an Associate Professor, University of Illinois at Chicago. He is also a volunteer social studies teacher at the Greater Lawndale High School for Social Justice, where he was a member of the design team.

Terrenda White is an Assistant Professor of sociology and education at the University of Colorado–Boulder. Her research focuses on market-based education reforms in urban communities and its cultural and pedagogical impact on teaching and learning, as well as the impact on teacher dispositions, teacher autonomy, and teacher professional identity. Particularly, White explores the organizational distinctions across community-based charter schools and privately managed charter schools, as well as institutional and community responses to market-based education restructuring.

Index

r

Darren E. Lund, Paul R. Carr, & Virginia Lea
GENERAL EDITORS

This book series seeks to engage a broad and cross-disciplinary range of students, scholars, activists, and others in a critical multicultural dialogue on the complex intersections of power, privilege, identity, and Whiteness. The series aims to link theory and practice to problematize key societal and educational concerns related to Whiteness. The series editors share the view that taking action for transformative change in and through education, in the spirit of what Paulo Freire called *conscientization*, is the role of educators who seek to address the needs of *all* their students. In focusing on Whiteness, we are concerned with social, economic, and environmental justice, the problematization of race, and the potential for education to be emancipatory in addressing power imbalances. Some of the questions of interest for this book series include:

- How do we engage in critical discussions related to power, privilege, identity, and Whiteness when many multicultural frameworks dissuade us from such work?

- How can we connect Whiteness to other intersecting and pivotal forms of being, marginalization, and identity?

- How can those categorized as White engage in dialogues and action about Whiteness that can positively contribute to addressing concerns of racialized and marginalized groups?

- How can we effectively contextualize and critique hegemony and globalized economic realities so as to be able to discuss race in a constructive and transformative manner?

For individual or group inquiries please contact:

Darren E. Lund | *dlund@ucalgary.ca*
Paul R. Carr | *prcarr@gmail.com*
Virginia Lea | *leav@uwstout.edu*
Christopher S. Myers, Acquisitions Editor | *chrism@plang.com*

To order other books in this series, please contact our Customer Service Department at:

(800) 770-LANG (within the U.S.)
(212) 647-7706 (outside the U.S.)
(212) 647-7707 FAX

Or browse online by series at www.peterlang.com